Bite
me

Cover credits:
Design: Mark Latter/Blue Dragonfly
Photography: Michael Alberstat

Published in 2010 by Kyle Books,
an imprint of Kyle Cathie Ltd.
www.kylebooks.com

Distributed by National Book Network
4501 Forbes Blvd., Suite 200
Lanham, MD 20706
Phone: (800) 462-6420 Fax: (301) 429-5746

First published in Canada in 2009 by Pinky Swear Press Inc.

ISBN 978-1-906868-44-4

Library of Congress Control Number: 2010932843

www.pinkyswearpress.com
www.bitemecookbook.com

Printed and bound by C & C Offset Printing Co., Ltd.

FSC
www.fsc.org
MIX
Paper from
responsible sources
FSC® C008047

Bite me

By the not-so-sweet, tiny-bit-salty sisters
Julie Albert & Lisa Gnat

Published by
KYLE BOOKS

Inscribe me

To Lisa

Your food's mother-forkin' great.
Love you like a sister.

To Julie

Nice going, Drama Queen.
Love you more than chocolate.

"After all the trouble you go to, you get about as much actual 'food' out of eating an artichoke as you would from licking 30 or 40 postage stamps." — Miss Piggy, entertainer

There's not a single thorny artichoke, scrawny quail or roasted chestnut to be peeled in this book. What you will find in **BITE ME** are 175 dependably delicious recipes created for the urban and suburban, the aspiring and well-seasoned home cook. You won't need an army of sous chefs, a pantry of guava paste or a blowtorch in order to turn a bag of groceries into a satisfying meal. We're all about making you confident in the kitchen and relaxed at the table.

"Anyone who eats three meals a day should understand why cookbooks outsell sex books three-to-one." — L.M. Boyd, journalist

We love poring over cookbooks, admiring the sublime combinations of celebrity chef Jean-Georges Vongerichten and the unmatched techniques of French chef Daniel Boulud. However, these haute tomes don't offer swift responses to the big question, "What's for dinner?" With the help of **BITE ME** you can stop gnawing your nails, forget all about mushroom foam and smile when someone asks you, "What's cooking, good looking?" Let **BITE ME**, a thoroughly tested cookbook, make filling yours and others' plates a piece of cake.

"Take me! I am the hallucinogenic!"

— Salvador Dali, artist

BITE ME speaks to more than your stomach. For us, the creation of food is intimately tied to the world outside the kitchen – family, art, music, movies and pop culture are constant sources of laughter and inspiration. What's a day without a grandmother-related guffaw or a cooking session without tunes blasting? Boring. And where else can you flip to a famous photo while cleaning a chicken breast? Yes, we hope that **BITE ME** will be your multi-sensory smorgasbord, a feast for your eyes, ears, mouth and nose.

Julie
Albert

I ADORE SUSHI CONVEYOR BELTS
PET PEEVES PANTYHOSE, AIR QUOTES
GUILTY PLEASURE SIZE 8½ HEELS
MUCH-LOVED MEAL LOMBARDI'S PIZZA, NYC
BEST FAUX PAS "WHEN'S THE BABY DUE?"
FAVORITE PAGE in "BITE ME" 111
IRVING PENN LEAVES ME SPEECHLESS
CHOICE CANDY LICORICE ALLSORTS
SUPERPOWER WISH TO HAVE BARBARELLA HAIR
MY FREEBIE DENIS LEARY
BEST QUOTE "NOBODY PUTS BABY IN THE CORNER"
AWARDS 1st PLACE, GRADE 7 HURDLE RELAY
SISTER'S BEST SECRET LISA CAN'T RIDE A BIKE
CURRENTLY WORKING ON GROWING UP

Lisa
Gnat

I ADORE MY MAC CHEF KNIFE
PET PEEVES WHISTLING, SNUFFLING
GUILTY PLEASURE CHOCOLATE BEFORE 9AM
MUCH-LOVED MEAL FRENCH TOAST DRENCHED IN MAPLE SYRUP
BEST FAUX PAS CAUGHT SINGING IN MY CAR
FAVORITE PAGE in "BITE ME" 245
ALICE WATERS LEAVES ME SPEECHLESS
CHOICE CANDY 3 MUSKETEERS
SUPERPOWER WISH TO BE INVISIBLE
MY FREEBIE GORDON RAMSAY
BEST QUOTE "C IS FOR COOKIE THAT'S GOOD ENOUGH FOR ME"
AWARDS BAKERY PRODUCTION CLUB AWARD
SISTER'S BEST SECRET JULIE CAN'T WINK
CURRENTLY WORKING ON FUDGY MARSHMALLOW CAKE

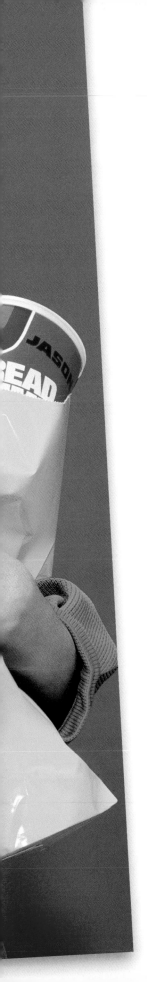

TGTBT Salad Rolls 14
Wild Mushroom Crostini with Mint and Parmesan 15
Slacker's Stacked Sushi 16
Mona Lisa's Fontina and Arugula Pizza 18
Sky-High Potato Skins 20
Crab Cakes with Creamy Mustard Sauce 21

Grab me

Little Nibbles

Creamy White Bean Spread with Asiago Crackers 22
Tuna Skewers with Wasabi Dip 24
Grilled Beef Satay with Peanut Sauce 25
Honey-Baked Coconut Shrimp 27
Piled-High Chicken Tostada Cups 28
Sweet and Sour Candied Salami 30
DYN-O-MITE! Asian Meatballs 31

TGTBT SALAD ROLLS
Too Good To Be True Salad Rolls

INGREDIENTS

Salad Rolls

6oz/175g rice stick noodles

10 round rice paper sheets

10 green curly lettuce leaves

1 medium carrot,
peeled and shredded

2 ripe mangos, peeled
and julienned

1 English cucumber, peeled,
seeded and julienned

3 tbsp plus 1 tsp
fresh chopped basil

Thai Dipping Sauce

¼ cup soy sauce

3 tbsp mirin

2 tbsp rice wine vinegar

1 tbsp sugar

1 tsp sesame oil

1 tsp grated fresh ginger

⅛ tsp hot sauce
(Sirachee brand)

Julie: RU there?
Are you there?

Lisa: S^?
What's up?

Julie: UCWAP. Din PT. Need GR8 AP PDQ.
Up the creek without a paddle.
Dinner party. Need great appetizer pretty darn quick.

Lisa: RPW. Duh. F&E2RL. TM. PFM.
Rice paper wrap. Duh. Fast and easy to roll. Trust me.
Pure freakin' magic.

Julie: N1. ^5. G2GLYS.
Nice one. High five. Got to go, love you so.

Lisa: LYLAS. OO.
Love you like a sister. Over and out.

DIRECTIONS

1) For the salad rolls, bring a medium pot of water to a boil. Add rice stick noodles and cook according to package directions. When tender, drain, rinse with cold water and drain well again. Set aside. 2) Place 1 rice paper sheet in a shallow bowl or pie plate of hot water until just softened, about 1 minute. Lay rice paper sheet on tea towel. Place a lettuce leaf down the center of the rice sheet leaving a 1-inch border at the top and bottom. Place ¼ cup rice noodles lengthwise on the lettuce leaf followed by 1 tbsp shredded carrots, 6 slices of mango, 4 slices of cucumber and 1 tsp chopped basil. Fold up the bottom 1-inch border of rice paper placing it over the filling. Fold in the right side, followed by the left side and then the top, forming a tight cylinder. Repeat with remaining rice paper sheets and filling. Serve with dipping sauce. 3) For the dipping sauce, in a medium bowl, whisk soy sauce, mirin, rice vinegar, sugar, sesame oil, ginger and hot sauce.

Yield: 10 large salad rolls

WILD MUSHROOM CROSTINI with MINT and PARMESAN

INGREDIENTS

Crostini

32 diagonal slices of baguette or Italian bread, cut into ¼-inch thick slices

4 tbsp olive oil

½ tsp kosher salt

Mushroom Topping

2 tbsp olive oil

2 tbsp finely chopped shallots

2 medium garlic cloves, minced

6 cups sliced mushrooms (a mix of shiitake, chanterelle and button mushrooms)

¼ cup dry white wine

¼ cup freshly grated Parmesan cheese

1 tbsp chopped fresh mint

½ tsp kosher salt

¼ tsp freshly ground black pepper

32 fresh Parmesan curls, made with vegetable peeler

It's time to put an end to the rumors. Jerry Garcia was NOT spotted eating oatmeal in my kitchen and do not call me at 2 a.m. asking me to "hook you up." Yes, I admit, there is magic in these mushrooms, but, c'mon neighborhood Narc, it's nothing illegal. Just a little garlic and white wine. So, to those of you who love these addictive bites, stop complimenting me on my "shroom-fests" in public...you're ruining my reputation.

DIRECTIONS

1) Preheat oven to 400°F. Place the bread slices on a non-stick baking sheet. Brush bread on both sides with olive oil and sprinkle salt evenly overtop. Bake 4 minutes, flip slices over and continue to bake 3 minutes more. Remove from oven and set aside. 2) For the mushroom topping, in a large skillet, heat olive oil over medium heat. Add shallots and garlic, sautéing for 1 minute. Stir in mushrooms and sauté until they soften and begin to brown, 5-6 minutes. 3) Turn heat to high, add white wine and stir 3-4 minutes until liquid evaporates. Remove from heat, stir in grated Parmesan, mint, salt and pepper. 4) To assemble, top each toast with 1 tbsp mushroom topping and a Parmesan curl. Serve immediately.

Yield: 32 pieces

BITE ME BIT

"The Smurfs are little blue people who live in magic mushrooms. Think about it."

– Author unknown, or was it that dude with the little baggy...forget it.

SLACKER'S STACKED SUSHI

INGREDIENTS

Rice

1 cup short grain sushi rice

1¼ cups water

2 tbsp rice vinegar

Egg

4 large eggs

2 tbsp chicken broth

1 tbsp sugar

1 tbsp soy sauce

2 tsp mirin

2 tsp vegetable oil

Mayonnaise Filling

½ cup mayonnaise

1 tbsp wasabi powder

4 sheets nori
(roasted seaweed)

3 tsp black sesame seeds

1 large avocado, peeled,
pitted and thinly sliced

½ large English
cucumber, peeled, cut
into half lengthwise,
centre scooped
out and cucumber
thinly sliced

Whoa, man. You know the Japanese epidemic, "death by overworking"? I don't want any "karoshi" on my conscience. Training to be a sushi chef STARTS with 3 years of meditation and rice washing, duuude. So forget it. Take a swig of warm sake and feast on this, our chillax-style sushi – you're going to dig these layers of seasoned rice, sweet egg, creamy avocado and crispy cucumbers.

DIRECTIONS

1) For the rice, place rice in colander and rinse thoroughly under cold water until the water runs clear. Drain. Place rice in a 2-quart saucepan with 1¼ cups water. Heat on high until boiling. Reduce heat to low, stir, cover tightly and simmer gently for 20 minutes without lifting the lid. Remove pan from heat, let stand 10 minutes. Place rice in a medium size bowl and gently stir in rice vinegar. 2) While the rice cooks, in a medium bowl, whisk together eggs, chicken broth, sugar, soy sauce and mirin. Heat a 10-inch skillet over low heat, add vegetable oil and using a paper towel, spread to cover sides and bottom. Pour egg mixture into the pan and cover tightly. Cook 4-5 minutes until omelet is somewhat set. Remove the lid and using a large spatula flip the omelet and continue to cook 2-3 minutes more. Remove from heat and set aside. 3) For the mayonnaise filling, in a small bowl, whisk together mayonnaise and wasabi powder. Set aside. 4) Line an 8-inch square baking pan with plastic wrap leaving a 6-inch overhang on opposite sides. Place 1 nori sheet in the base of the

Wasabi Mayonnaise Sauce

2 tbsp wasabi powder

2 tbsp water

¾ cup mayonnaise

2 tbsp soy sauce

1 tbsp rice wine vinegar

pan. Top with a generous ¾ cup of cooked rice, spreading evenly. Sprinkle with 1 tsp black sesame seeds. Top with 4 tbsp mayonnaise mixture, followed by a single layer of sliced cucumber. Top with another sheet of nori. Spread another generous ¾ cup cooked rice over the nori sheet. Sprinkle with 1 tsp black sesame seeds followed by the remaining 4 tbsp of mayonnaise mixture. Lay a single layer of avocado on top and place cooked egg omelet on top of avocado. Cover with nori sheet. Spread remaining rice evenly overtop and sprinkle with remaining teaspoon of black sesame seeds. Top with final nori sheet. Cover with plastic wrap, weigh down with a few small books and refrigerate 1 hour. Use plastic overhang to remove sushi from the baking pan. Trim the edges and cut into 6 generous portions. Serve each portion with wasabi mayonnaise sauce. **5)** For the wasabi mayonnaise, in a small bowl, whisk wasabi powder and water to form a smooth paste. Add mayonnaise, soy sauce and rice vinegar. Whisk to combine and refrigerate covered until ready to use.

Serves 6

BITE ME BIT

"Who's ever written a great work about the immense effort required in order not to create?"

– The Dostoyevsky Wannabe (actor Brecht Andersch) in the 1991 movie "Slacker"

MONA LISA'S FONTINA and ARUGULA PIZZA

INGREDIENTS

Dough

1 tsp olive oil

1 cup warm water (105°F to 115°F)

1 package (2¼ tsp) active dry yeast

2¾ cups flour

1 tbsp honey

2 tsp kosher salt

2 tbsp olive oil

Yellow cornmeal to dust pizza pans or baking sheets

Pizza Topping

2 tbsp olive oil

½ tsp kosher salt

1 cup shredded Fontina cheese

1 cup shredded mozzarella cheese

1 tsp chopped fresh thyme

Why the big fuss over Da Vinci's painting? I mean, my sister is THE Mona Lisa – she's got the brown eyes that follow me everywhere, the corners of her mouth in a slight upturn and a constant air of mystery. But she melts down like the Dali clock when I ask her how much longer until her master-piece – this crispy thin-crust pizza topped with nutty-tasting Fontina and arugula – comes out of the oven.

DIRECTIONS

1) Brush a large bowl with 1 tsp olive oil. Set aside. 2) For the dough, pour 1 cup warm water into a small bowl. Sprinkle yeast over top and set aside until yeast dissolves and becomes foamy, 5-10 minutes. 3) Meanwhile, place flour, honey and salt in a food processor fitted with the steel blade and process to mix. With the machine running, add the yeast mixture and 2 tbsp olive oil in a steady stream. Process until dough forms a sticky ball, about 10 seconds. Transfer to a lightly floured surface and knead dough until smooth and elastic, about 2 minutes. Add more flour if dough is too sticky, 1 tbsp at a time. Place dough in oil-coated bowl and cover with plastic wrap, letting the dough rise in a warm, draft-free area until almost double in size, about 1 hour. 4) Preheat oven to 475°F. Dust pizza pan or baking sheet with yellow cornmeal. 5) Once dough has doubled in size, punch down dough and divide into 2 equal pieces. On a lightly floured surface, roll out one piece at a time, starting in the center of the dough and rolling outwards to form a 12-inch circle. Transfer to pizza pan or baking sheet. Repeat with other half of the pizza dough. 6) Brush 1 tbsp olive oil on each pizza base and sprinkle each with ¼ tsp salt. On

Arugula Topping

8 cups baby arugula

4 tbsp olive oil

2 tbsp fresh lemon juice

½ tsp kosher salt

½ tsp freshly ground black pepper

each pizza, sprinkle the Fontina, mozzarella and thyme, dividing evenly between the two. **7)** Bake 10-12 minutes, until the edges are golden. Let sit 5 minutes before slicing. Slice each pizza into 8 pieces. **8)** For arugula topping, in a medium bowl, toss baby arugula with olive oil, lemon juice, salt and pepper. Divide arugula between both pizzas, topping each slice with a generous handful. Serve immediately.

Yield: 16 slices

SKY-HIGH POTATO SKINS

INGREDIENTS

4 medium russet potatoes

2 tbsp olive oil

4 tbsp melted butter

½ tsp kosher salt

¼ tsp freshly ground
black pepper

6 turkey bacon slices, cooked
crisp and crumbled

1 cup shredded cheddar cheese

1 cup shredded Monterey
Jack cheese

½ cup sour cream, for topping

I don't bother calling Lisa's house on Sunday. No one ever answers. Her husband is probably preoccupied painting his face Dolphins' orange and teal. Her kids are scurrying to get the TV room ready for hours of hibachi-free tailgating. As for my sister, she has the privilege of preparing the ultimate football fare – crispy potato skins. The perennial champs of couch-potato cuisine, these addictive skins are mounded high with crunchy turkey bacon and gooey melted cheese.

DIRECTIONS

1) Preheat oven to 425°F. Line a baking sheet with aluminum foil. Scrub potatoes, pat dry and pierce with a fork several times. Rub each potato with ½ tbsp olive oil and place on prepared baking sheet. Bake 50-60 minutes or until potatoes are tender. Remove from oven, allowing potatoes to cool just enough to handle comfortably. 2) Turn the oven up to 450°F. 3) Cut each potato in half lengthwise and scoop out the cooked potato leaving a ½-inch thick layer of potato along the sides and bottoms of the skins. Discard scooped out potato or use for mashed potatoes. 4) Brush the hollowed potato skins (inside and outside) with melted butter and sprinkle with salt and pepper. Place potatoes skin-side-up on baking sheet and return to oven for 10 minutes. Flip the skins and bake another 8 minutes. 5) Remove from oven, sprinkle skins with crumbled turkey bacon, cheddar and Monterey Jack. Return to oven and bake 2 minutes longer or until cheese is melted. Serve warm, topped with sour cream.

Yield: 8 potato skins

CRAB CAKES with CREAMY MUSTARD SAUCE

INGREDIENTS

Crab Cakes

1 large egg, lightly beaten

1 cup soft fresh breadcrumbs (4-5 slices of crustless bread processed in food processor until coarse crumbs)

¼ cup mayonnaise

1 tbsp Dijon mustard

1 tsp fresh lemon juice

1 tsp Worcestershire sauce

1 tsp chopped fresh thyme

½ tsp kosher salt

¼ tsp freshly ground black pepper

⅛ tsp cayenne pepper

1 lb (approx. 3 cups) crabmeat, drained well, cartilage removed, crabmeat flaked

¼ cup yellow cornmeal

2 tbsp olive oil

Creamy Mustard Sauce

2 tsp vegetable oil

1 small shallot, finely diced

¼ cup dry white wine

½ cup mayonnaise

½ cup sour cream

1 tbsp Dijon mustard

1 tbsp seed mustard

1 tbsp honey

¼ tsp kosher salt

Maryland gave us Babe Ruth, Frank Zappa, and the golden glory of crab cakes. It might be difficult to compete with the masters of the Chesapeake – Faidleys, G&M, Angelina's, Timbuktu – but our delectable version strikes the perfect balance between seasoning and the stuffing that keeps this sweet delicacy from falling apart while still showcasing the luscious lump meat.

DIRECTIONS

1) For the crab cakes, preheat oven to 375°F. Line a baking sheet with aluminum foil and coat with non-stick cooking spray. 2) In a medium bowl, combine egg, breadcrumbs, mayonnaise, Dijon mustard, lemon juice, Worcestershire sauce, thyme, salt, pepper and cayenne pepper; stir to combine ingredients. Add crabmeat and mix well. 3) Using moistened hands, shape crab mixture into 12 patties, ½-inch thick. Place cornmeal in a shallow dish, dip patties in cornmeal, turning to coat both sides. Place on prepared baking sheet, bake 10 minutes, flip and bake another 10 minutes, until slightly golden. 4) Remove from oven. In a large skillet, heat olive oil over high heat. Add crab cakes and brown 1 minute on each side to get a golden crust. Remove and serve with creamy mustard sauce. 5) For the creamy mustard sauce, in a small saucepan, heat vegetable oil over medium heat. Add shallots and sauté until softened, about 2 minutes. Add white wine and simmer until wine is almost evaporated, about 3 minutes. Set aside to cool. 6) In a blender, combine mayonnaise, sour cream, Dijon mustard, seed mustard, honey and salt. Add shallots and blend until smooth. Serve with crab cakes.

Yield: 12 appetizer crab cakes and 1¼ cups mustard sauce

CREAMY WHITE BEAN SPREAD with ASIAGO CRACKERS

INGREDIENTS

Asiago Crackers

1½ cups flour

½ tsp kosher salt

½ cup cold butter, cut into pieces

2 cups grated Asiago cheese

½ cup sour cream

White Bean Spread

¼ cup olive oil

2 large garlic cloves, minced

1½ cups canned white kidney (cannellini) beans, rinsed well and drained

1 tbsp fresh lemon juice

1 tbsp water

1 tsp chopped fresh thyme

½ tsp kosher salt

¼ tsp freshly ground black pepper

⅛ tsp cayenne pepper

Some might have looked upon Jack as a most unsavvy businessman – trading a cow for 5 magic beans? Heck, even his mother sent him to bed with no supper. But I applaud him for his astute vision. I, too, think there's nothing better than miraculous white beans, especially when mashed with garlic and piled atop savory cheese crackers. Fee-fi-fo-fum, I smell a scrumptious swap to come... my brother for 3 beans?

DIRECTIONS

ASIAGO CRACKERS

1) In a large bowl, combine flour and salt. Using a pastry blender or your fingers, cut in cold butter until you have coarse crumbs. Toss in Asiago cheese. Add sour cream and stir until dough comes together. Turn onto a lightly floured surface, divide dough into 2 and roll each half into a 1½-inch diameter log. Wrap each log in plastic wrap and refrigerate at least 2 hours before slicing. 2) Preheat oven to 325°F. Cover a baking sheet with parchment paper. 3) Slice logs into ⅛-inch thick slices and place on prepared baking sheet, leaving some space between each. Bake for 10 minutes, flip crackers over and bake another 10 minutes until golden. Remove from oven and cool completely on a wire rack. Can be prepared ahead of time, cooled and stored in an airtight container.

Yield: 50 crackers

WHITE BEAN SPREAD

1) In a small skillet, heat oil over medium heat. Add minced garlic and turn heat off immediately. Allow garlic to sit in the oil for 30 seconds and then strain out garlic pieces, reserving the flavored oil. Set aside to cool slightly and discard garlic from the sieve. 2) In a food processor, combine white beans, reserved garlic flavored olive oil, lemon juice, water, thyme, salt, black pepper and cayenne. Process until smooth, about 20 seconds. The dip may be refrigerated a few hours ahead of serving. Bring to room temperature before serving.

Yield: 1½ cups

BITE ME BIT

"He's so cheesy, I can't watch him without crackers."

– Lelaina Pierce (actress Winona Ryder) in the 1994 movie "Reality Bites"

TUNA SKEWERS with WASABI DIP

INGREDIENTS

1½ lbs fresh tuna,
cut into 1-inch cubes

4 tbsp soy sauce

1 tsp freshly ground black pepper

1½ tbsp vegetable oil

Wasabi Dip

3 tbsp water

2 tbsp wasabi powder

¾ cup mayonnaise

30 toothpicks or small
cocktail sticks

30 slices of pickled ginger

Canned tuna has its charms. Given the right mood we can even go for some Hot Tuna, especially their 1972 album "Burgers." But nothing tinned can top this recipe for fresh tuna, a tasty and exotic way to gussy up this deliciously mild, firm fish. Soak it in savory soy sauce, sear it to perfection, add a sliver of spicy ginger and dunk it in the piquant mayonnaise and, ta-dah, your guests will think, however mistakenly, that you're the classiest.

DIRECTIONS

1) In a medium bowl, combine tuna and soy sauce. Marinate for 1 hour at room temperature. 2) For the dip, in a small bowl, combine water and wasabi powder. Stir to dissolve the powder and add mayonnaise. Refrigerate until ready to serve. 3) Once finished marinating, drain the tuna and pat dry with paper towel. Return to bowl and toss tuna with black pepper. 4) In a large skillet, heat oil over medium-high heat. Add tuna, stirring constantly until browned on the outside but still pink inside, 3-5 minutes. Remove from heat. 5) Skewer 1 piece of tuna and 1 slice of ginger on each cocktail stick. Serve with wasabi dip.

Serves 6-8

GRILLED BEEF SATAY with PEANUT SAUCE

INGREDIENTS

1¼ lbs beef tenderloin, cut into 2-inch strips

¼ cup soy sauce

2 tbsp packed brown sugar

1 tbsp fresh lime juice

1 small garlic clove, minced

1 (1-inch) piece of lemongrass, finely minced

1 tsp ground cumin

¼ tsp ground ginger

½ tsp kosher salt

¼ tsp freshly ground black pepper

Peanut Dipping Sauce

1¼ cups chicken broth

1 cup smooth peanut butter

2 tbsp packed brown sugar

2 tbsp fresh lime juice

2 tbsp soy sauce

½ tsp grated fresh ginger

Wooden skewers, soaked in warm water for 20-30 minutes before threading on the meat

Whether you're eating yakitori in Japan, shish kebab in Turkey or chuanr in China, there is a universal caveman-thrill from eating meat off a stick. Looking for inspiration we bypassed the North American corn dog and traveled East – aromatic lemongrass and smooth peanut sauce lend our easy beef satay full-bodied flavor.

DIRECTIONS

1) Place beef strips in a large resealable bag. In a small bowl, stir together soy sauce, brown sugar, lime juice, garlic, lemongrass, cumin, ginger, salt and pepper. Pour marinade over beef and toss to coat. Refrigerate 1-2 hours. 2) Preheat barbeque to medium-high. 3) Remove meat from refrigerator. Thread meat on to prepared skewers and discard marinade. 4) Grill over medium-high heat, 2-3 minutes per side or until browned and cooked to desired doneness. 5) For the peanut sauce, in a medium saucepan, whisk chicken broth, peanut butter, brown sugar, lime juice, soy sauce and ginger over medium-high heat. Whisk until smooth and thickened, about 6 minutes. Serve with cooked beef skewers. This sauce yields 2 cups and leftovers can be stored in the refrigerator for up to 1 week.

Serves 8-10

HONEY-BAKED COCONUT SHRIMP

INGREDIENTS

Coconut Shrimp

½ cup honey

1½ cups panko (Japanese breadcrumbs)

1 cup flaked sweetened coconut

½ tsp ground cumin

½ tsp kosher salt

¼ tsp freshly ground black pepper

26 large raw shrimp, peeled and de-veined

Apricot Dipping Sauce

⅔ cup apricot jam

3 tbsp Heinz chili sauce

2 tsp Dijon mustard

Back in the day, we didn't go to bars for the Tequila shooters or the boys. We went to get our greasy food fix. Despite not doing barstool banquets these days, we still long for the tantalizing tastes – we've brought the feast home, but we've left behind the oily glory of the deep fryer and created juicy, coconut-coated, golden-baked shrimp dipped in a sweet apricot sauce.

DIRECTIONS

1) Preheat oven to 425°F. Line a large baking sheet with aluminum foil and coat with non-stick cooking spray. 2) For the shrimp, pour honey in a medium bowl and warm on high in the microwave, 20-25 seconds. 3) On a large plate, combine panko, coconut, cumin, salt and pepper. 4) Taking shrimp one at a time, dip in honey and then coat in coconut mixture. Place on prepared baking sheet and bake 14 minutes, gently flipping shrimp halfway through baking. 5) For the sauce, place jam in a medium bowl. Warm in the microwave for 45 seconds. Add chili sauce and Dijon mustard, stirring to combine. Serve with baked coconut shrimp.

Serves 4-6

BITE ME BIT

Save a tree, send a coconut. Affixed with mailing label and correct postage, the U.S. Postal Service will deliver coconut mail.

PILED-HIGH CHICKEN TOSTADA CUPS

INGREDIENTS

Tortilla Cups

4 (8-inch) tortilla wrappers

2 tbsp olive oil

1 tsp kosher salt

Chicken

4 boneless, skinless chicken breast halves

1 small white onion, quartered

2 large garlic cloves, peeled and smashed

¼ cup coarsely chopped fresh flat-leaf parsley

3 fresh mint leaves

1 dried bay leaf

1 tsp kosher salt

Bean Mixture

1 tbsp vegetable oil

2 cups canned black beans, rinsed and drained

1 tsp ground cumin

1 cup ketchup

2 tbsp honey

2 tbsp orange juice

2 tbsp soy sauce

2 tbsp sherry vinegar

1 tbsp chipotle chilis in adobo sauce, chopped

Traditionally, tostadas are flat, deep-fried tortillas topped with refried beans, cheese and other fixings. Tasty, but try balancing a greasy "open face" taco in one hand while not spilling your drink from the other...awkward. We won't let your fiesta flop – these tortilla cups mounded with Mexican-spiced chicken and creamy guacamole guarantee the only thing to hit the deck will be your Corona-crocked amigos.

DIRECTIONS

1) Preheat oven to 400°F. Coat a standard size muffin tin with non-stick cooking spray. 2) Brush both sides of the tortillas with olive oil and sprinkle with salt. Cut each tortilla into 8 wedges. Working in batches, mold each tortilla triangle to fit the muffin cups and bake 7-8 minutes until crisp and golden. Remove from muffin tin and set aside. 3) For the chicken, in a large pot, combine chicken breasts, onion, garlic, parsley, mint, bay leaf and salt. Add 8 cups of water and bring to a boil over high heat. Reduce heat and simmer covered for 10 minutes. Turn heat off and let sit covered an additional 10 minutes. Remove chicken from broth, allow to cool slightly and then shred chicken. 4) For the bean mixture, in a medium saucepan, heat oil over high heat. Add beans and cumin, stirring 1 minute. Add ketchup, honey, orange juice, soy sauce, sherry vinegar and chopped chipotles. Lower heat to medium and continue to cook until sauce is syrupy, about

Guacamole

2 large ripe avocados,
pitted and peeled

2 large Roma tomatoes,
seeded and diced

1 tbsp fresh lime juice

1 tbsp fresh lemon juice

½ tsp ground cumin

½ tsp kosher salt

⅛ tsp cayenne pepper

5 minutes. Add shredded chicken, stir to coat, and remove from heat. **5)** For the guacamole, cut avocados in large chunks and mash in a medium bowl with a fork. Stir in tomatoes, lime juice, lemon juice, cumin, salt and cayenne pepper. **6)** To assemble, top each baked tortilla cup with a heaping spoonful of the chicken and bean mixture followed by a dollop of guacamole. Serve immediately.

Yield: 32 tostadas

BITE ME BIT

"You're not drunk if you can lie on the floor without holding on."

– Dean Martin, entertainer

SWEET and SOUR CANDIED SALAMI

INGREDIENTS

7 cups kosher beef salami, cut into 1-inch cubes

3½ cups Heinz chili sauce

1 cup apricot jam

2 lemons, juiced

3 tbsp Worcestershire sauce

Watch your backs, fussy, flaky puff pastries. Slash your prices, conceited caviar. Salami, once considered déclassé in the haute hors d'oeuvres world, is taking pompous parties by storm. A snap to put together, this salty and spicy beef is baked into a sticky, syrupy scene-stealer. Take that, smug smoked salmon.

DIRECTIONS

1) Preheat oven to 350°F. 2) Place cubed salami in a 13x9-inch baking dish. 3) In a medium bowl, whisk chili sauce, jam, lemon juice and Worcestershire sauce. Pour over salami. 4) Bake uncovered, stirring every 20 minutes, for 1½ to 2 hours, until the sauce is reduced by half and thickened. Serve with toothpicks.

Serves 8-10

BITE ME BIT

"Wait up, girls. I got a salami I gotta hide still."

– Carl Spackler (actor Bill Murray) in the 1980 movie "Caddyshack"

DYN-O-MITE! ASIAN MEATBALLS

INGREDIENTS

Meatballs

2 lbs lean ground beef

2 large eggs

½ cup breadcrumbs

½ cup hoisin sauce

1 tsp grated fresh ginger

Asian Sauce

1 cup apricot jam

½ cup hoisin sauce

½ cup rice vinegar

½ tsp grated fresh ginger

⅛ tsp cayenne pepper

The cocktail meatball is one 1970s culinary delight we're thrilled has made a comeback. With a Harvey Wallbanger in one hand and this hoisin one-biter in the other, you get all the sweetness and flavor of the "Me Decade" without having to shimmy into a spandex halter-neck catsuit.

DIRECTIONS

1) Preheat oven to 375°F. Line two baking sheets with aluminum foil and coat with non-stick cooking spray. 2) For the meatballs, in a large bowl, combine beef, eggs, breadcrumbs, hoisin sauce and ginger. Shape the meat mixture into walnut-sized balls, making approximately 60 meatballs. Place on prepared baking sheets and bake for 24 minutes, turning meatballs halfway through baking time. Remove from oven and let meatballs sit on paper towel to drain. 3) For the Asian sauce, in a large saucepan, bring jam, hoisin sauce, rice vinegar, ginger and cayenne pepper to a boil over medium-high heat. Reduce heat to low and simmer for 5 minutes. Add cooked meatballs to the sauce, heat through and serve.

Yield: approximately 60 meatballs

BITE ME BIT

Archie: You are a Meathead.

Mike: What did you call me?

Archie: Meathead. Dead from the neck up. Meathead.

– From the 1971 television show "All in the Family"

Traditional Chicken Soup with Matzo Balls 34
Bestowed (mushroom) Barley Soup 35
Roasted Carrot Soup with Candied Pistachios 36
Restorative Roasted Vegetable Soup 38
Potato Soup with Spiced Chickpeas 39
Tomato Soup with Grilled Cheese Croutons 41
Incroyable French Onion Soup 42

Spoon
me

Steamy Soups

Southwestern Chicken Corn Chowder 43
White Bean Soup with Spinach and Couscous 46
Nutty Butternut Squash Soup 47
Minestrone with Pesto Drizzle 49
Raj's Vegetable Lentil Soup 50
Moroccan Spiced Chicken Soup 51
Ian Muggridge's Tuscan Bread Soup 52

TELEGRAM

URGENT, DELIVER WITHOUT DELAY

January 22, 1907
SICK OF BORSCHT STOP FREEZING MY MATZO BALLS IN
VLADIVOSTOK STOP HOPPING ON SLOW BOAT TO ELLIS ISLAND STOP
HEARD THEY HAVE NICE SOUP ON LOWER EAST SIDE STOP

TRADITIONAL CHICKEN SOUP with MATZO BALLS

INGREDIENTS

Chicken Soup

1 (4 lb) whole chicken, well rinsed

8 chicken wings, split, tips removed

5 large carrots, peeled and cut into 2-inch pieces

5 large celery stalks, cut into 2-inch pieces

2 medium parsnips, peeled and sliced

1 large yellow onion, peeled and quartered

3 garlic cloves, peeled and left whole

1 large bunch of fresh flat-leaf parsley

1 large bunch of fresh dill

10 black peppercorns

1 tbsp kosher salt

Matzo Balls

4 large eggs, lightly beaten

2 tbsp vegetable oil

1 tsp kosher salt

A pinch of freshly ground black pepper

1 cup matzo meal

DIRECTIONS

1) For the soup, place the whole chicken and chicken wings in a very large soup pot. Fill with enough cold water to cover the chicken and fill the pot to ¾ full. Bring to a boil over high heat and skim off the foam that accumulates on the top. Reduce heat to a simmer and add carrots, celery, parsnips, onion, garlic, parsley, dill, peppercorns and salt. Return to a boil, reduce heat and cover, simmering gently for 2 hours. Remove lid and continue to simmer for 1 hour. 2) Strain the soup into another pot through a very fine sieve or a strainer lined with cheesecloth. Shred the meat from the chicken breast and put it in the strained soup or save for another time. Discard the remaining chicken and solids. 3) Salt the soup to taste. Cool soup and skim off any fat that has risen to the surface (the easiest way is to refrigerate the soup overnight and then discard solidified fat from the surface). Serve hot with shredded chicken, matzo balls and/or cooked egg noodles. 4) For the matzo balls, in a medium bowl, whisk together eggs, vegetable oil, salt and pepper. Whisk in matzo meal just until combined. Cover mixture lightly with plastic wrap and refrigerate 1 hour until slightly firm. 5) Bring a large pot of salted water to a boil. Remove matzo ball mixture from refrigerator. Gently roll a heaping tablespoon of the matzo mixture into balls; too much pressure when rolling the balls will make them too hard. Add to boiling water, cover and reduce heat to low, simmering until doubled in size, 25-30 minutes. Using a slotted spoon, transfer matzo balls to prepared soup.

Yield: 20-24 matzo balls
Serves 10-12

BESTOWED (mushroom) BARLEY SOUP

INGREDIENTS

1 (1.1oz/30g) package dried porcini mushrooms

1 cup boiling water

2 tbsp olive oil

2 medium celery stalks, chopped

2 medium carrots, peeled and chopped

1 medium yellow onion, finely chopped

3 cups assorted mushrooms (shiitake, cremini, button, portobello), coarsely chopped

8 cups beef broth

½ cup pearl barley, rinsed and drained

½ tsp dried thyme

½ tsp dried basil

½ tsp kosher salt

½ tsp freshly ground black pepper

2 tbsp minced fresh flat-leaf parsley

Did your ancestors bring recipes from the old country that "by accident" omitted the main ingredient? A beloved relative of ours was famous for her meatless meatballs, fruit-free cherry cake, and, of course, her impeccable mushroom-less mushroom barley soup. We've done little to improve her genius. We just added an ingredient.

DIRECTIONS

1) Place dried porcini mushrooms in a small bowl and cover with boiling water, letting stand for 20 minutes or until softened. Drain mushrooms, rinse well and finely chop. Set aside. 2) Heat olive oil in a large soup pot over medium heat. Add celery, carrots and onions. Stirring frequently, cook for 5 minutes until tender. Add the 3 cups of fresh assorted mushrooms and cook for another 5 minutes until they begin to brown and release their liquid. Raise heat to high and add broth, chopped porcini mushrooms, barley, thyme, basil, salt and pepper. Bring to a boil. Reduce heat to low, cover partially and simmer for 1 hour, until barley is tender. Stir in fresh parsley and serve.

Serves 8

BITE ME BIT

Freud had a fetish for fungi. "On an expedition for the purpose, he would often leave the children and...then creep silently up to it and suddenly pounce to capture the fungus with his hat as if it were a bird or butterfly," wrote biographer Ernest Jones. We'll let you interpret the meaning.

ROASTED CARROT SOUP TOPPED with CANDIED PISTACHIOS

INGREDIENTS

Candied Pistachios

3 tbsp corn syrup

1 tbsp sugar

¼ tsp kosher salt

1¼ cups shelled pistachio nuts

Carrot Soup

2 lbs carrots, peeled and cut into 1½-inch cubes

2 large parsnips, peeled and cut into 1½-inch cubes

2 tbsp olive oil

2 tbsp honey

½ tsp kosher salt

1 tbsp butter

¾ cup chopped red onion

8 cups chicken broth

¼ tsp kosher salt

Beep, beep, beep. Our carotene-enhanced bionic eyesight is at labor. We spy nutrient-rich, sweet roasted carrot and golden parsnip soup sprinkled with crunchy candied pistachios. Diners are taking spoons. Inserting them into beta-carotene bowls. They are smiling. Over.

DIRECTIONS

1) For the pistachios, preheat oven to 325°F. Line a baking sheet with parchment paper. In a small bowl, combine corn syrup, sugar, salt and nuts. Spread nuts on prepared baking sheet and bake 15 minutes, stirring every 5 minutes. Remove from oven, cool completely and chop into coarse pieces. These can be made up to 2 days ahead and stored in an airtight container. 2) For the soup, preheat oven to 400°F. Line a baking sheet with aluminum foil and coat with non-stick cooking spray. 3) In a large bowl, toss carrots, parsnips, olive oil, honey and ½ tsp salt. Pour onto prepared baking sheet in a single layer. Bake 35-40 minutes, stirring once halfway through. Remove from oven when carrots and parsnips are tender and lightly browned. Set aside. 4) In a large soup pot, melt butter over medium heat. Add onion and cook until tender but not browned, about 3-4 minutes. Add the roasted carrots, parsnips and chicken broth. Bring to a boil, reduce heat to low, cover and cook until carrots and parsnips are extremely tender, about 40 minutes. Remove from heat and allow to cool slightly. 5) Using a hand held or countertop blender, puree the soup until smooth. Season with ¼ tsp salt and garnish each serving with a tablespoon of chopped candied pistachios.

Serves 6-8

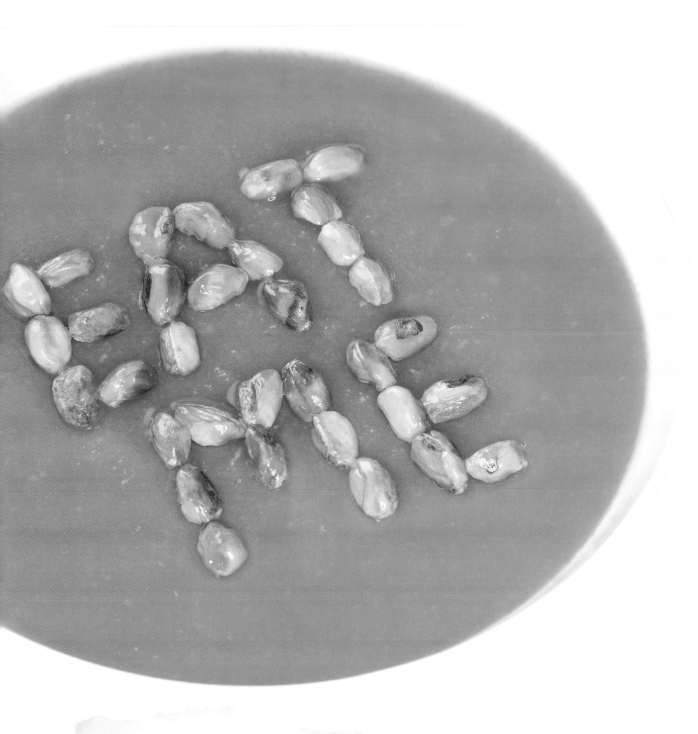

BITE ME BIT

"A fool bolts a door with a boiled carrot."

– Proverb

RESTORATIVE ROASTED VEGETABLE SOUP

INGREDIENTS

2 large carrots, peeled and cut into 1-inch cubes

1 large sweet potato, peeled and cut into 1-inch cubes

2 medium zucchini, cut into 1-inch cubes

1 large red bell pepper, cut into 1-inch cubes

1 medium red onion, cut into 1-inch cubes

1 cup mushrooms, peeled and quartered

3 tbsp olive oil

½ tsp kosher salt

3 sprigs fresh rosemary

1 cup water

8 cups chicken broth

3 boneless, skinless chicken breast halves, cut into ½-inch cubes

2 cups cooked bowtie pasta

These days everything from souvlaki to astrology is considered good for the soul. Though we love Greek food and stargazing, our souls get fully nourished by this satisfying soup packed with roasted vegetables, succulent chicken and bowtie pasta.

DIRECTIONS

1) Preheat oven to 375°F. Line a baking sheet with aluminum foil and coat with non-stick cooking spray. 2) In a large bowl, combine carrots, sweet potato, zucchini, red pepper, onion and mushrooms. Add olive oil and salt, tossing well to coat. Spread vegetables out on prepared baking sheet and nestle rosemary sprigs among the vegetables. Bake for 40-45 minutes, stirring occasionally. When vegetables are done cooking, discard rosemary sprigs. 3) In a large soup pot, combine 1 cup of water, chicken broth and cubed chicken breasts. Bring to a boil over high heat. Reduce heat to medium-low and simmer for 10 minutes. Add the roasted vegetables and simmer another 10 minutes. Add cooked pasta and heat through.

Serves 8

BITE ME BIT

"It takes more than just a good looking body. You've got to have the heart and soul to go with it."

– Epictetus, Greek philosopher

POTATO SOUP with SPICED CHICKPEAS

INGREDIENTS

Roasted Chickpeas

1¾ cups canned chickpeas, drained, rinsed and patted dry

1 tbsp olive oil

1 tbsp soy sauce

1 tsp sesame oil

½ tsp chili powder

Potato Soup

2 tbsp butter

1 small yellow onion, diced

½ tsp kosher salt

¼ tsp freshly ground black pepper

2 large Yukon Gold potatoes, peeled and diced

2 cups diced zucchini

4 cups chicken broth

2 tsp chopped fresh mint leaves

Our Dad often refers to Lisa and me as "The Twisted Sisters." We can't disagree. We're two girls who like surprises. Take our silky smooth potato soup. We've added zucchini, which, much like Lisa's personality, lends a mellow and delicate flavor, enhancing the traditional soup. As for myself, I'm more like the spice-roasted chickpeas scattered atop – zippy, biting and salty.

DIRECTIONS

1) For the chickpeas, preheat oven to 400°F. Line a baking sheet with aluminum foil and coat with non-stick cooking spray. Spread chickpeas on baking sheet and drizzle with olive oil. Roast for 30 minutes, shaking the pan once or twice during baking. Remove from oven. 2) In a small bowl, stir together soy sauce, sesame oil and chili powder. Toss with chickpeas and set aside to serve as soup garnish. 3) For the soup, in a large soup pot, melt butter over medium-low heat. Add onion, salt and pepper and cook covered, stirring occasionally for 4-5 minutes, until onion begins to soften but not brown. Add potatoes, cooking uncovered for 3 minutes. Stir in zucchini and chicken broth, bringing to a boil over high heat. Cover and turn down to low, simmering until potatoes are tender, about 20 minutes. 4) Remove from heat and puree the soup (using a hand held or countertop blender) until smooth. Re-warm soup if necessary. Taste for additional salt or pepper. Stir in chopped mint. Garnish each serving with a spoonful of roasted chickpeas.

Serves 6-8

BITE ME BIT

"He was so twisted he could eat soup with a corkscrew."

– Myra Langtry (actress Annette Bening) in the 1990 movie "The Grifters"

TOMATO SOUP with GRILLED CHEESE CROUTONS

If Andy Warhol had tasted our deeply flavored roasted tomato soup, we're confident he would have chosen it over the bland canned variety. We can picture the canvas…bowl after bowl of velvety, steaming tomato puree topped with crispy mini grilled cheese croutons…a comfort-food masterpiece that'll be remembered long past 15 minutes.

INGREDIENTS

Tomato Soup

2 (28oz/796ml) cans diced tomatoes

2 tbsp olive oil

¼ tsp kosher salt

⅛ tsp freshly ground black pepper

2 tbsp olive oil

1 small yellow onion, diced

2 medium carrots, peeled and diced

2 medium celery stalks, diced

1 large garlic clove, minced

2 tbsp flour

3 cups chicken broth

1 dried bay leaf

2 tsp sugar

¼ tsp kosher salt

¼ tsp freshly ground black pepper

2 tbsp butter

2 tbsp chopped fresh basil

Grilled Cheese Croutons

4 slices white bread

2 tbsp margarine

2 slices cheddar cheese

DIRECTIONS

1) Preheat oven to 425°F. Cover a baking sheet with aluminum foil and coat with non-stick cooking spray. Strain tomatoes, reserving their juices in a medium bowl. Spread strained tomatoes on prepared baking sheet, drizzle with 2 tbsp olive oil and season with ¼ tsp salt and ⅛ tsp pepper. Roast in oven for 15 minutes.
2) While the tomatoes are roasting, in a large soup pot, heat remaining 2 tbsp olive oil over medium-low heat. Add onion, carrots, celery and garlic, cooking until softened, about 8 minutes. Add flour and stir to coat. Over high heat, add the roasted tomatoes, reserved tomato juices, chicken broth, bay leaf, sugar, salt and pepper. Bring to a boil and reduce to a gentle simmer, cover and continue to simmer for 30 minutes. 3) Remove from heat, discard bay leaf and puree the soup (using a hand held or countertop blender) until smooth. Stir in 2 tbsp butter and chopped basil.
4) For the croutons, spread margarine on both sides of bread slices. Heat a frying pan over medium heat and place 2 slices in the pan. Top each with 1 slice of cheese and place remaining bread slices on the cheese. Cook for 2 minutes, until underside is golden brown, flip and cook 1-2 minutes more. Remove from pan, cooling a few minutes before slicing. Cut into 1-inch squares and sprinkle a small handful on each bowl of soup.

Serves 10-12

INCROYABLE FRENCH ONION SOUP

INGREDIENTS

2 tbsp olive oil

2 tbsp butter

6 medium white onions, halved and thinly sliced (about 9 cups sliced)

2 tsp flour

1 tsp sugar

½ tsp kosher salt

½ tsp freshly ground black pepper

2 sprigs of fresh thyme

2 dried bay leaves

⅓ cup port wine

1 cup dry red wine

4½ cups beef broth

1 cup chicken broth

¼ tsp kosher salt

Topping

6-8 baguette slices, cut crosswise ½-inch thick, lightly toasted on both sides (350°F oven, 5 minutes per side)

½ lb Gruyère cheese, thinly sliced (easily done with cheese slicer)

2 tbsp freshly grated Parmesan cheese

Bonjour! Je suis Laurence, la meilleure amie française de Julie. Lorsqu'elle m'a demandé de goûter à sa soupe à l'oignon française, sans rire, je me suis inquiétée. Elle n'a tellement rien à voir avec la France et le fait qu'elle porte un béret ne veut pas dire qu'elle soit capable de réussir cet emblème gastronomique national. En fait, je n'avais pas à m'inquiéter. Sa soupe était aussi authentique que celles que l'on peut déguster dans les environs de la Tour Eiffel. Le bouillon était riche, le Gruyère absolument savoureux et les oignons caramélisés à la perfection. Bien joué, mon amie anglophone, bien joué! (transl. This onion soup is great.)

DIRECTIONS

1) For the onion soup, in a large cast iron soup pot, heat olive oil and butter over high heat. Add onions, continuing to cook on high heat for 5 minutes, stirring occasionally. Reduce heat to medium-low, cooking 40-45 minutes, stirring often until the onions are tender and caramelized. 2) Stir in flour, sugar, salt, pepper, thyme and bay leaves, cooking for 1 minute. Increase heat to high, add port and red wine and bring to a boil. Boil for 2 minutes. Add beef broth and chicken broth and return to a boil. Reduce heat to low. Cook covered for 15 minutes, remove cover and continue cooking 30-35 minutes more. Remove and discard thyme sprigs and bay leaves. Adjust seasoning with an additional ¼ tsp kosher salt if desired. 3) To serve, adjust an oven rack to the upper-middle position. Preheat broiler. 4) Set 6 oven-safe crock bowls on a baking sheet. Fill each dish with hot soup, top with toasted baguette slice, cover with sliced Gruyère cheese and sprinkle with Parmesan. Broil until the cheese is golden and bubbly, 2-3 minutes.

Serves 6 (large bowls) or 8 (smaller bowls)

SOUTHWESTERN CHICKEN CORN CHOWDER

INGREDIENTS

1 tbsp butter

1 small yellow onion, chopped

1 large red bell pepper, chopped

1 (28oz/796ml) can diced tomatoes, drained

½ cup canned chopped green chilies

3 cups creamed corn

2 cups frozen corn kernels, defrosted

2 cups chicken broth

¼ tsp kosher salt

¼ tsp freshly ground black pepper

3 boneless, skinless chicken breast halves, cooked and shredded

1 cup milk

¾ cup shredded Monterey Jack cheese

1 cup crumbled tortilla chips, for topping

New England and Manhattan have hogged the spotlight long enough. There's a new chowder in town – say goodbye to clams and crackers and ¡hola! to corn and tortillas. The taste of this creamy, flavor-packed chowder comes from the combo of sweet yellow kernels and nacho toppings. For an added Southwestern kick drizzle on some hot sauce and you'll be warmed from your nose down to your toes.

DIRECTIONS

1) In a large soup pot, melt butter over medium-high heat. Add onion and bell pepper, cooking until softened, about 5 minutes. Add the diced tomatoes and chopped chilies, mixing well. 2) Stir in the creamed corn, corn kernels, chicken broth, salt, pepper, shredded chicken and milk. Increase heat to high, bring to a boil and then reduce heat to low, simmering for 25 minutes. 3) Stir in the cheese, mixing until melted. Top each portion with crushed chips.

Serves 6

BITE ME BIT

"Corn chowder. That's an interesting choice. You do know that cellulite is one of the main ingredients in corn chowder."

– Nigel (actor Stanley Tucci) in the 2006 movie "The Devil Wears Prada"

Whoopsie

Recipes for Disaster

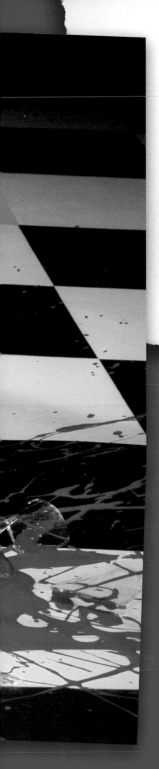

Curse you, telephone, for ringing. Without fail, I say "hello" and instantly morph into Blunder Woman. A great convo has caused me to: use coriander instead of parsley, salt in place of sugar, burn everything from toast to rice and has led to the top getting blown off a pressure cooker. Friends, if you're reading this, don't call me during cooking time. But, if you must, here's what I'll do should (read: when) things go wrong…

THE SOUP IS A SALT MINE You read tablespoon instead of teaspoon and end up with a pot of sodium soup. You can add a raw potato (peeled and cut into chunks) to soak up some of the salt by simmering for 15 minutes and then removing the potato. As well, sugar and cider vinegar (1 teaspoon of each) can also neutralize the damage. Finally, adding extra vegetables will go far in diluting the excess.

MY MOUTH IS A 10-ALARM BLAZE Spice is nice in salsa, chili and curry, but, if there's too much, here are a few handy-dandy extinguishers: sugar (a can of crushed pineapple in the salsa or chili), acids (lime juice in the salsa) or dairy (yogurt in the curry, sour cream to top the chili).

THE VEGETABLES ARE OVERCOOKED If only there was Viagra for limp vegetables. But until that invention comes around – and we hope Bob Dole will be plugging it – we will have to put them in the food processor and puree. Some suggestions include broccoli or cauliflower with cheddar and fresh herbs, carrots with cream and salt or sweet potatoes with maple syrup and a touch of cinnamon.

THE COOKIES ARE BAKING UNEVENLY Remove the slightly brown cookies to a cooling rack. Return the under-baked cookies to the oven; make sure the tray is placed in the center of the oven to allow heat to circulate. Rotating your baking sheet from front to back halfway through baking is another option if your cookies are browning unevenly. As well, reduce the risk of burned bottoms by baking your cookies on light-colored cookie sheets with a dull finish.

WHITE BEAN SOUP with SPINACH and COUSCOUS

INGREDIENTS

2 tsp olive oil

2 leeks, rinsed well, white portions chopped and green discarded

2 large garlic cloves, minced

2 tsp ground cumin

8 cups chicken broth

3 cups canned white kidney (cannellini) beans, rinsed and drained

2 dried bay leaves

½ cup whole-wheat couscous

2 cups fresh spinach leaves, packed tight

Kosher salt and freshly ground black pepper to taste

Bean soups can be like exercise bikes. They're healthy, convenient and make you feel virtuous. But sometimes you want to feel like you're going places, having new experiences. This exotic spin on a Tuscan tradition relies on leeks, the mild cousin of the onion, for their subtle flavor, creamy beans for their rich texture, and couscous, with a nutty taste that makes every trip to the bowl delightful and surprising.

DIRECTIONS

1) Heat oil in a large soup pot over medium-high heat. Add leeks and garlic, sautéing 2 minutes or until tender. 2) Stir in cumin. Add broth, white beans and bay leaves. Over high heat, bring to a boil. 3) Add couscous, reduce heat to low, cover and simmer for 5 minutes. 4) Remove bay leaves and discard. Stir in spinach and cook until wilted, about 30 seconds. Season with salt and pepper.

Serves 6

BITE ME BIT

"He couldn't ad-lib a fart after a baked bean dinner."

– Johnny Carson, TV talk show host and comedian

NUTTY BUTTERNUT SQUASH SOUP

INGREDIENTS

2 tsp vegetable oil

1 small yellow onion, diced

1 large garlic clove, minced

1 tbsp mild curry powder

2 tsp ground cumin

½ tsp kosher salt

6 cups chicken broth

3 cups peeled and chopped butternut squash

1 cup peeled and shredded carrots

1½ cups cooked white rice (basmati, jasmine or instant rice)

1 cup frozen green peas, thawed

6 tbsp smooth peanut butter

½ tsp kosher salt

This unusual combination could be billed as a gastronomic prizefight, peanut butter in one corner, butternut squash in the other. But the heavyweights come together amazingly on the palate, the smooth peanut butter lending a luscious tinge to the full-flavored squash.

DIRECTIONS

1) In a large soup pot, heat oil over medium-low heat. Add onion and garlic, cooking 4-5 minutes, or until softened, stirring occasionally. Add curry powder, cumin and ½ tsp salt. Cook for 1 minute, stirring constantly. 2) Add chicken broth, butternut squash and carrots. Over high heat, bring to a boil. Reduce heat to low, cover and simmer for 20 minutes until the squash has softened. 3) Stir in the rice, peas, peanut butter and ½ tsp salt. Cook uncovered for 3 minutes until ingredients are blended.

Serves 6

BITE ME BIT

"C'mon, he's insane. Look. Right now he's probably dancing around in his grandma's panties, yeah, rubbing himself in peanut butter."

– Detective Dave Mills (actor Brad Pitt) in the 1995 movie "Se7en"

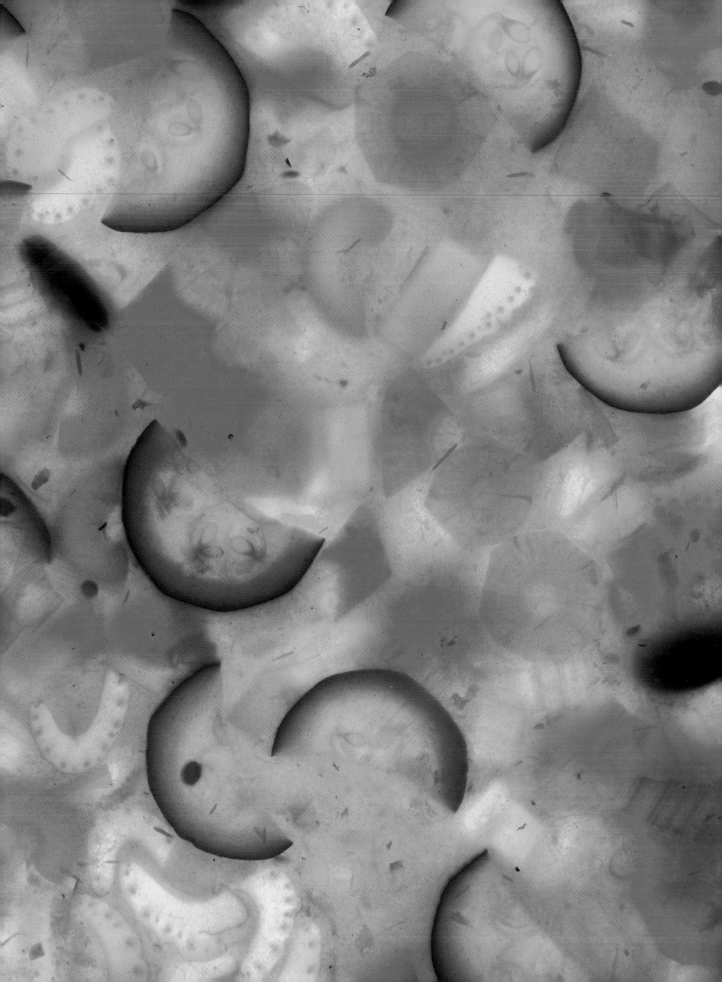

MINESTRONE SOUP with PESTO DRIZZLE

INGREDIENTS

Minestrone Soup

3 tbsp olive oil

2 large garlic cloves, chopped

1 medium yellow onion, chopped

5 medium celery stalks, chopped

5 medium carrots, peeled and chopped

5 cups chicken broth

1 (28oz/796ml) can diced tomatoes, with liquid

2 cups tomato sauce

½ cup dry red wine

2 cups fresh baby spinach

1½ cups canned red kidney beans, rinsed and drained

2 large zucchini, chopped

2 tbsp chopped fresh basil

1 tbsp chopped fresh oregano

1 tbsp sugar

½ tsp kosher salt

¼ tsp freshly ground black pepper

1 cup cooked seashell pasta

Pesto Drizzle

1 cup loosely packed fresh basil leaves

1 small garlic clove

¼ cup pine nuts

¼ cup freshly grated Parmesan cheese

½ tsp kosher salt

¼ cup olive oil

As typically Italian as Fiat and Benetton, this rich-tasting soup transports us to Firenze. No, not Florence, Italy, but the strip mall ristorante that ignited our childhood love for all things Italian, especially frescos of naked and boozing burly men and voluptuous women. Titillating for sure, but nothing grabbed our attention more than Mary's minestrone. As soon as she'd set down the steaming, vegetable-packed rich broth, focus turned to the full-bodied soup. Now, though Mary and her minestrone are gone, we've got her legendary soup recreated to perfection...only thing missing is the bacchanalian mural.

DIRECTIONS

1) In a large soup pot, heat olive oil over medium-low heat and sauté garlic and onion for 4-5 minutes. Add celery and carrots, sautéing for an additional 5 minutes. 2) Add broth, diced tomatoes (with liquid) and tomato sauce. Bring to a boil over high heat. Turn to low and add red wine, spinach, kidney beans, zucchini, basil, oregano, sugar, salt and pepper. Simmer uncovered for 30 minutes. 3) Add cooked pasta and simmer for 2-3 minutes to combine flavors. 4) For the pesto sauce, place basil leaves and garlic in a food processor and process until leaves are finely chopped. Add pine nuts and process until nuts are finely chopped. Add cheese and salt, processing until combined. With the machine running, add olive oil in a slow, steady stream until the oil is incorporated. This sauce yields ⅓ cup and, if you're not using it immediately, store it covered in the refrigerator to prevent the sauce from turning brown. 5) Drizzle 1 tsp of pesto sauce over each bowl of soup.

Serves 8-10

RAJ'S VEGETABLE LENTIL SOUP

INGREDIENTS

2 tbsp olive oil

1 large celery stalk, chopped

1 large carrot, peeled and chopped

1 medium parsnip, peeled and chopped

1 small shallot, diced

1 large garlic clove, minced

1 tsp grated fresh ginger

1½ tsp curry powder

½ tsp ground cumin

⅛ tsp crushed red pepper flakes

5 cups chicken broth

1 cup dried green lentils

½ tsp kosher salt

¼ tsp freshly ground black pepper

½ cup sour cream

2 tbsp chopped fresh mint

I've been Punk'd, Bollywood style. After teaching me all I ever wanted to know about cricket and Shah Rukh Khan films, my friend Raj moved on to Indian cuisine. I felt honored to get this spiced, vegetable-packed lentil soup recipe "straight from grandmother's Calcutta kitchen." Turns out, his grandmother learned it from her Mahjong partner in Fort Lauderdale.

DIRECTIONS

1) In a large soup pot, heat oil over medium heat. Add celery, carrot, parsnip, shallot, garlic and ginger. Cook stirring until softened, about 5 minutes. Add curry powder, cumin and crushed red pepper flakes. Stir constantly until spices are fragrant, about 1 minute. 2) Add the chicken broth, lentils, salt and pepper. Bring to a boil over high heat. Reduce heat to low and simmer covered until lentils are tender, about 25 minutes. 3) Remove 2 cups of soup and puree using a hand held or countertop blender. Return smooth puree back into the remaining soup in the pot. Stir well, adjusting salt and pepper to taste. 4) Ladle soup into bowls and top each serving with a spoonful of sour cream and a sprinkle of fresh mint.

Serves 6

BITE ME BIT

"These can never be true friends: hope, dice, a prostitute, a robber, a cheat, a goldsmith, a monkey, a doctor, a distiller."

– Indian proverb

MOROCCAN SPICED CHICKEN SOUP

INGREDIENTS

2 tbsp butter

1 medium yellow onion, chopped

2 large celery stalks, chopped

2 large carrots, peeled and chopped

1 tsp ground cinnamon

1 tsp ground turmeric

1 tsp ground cumin

½ tsp kosher salt

¼ tsp freshly ground black pepper

1 (28oz/796ml) can crushed tomatoes

3½ cups canned chickpeas, rinsed and drained

7 cups chicken broth

1 cup dried green lentils

1 cup uncooked angel hair pasta, broken into 1-inch pieces

2 boneless, skinless chicken breast halves, cooked and shredded

¼ cup chopped fresh flat-leaf parsley

I'm pretty literal. When The Clash tells me to "Rock The Casbah" who am I to refuse this invitation? I called on the conductor (aka Lisa) to compose a big hit – a thick, hearty and full-bodied soup that would deliver all the allure and rich spices of Morocco. Packed with chickpeas, lentils, noodles and North African flavors, this fragrant soup will take you right to the narrow alleyways and bustling bazaars. Gotta go – London's Calling.

DIRECTIONS

1) In a large soup pot, melt butter over medium-low heat. Add onion, celery and carrots, cooking until softened, about 8-10 minutes. Add cinnamon, turmeric, cumin, salt and pepper and cook, stirring for 2 minutes. 2) Stir in crushed tomatoes, chickpeas, chicken broth and lentils. Bring to a boil and then reduce heat to low, simmering uncovered until lentils are tender, about 30-35 minutes. 3) Add pasta and cook for 5 minutes or until softened. Stir in shredded chicken and parsley, cooking until heated through.

Serves 6

IAN MUGGRIDGE'S TUSCAN BREAD SOUP

INGREDIENTS

1 French bread (about ½ lb, preferably day-old), cut into 1½-inch cubes

2 tbsp olive oil

¼ tsp kosher salt

2 tbsp olive oil

1 medium white onion, chopped

2 medium garlic cloves, minced

3 lbs plum tomatoes cut into wedges (reserve 6 wedges for garnish at the end)

2 large red bell peppers, chopped

1 cup dry white wine

6 cups chicken broth

2 dried bay leaves

¼ tsp kosher salt

¼ tsp freshly ground black pepper

Poached Eggs

2 cups water

¼ cup distilled white vinegar

6 large eggs

¼ cup sliced fresh basil

1 cup fresh Parmesan cheese, shaved with a vegetable peeler

We confess – we fancy this man we call "Mugsy." He's a great bloke, superb food stylist and chef extraordinaire. Though he doesn't have a Tuscan bone in his body (Brit to the core), he has generously shared his smashing soup of rustic bread, hearty tomato broth and garlic, finished with a fab poached egg on top. Cheerio, Chap.

DIRECTIONS

1) Preheat oven to 300°F. In a large bowl, combine bread cubes with 2 tbsp olive oil and ¼ tsp kosher salt. Toss to coat and spread out on a baking sheet. Bake 30-40 minutes, until the cubes are crisp all the way through. Remove from oven and set aside. 2) In a large soup pot, heat 2 tbsp olive oil over medium heat. Add onion and sauté until softened, about 4 minutes. Add minced garlic, cooking until fragrant, about 1 minute. Add tomato wedges and sauté until they start to break down, about 3 minutes. Stir in red peppers and white wine, continuing to cook on medium heat for 15 minutes. Add chicken broth and bay leaves. Bring to a boil, reduce heat to a gentle simmer and cook another 15 minutes. Remove from heat and strain liquid through a fine mesh sieve, discarding solids. Return soup to pot, season with salt and pepper and keep hot. 3) For the poached eggs, in a small saucepan, heat the water and vinegar over low heat. When water is simmering, gently crack 2 eggs at a time into the water and poach for 2-3 minutes. Remove and plunge into a bowl filled with ice water. Yolks should be runny. Repeat with remaining eggs. 4) To serve, ladle soup into bowls. Add toasted bread cubes, reserved tomato wedges, basil and poached egg. Finish with shaved Parmesan cheese. Serve immediately.

Serves 6

unDress me

Eye-Popping Salads

STRAWBERRY SALAD with SUGARED ALMONDS

INGREDIENTS

Sugared Almonds

¼ cup sugar

2 tsp water

¾ cup slivered almonds

Poppy Seed Dressing

¼ cup sugar

¼ cup mayonnaise

2 tbsp milk

1 tbsp white vinegar

2 tsp poppy seeds

8 cups romaine lettuce torn into bite-size pieces

1 cup sliced strawberries

½ cup dried cranberries

Some people believe strawberries are an aphrodisiac, others, that almonds bring good fortune. So get lucky with our "perfect bite" — a fork crammed with crisp lettuce, scarlet strawberries and sugared almonds, all coated in a sweet-and-sour poppy seed dressing.

DIRECTIONS

1) For the almonds, in a medium saucepan, combine sugar and water. Cook over medium heat until sugar dissolves. Add slivered almonds and stir to coat. Continue to cook and stir until sugar and almonds turn golden. Remove from heat and place almonds on a piece of aluminum foil that has been coated with non-stick cooking spray. 2) For the dressing, in a small bowl, whisk sugar, mayonnaise, milk, vinegar and poppy seeds. 3) In a large bowl, combine lettuce, strawberries, cranberries and sugared almonds. Toss with dressing and serve.

Serves 6

BITE ME BIT

A recent U.S. survey found that strawberry-lovers are happy, fun-loving and smart people; strawberry-haters are weird, dull and picky. Did we mention that we love strawberries?

MIXED GREENS with SQUASH, PECANS and PEARS

INGREDIENTS

Spicy Pecans

1 cup coarsely chopped pecans

1 tbsp olive oil

¼ tsp ground cumin

¼ tsp ground cinnamon

¼ tsp chili powder

⅛ tsp cayenne pepper, optional

Sweet Squash

3 cups peeled and cubed butternut squash

2 tbsp olive oil

2 tbsp maple syrup

¾ tsp kosher salt

Vinaigrette

3 tbsp balsamic vinegar

1 tbsp Dijon mustard

1 tbsp packed brown sugar

¼ tsp kosher salt

¼ cup olive oil

8 cups loosely packed mixed salad greens

2 large pears, cored and thinly sliced

½ cup dried cranberries

DIRECTIONS

1) Preheat oven to 450°F. Line a baking sheet with aluminum foil and coat with non-stick cooking spray. 2) For the pecans, in a small bowl, toss pecans with olive oil, cumin, cinnamon, chili powder and cayenne. Spread pecans out on prepared baking sheet. Bake 5 minutes or until lightly toasted. Set aside to cool. 3) For the squash, line a baking sheet with aluminum foil and coat with non-stick cooking spray. In a medium bowl, toss cubed squash with olive oil, syrup and salt. Spread on prepared baking sheet and roast for 20 minutes, stir and continue to cook for an additional 5-10 minutes until squash is tender and lightly browned. Set aside to cool.
4) For the dressing, in a small bowl, whisk vinegar, Dijon mustard, brown sugar and salt. Continue to whisk, slowly adding olive oil until combined. 5) In a large serving bowl, gently toss salad greens with 2 tbsp of dressing to lightly coat. Add pecans, squash, pears and dried cranberries. Drizzle salad with remaining dressing.

Serves 6-8

116 SEDUCED BY THE SALAD

It was a dark and stormy night. The Duke's eyes were locked on her cascading hair and heaving bosom. He knew the scandal could ruin him, but he couldn't look away. The innocent country girl set down his salad, her tapered fingers brushing his arm, igniting his forbidden desire. She remained at his side as he picked up his fork and took a mouthful of the sweet roasted squash, spicy pecans and juicy pears. He took another bite as she ripped off her bodice. He took another bite as she beckoned him. He took another bite as she got her clothes back on and ran off sobbing. His heart swelled for the salad, and the salad alone.

MANGO and CRANBERRY SALAD with HONEY MUSTARD DRESSING

INGREDIENTS

Sugared Pecans

1 large egg white

1 tbsp water

4 cups pecan halves

1 cup sugar

1 tsp ground cinnamon

¾ tsp kosher salt

* Put half the sugared pecans in the salad – save the rest for a sweet snack.

Honey Mustard Dressing

¼ cup honey

¼ cup seed mustard

¼ cup honey mustard

¼ cup rice vinegar

¼ cup canola oil

2 tbsp orange juice

¼ tsp kosher salt

10 cups romaine lettuce torn into bite-size pieces

2 mangoes, peeled and diced

¼ cup dried cranberries

How is this sweet and savory salad like a little black dress? Indispensable, versatile and timeless, it too will be a dramatic statement at brunch or an elegant complement to a dinner party. Though both the greens and the frock are easily dressed up, only one will look good with chicken and goat cheese on it.

DIRECTIONS

1) For the pecans, preheat oven to 250°F. Coat a baking sheet with non-stick cooking spray. In a large bowl, whisk the egg white and water until bubbles form. In a medium bowl, mix sugar, cinnamon and salt. Add pecans to egg whites, mixing to coat. Add sugar mixture, tossing pecans until they are coated. Spread pecans on prepared baking sheet and bake for 1 hour, stirring every 20 minutes. 2) For the dressing, in a medium bowl, whisk honey, seed mustard, honey mustard, vinegar, oil, orange juice and salt. 3) In a large bowl, place lettuce, diced mango and cranberries. Add ½ cup sugared pecans and salad dressing, tossing well to combine.

Serves 6

TLT (The Larry T) SALAD

INGREDIENTS

Croutons

8 slices French baguette, cut into ½-inch cubes

1 tbsp olive oil

¼ cup freshly grated Parmesan cheese

1 tsp kosher salt

Creamy Basil Dressing

¾ cup mayonnaise

¼ cup finely chopped fresh basil

3 tbsp white wine vinegar

10 cups romaine lettuce torn into bite-size pieces

3 cups cherry tomatoes, halved

8 slices turkey bacon, cooked crisp and crumbled

1 avocado, peeled and diced

Our Dad has taught us a lot about eating – in Larry-Land, meatloaf is an appetizer and there's always room for a hot dog. So, in his honor we've named this dish after him. He might be surprised (read: aghast) that we chose a bowl of greens, but, since this He-man-sized salad is a deconstructed BLT coated in creamy basil dressing, we're confident we'll have his blessing.

DIRECTIONS

1) For the croutons, preheat oven to 350°F. Coat a baking sheet with non-stick cooking spray. In a large bowl, toss bread cubes with olive oil. Add Parmesan and salt, tossing well. Spread pieces on baking sheet and bake 15 minutes, stirring frequently. 2) For the dressing, in a small bowl, whisk mayonnaise, basil and vinegar. 3) In a large bowl, combine lettuce, tomatoes, turkey bacon, avocado and croutons. Add dressing and toss to coat.

Serves 6

BITE ME BIT

"After a good dinner one can forgive anybody, even one's own relatives."

– Oscar Wilde, playwright

COBB SALAD featuring TINSELTOWN (aka Thousand Island) DRESSING

INGREDIENTS

Dressing

1 cup mayonnaise

4 tbsp ketchup

2 tbsp white vinegar

1 tbsp sugar

2 tsp sweet green relish

¼ tsp kosher salt

¼ tsp freshly ground black pepper

Cobb Salad

8 cups romaine lettuce torn into bite-size pieces

6 turkey bacon slices, cooked crisp and crumbled

5 boneless, skinless chicken breast halves, cooked and diced

3 large eggs, hard boiled and finely chopped

3 large tomatoes, seeded and diced

2 avocados, pitted, peeled and diced

¾ cup crumbled blue cheese

DIRECTIONS

1) For the dressing, in a medium bowl, whisk mayonnaise, ketchup, vinegar, sugar, relish, salt and pepper. Set aside until ready to use (this recipe makes extra dressing for you to keep in the refrigerator for up to 1 week). 2) In a large bowl, combine lettuce, turkey bacon, diced chicken, egg, tomatoes, avocado and blue cheese. Gently toss with desired amount of dressing.

Serves 6

1937, Hollywood

BROWN DERBY - MIDNIGHT:

BOB COBB stands in his empty restaurant kitchen. Hungry. Alone. Chefless. He opens the fridge and pulls out handfuls of produce, eggs, chicken, bacon and cheese. Chops them up and tosses them together. Takes a large forkful, chews and swallows.

BOB (voice-over) Hey, this is a good salad. Wonder what I should call it?

CUT TO

2009, Toronto

ALBERT KITCHEN - 5:55pm:

JULIE ALBERT stands in the empty kitchen. Alone. Chefless. Five minutes until the hungry horde descends. She opens the fridge and pulls out handfuls of produce, eggs, chicken, turkey bacon and cheese. She chops them up and tosses them together.

JULIE (in a loud voice) Dinner's ready.

JULIE (whispering to the camera) I love you, Bob Cobb.

CREAMY CAESAR CARDINI SALAD

INGREDIENTS

8 cups romaine lettuce torn into bite-size pieces

1½ cups croutons

½ cup freshly grated Parmesan cheese

Creamy Caesar Dressing

¼ cup mayonnaise

¼ cup buttermilk

½ small garlic clove, finely minced

2 tsp fresh lemon juice

½ tsp Dijon mustard

¼ tsp Worcestershire sauce

¼ tsp kosher salt

¼ tsp freshly ground black pepper

¼ cup olive oil

¾ cup freshly grated Parmesan cheese

A message to all friends, Romans and countrymen: Stop stealing our thunder. You can have your Coliseum, keep your ravioli, but you can't take credit for the all-powerful Caesar. It was Mexican restaurateur Caesar Cardini who, in 1924, tossed together crisp romaine and creamy dressing. All hail Cardini.

Sincerely, Concerned Citizens of the Tijuana Salad Society

PS. We'd also be open to crediting these two sisters for their version, an inspired, perfectly blended, creamy dressing with crunchy croutons and premium Parmesan.

DIRECTIONS

1) Place lettuce and croutons in a large bowl. 2) For the dressing, in a medium bowl, whisk mayonnaise, buttermilk, garlic, lemon juice, Dijon mustard, Worcestershire, salt and pepper until combined. Gradually add olive oil, continuing to whisk until incorporated. Fold in ¾ cup Parmesan cheese. Spoon dressing on lettuce and croutons, tossing to coat. Sprinkle with remaining ½ cup Parmesan cheese.

Serves 6

BITE ME BIT

"Why should Caesar get to stomp around like a giant, while the rest of us try not to get smushed under his big feet? What's so great about Caesar? Hm? Brutus is just as cute as Caesar. Brutus is just as smart as Caesar. People totally like Brutus just as much as they like Caesar."

– Gretchen (actress Lacey Chabert) in the 2004 movie "Mean Girls"

FIESTA BOWL SALAD

INGREDIENTS

1 head iceberg lettuce, chopped

4 tomatoes, seeded and diced

1 avocado, peeled and diced

1 roasted deli chicken, breast meat shredded

¾ cup shredded cheddar or Monterey Jack cheese

Salsa Dressing

½ cup sour cream

½ cup salsa

¼ cup mayonnaise

½ cup canned chopped green chilies

1 lime, juiced

1 tbsp sugar

½ tsp ground cumin

¼ tsp chili powder

2 cups crumbled tortilla chips, for topping

Lisa knows when to draw the line. Though she refused to name her twin girls Peyton and Eli, she continues to elate her husband with the best gridiron grub. Citrus-glazed wings for the Orange Bowl, creamy fudge for the Sugar Bowl and, whenever it's the Fiesta Bowl, she turns out this amazing Southwestern salad of chunky avocado, roasted chicken and a hearty dose of cheese and tortilla chips tossed in a spicy salsa dressing. Darling brother-in-law, you're in charge of the Rose Bowl.

DIRECTIONS

1) Place lettuce, tomatoes, avocado, chicken and grated cheese in a large bowl. 2) For the dressing, in a medium bowl, whisk sour cream, salsa, mayonnaise, chopped green chilies, lime juice, sugar, cumin and chili powder. 3) Add dressing to salad bowl, tossing well to coat. Sprinkle salad with crumbled tortilla chips.

Serves 4

BITE ME BIT

"The house does not rest upon the ground, but upon a woman."

— Mexican proverb

SWEET CHUTNEY CHICKEN SALAD

INGREDIENTS

5 boneless, skinless chicken breast halves

1 Granny Smith apple, diced

1 mango, peeled and diced

1 cup seedless red grapes, halved

1 cup chopped celery

¼ cup raisins

¼ cup salted cashews

Chutney Dressing

½ cup mayonnaise

¼ cup sour cream

3 tbsp mango chutney

2 tbsp fresh lime juice

1 tsp lime zest

1 tsp mild curry powder

1 tsp honey

¼ tsp kosher salt

Taking its cues from the sweet side of Indian cuisine, this healthy and refreshing chicken salad mingles sugary mango, juicy grapes and plump raisins with tart lime and crunchy apples. A winning, timeless and trouble-free marriage of East-West flavors.

DIRECTIONS

1) Place chicken in a medium saucepan, cover with cold water and bring to a boil over high heat. Reduce heat, cover saucepan and simmer for 13 minutes or until chicken is no longer pink inside. If you have the time, allow the chicken to cool in the water, but if not, remove cooked chicken and chop into bite-size pieces. 2) In a large bowl, combine chicken, apple, mango, grapes, celery, raisins and cashews. 3) For the dressing, in a medium bowl, whisk mayonnaise, sour cream, chutney, lime juice, lime zest, curry powder, honey and salt. Pour over chicken and toss well.

Serves 6

BITE ME BIT

"All you have to do is hold the chicken, bring me the toast, give me a check for the chicken salad sandwich and you haven't broken any rules."

– Bobby Dupea (actor Jack Nicholson) in the 1970 movie "Five Easy Pieces"

SOY-GLAZED CHICKEN SALAD with MAGICAL MANDARINS

INGREDIENTS

Soy-Glazed Chicken

6 boneless, skinless chicken breast halves, cubed

2 tbsp cornstarch

1 tbsp vegetable oil

¾ cup packed brown sugar

¾ cup soy sauce

½ cup water

¼ cup honey

2 tbsp cornstarch

1 tsp grated fresh ginger

Dressing

½ cup mayonnaise

¼ cup rice vinegar

2 tbsp sugar

1 tbsp sesame oil

1 tbsp soy sauce

1 head iceberg lettuce, shredded

2 medium carrots, peeled and grated

2 cups chow mein salad noodles

1½ cups canned mandarin orange segments, drained

¾ cup sliced water chestnuts, rinsed, drained and halved

2 tbsp toasted sesame seeds

If we need to go to our "happy place," Lisa and I know exactly what to do. We crack open a few cans of syrupy mandarin slices. Sweet, cold and juicy, they transport us back to the cozy living room of our beloved grandparents in the Big Apple, to dreamy childhood visits and hours spent slurping from little glass bowls. Now, thanks to this mandarin-topped, Asian-dressed salad of crispy lettuce, shredded carrots, water chestnuts and succulent soy-glazed chicken, we can easily slip into that bygone New York state of mind.

DIRECTIONS

1) Preheat oven to 425°F. Coat an 11x7-inch baking dish with non-stick cooking spray. 2) For the chicken, in a medium bowl, toss cubed chicken with 2 tbsp cornstarch. 3) In a large skillet, heat oil over medium heat. Add chicken and stir until lightly browned (but not cooked through), about 5 minutes. Transfer chicken to baking dish. 4) For the sauce, in a small bowl, whisk brown sugar, soy sauce, water, honey, cornstarch and ginger. Pour over chicken. Bake uncovered 18-20 minutes, stirring once halfway through baking. Remove from oven and let cool to room temperature. 5) For the salad dressing, in a medium bowl, whisk mayonnaise, rice vinegar, sugar, sesame oil and soy sauce. Chill until ready to use. 6) For the salad, spread shredded lettuce on a large platter. Add carrots, chow mein noodles, mandarins, water chestnuts and sprinkle with toasted sesame seeds. Place soy chicken in center and drizzle entire salad with dressing.

Serves 6-8

APPEL KOOLSLA (transl. APPLE COLESLAW)

INGREDIENTS

Spiced Pecans

1½ cups pecan halves

2 tbsp packed brown sugar

1 tbsp melted butter

1 tsp Worcestershire sauce

¼ tsp kosher salt

⅛ tsp garlic powder

Dressing

2 tbsp rice vinegar

1 tbsp apple cider vinegar

1 tsp Dijon mustard

1 tsp sugar

¼ tsp kosher salt

¼ cup olive oil

2 Granny Smith apples, peeled and cubed

1 tbsp fresh lemon juice

3 cups thinly sliced Napa cabbage

3 cups thinly sliced red cabbage

1 cup dried cherries or dried cranberries

1 medium mango, peeled and cut into ½-inch cubes

I tip my hat to the Dutch. Love their cheese, tulips and the way they make the uninviting word "COLE-slaw" sound appetizing. Pleasant to the ear and pleasing to the palate, this salad isn't your traditional limp, fluorescent mush – it's a sweet, tart and crunchy combo of apples, mango and spiced pecans tossed in a tangy vinaigrette. I'd say "smakelijk eten" but "bon appétit" sounds better.

DIRECTIONS

1) Preheat oven to 350°F. 2) For the pecans, in a large bowl, combine pecans, brown sugar, butter, Worcestershire, salt and garlic powder. Mix well. Spread mixture on a baking sheet and bake 12-15 minutes, stirring every 5 minutes, until lightly toasted. Set aside and cool completely. 3) For the dressing, in a small bowl, whisk rice vinegar, cider vinegar, Dijon mustard, sugar and salt. Gradually whisk in olive oil. 4) In a large bowl, toss sliced apples with lemon juice. Add the cabbage, mango and dried fruit to the apples. Mix with the dressing and chill for 30 minutes before serving to blend flavors. Add pecans just before serving.

Serves 6-8

CHINESE CHICKEN SALAD with CRUNCHY NOODLES

INGREDIENTS

Peanut Butter Chicken

6 boneless, skinless chicken breast halves, cubed

¼ cup smooth peanut butter

¼ cup soy sauce

1 tbsp honey

1 tbsp sesame oil

½ tsp grated fresh ginger

Hoisin Peanut Dressing

6 tbsp hoisin sauce

¼ cup rice vinegar

¼ cup packed brown sugar

¼ cup smooth peanut butter

1 tbsp sesame oil

1 tsp grated fresh ginger

Crunchy Noodles

1 (3oz/85g) package ramen noodles, crushed

¾ cup slivered almonds

1 tbsp melted butter

2 cups snow peas, trimmed and cut on the diagonal

2 cups peeled and grated carrots

1½ cups corn kernels

12 cups shredded iceberg lettuce

Chinese chicken salad wasn't the glorious creation of a steamed-out Shanghai kitchen – it came from big box, suburban restaurant chains that keep you waiting hours to eat their gooey food. That doesn't mean we don't like them but let's just say this, our homemade healthful rendition – a towering salad topped with peanuty chicken, crunchy baked noodles and golden almonds tossed in a sweet hoisin dressing – beats a trip to the mall any day.

DIRECTIONS

1) For the chicken, preheat oven to 350°F. Coat an 11x9-inch baking dish with non-stick cooking spray. Place cubed chicken in baking dish. 2) In a small bowl, whisk peanut butter, soy sauce, honey, sesame oil and ginger. Pour sauce over cubed chicken and bake for 25 minutes or until cooked through. Remove from the oven and cool to room temperature before adding to salad. 3) For the dressing, in a medium bowl, whisk hoisin, rice vinegar, brown sugar, peanut butter, sesame oil and ginger. Set aside. 4) For the crunchy noodles, preheat oven to 350°F and line a baking sheet with aluminum foil. In a small bowl, toss ramen noodles, slivered almonds and melted butter until evenly coated. Spread mixture on prepared baking sheet and bake for 8 minutes or until toasted. Remove from the oven and cool. 5) Fill a medium saucepan with water and bring to a boil over high heat. Add snow peas, turn off heat and cover saucepan for 3 minutes. Drain snow peas and rinse under cold water to prevent further cooking. Drain and set aside. 6) On a large platter, top shredded lettuce with snow peas, carrots and corn. Pile cooked chicken in the center of the platter. Scatter noodle and almond mixture on top of the lettuce, vegetables and chicken. Drizzle with salad dressing and serve.

Serves 8

BROCCOLI, GRAPE and CRANBERRY SALAD

INGREDIENTS

2 large heads of broccoli, chopped into small florets

1½ cups red or green grapes, halved

1 cup chopped celery

1 cup dried cranberries

¼ cup salted sunflower seeds

Dressing

⅔ cup mayonnaise

½ cup sour cream

5 tbsp sugar

2 tbsp white vinegar

"Raw? Broccoli? Salad?" my husband asked as I set down his plate. "I might not be an ex-Prez, but if George Bush doesn't have to eat broccoli, neither do I." He was skeptical and I couldn't really blame the guy — he's not a vegetable lover and, to his ears, this sounded like spa food. But, one bite of this creamy, crispy, sweet, sour and salty broccoli salad was all it took to make him a believer.

DIRECTIONS

1) In a large bowl, combine uncooked broccoli, grapes, celery, cranberries and sunflower seeds. Set aside. 2) For the dressing, in a medium bowl, whisk mayonnaise, sour cream, sugar and white vinegar. Pour dressing over broccoli mixture and mix well. Refrigerate at least 1 hour before serving.

Serves 6-8

BITE ME BIT

"Beulah, peel me a grape."

– Tira (actress Mae West) in the 1933 movie "I'm No Angel"

PITA in SALAD!

INGREDIENTS

3 large pitas, cut into
1-inch pieces

1 tbsp olive oil

½ tsp kosher salt

1 English cucumber, peeled,
seeded and chopped

4 large tomatoes, seeded
and chopped

1 large green pepper, chopped

2 tbsp chopped fresh
flat-leaf parsley

2 tbsp chopped fresh mint

Dressing

¼ cup fresh lemon juice

⅓ cup olive oil

1 large garlic clove, minced

½ tsp kosher salt

¼ tsp freshly ground
black pepper

Oh pita! Oh pita! You are so nice.
A lovely pocket of paradise!
Say! Let's add, add, add in some more.
Veggies and herbs will make you soar!
Up! Up! Up! You go.
A refreshing salad for all to love so!
Gather Flummox, Horton and even the Grinch,
This savory salad to make is a cinch!

DIRECTIONS

1) Preheat oven to 350°F. Coat a baking sheet with non-stick cooking spray. 2) In a medium bowl, toss cut pita with olive oil and salt. Spread on prepared baking sheet and bake 10-15 minutes, until crisp. Set aside and let cool. 3) In a large bowl, toss cucumbers, tomatoes, green pepper, parsley and mint. 4) For the dressing, in a small bowl, whisk lemon juice, olive oil, garlic, salt and pepper. 5) Just before serving, toss the cucumber-tomato mixture with the dressing. Gently add toasted pita and let stand for 5-10 minutes, allowing flavors to blend. Add salt to taste.

Serves 8

BITE ME BIT

"Three tomatoes are walking down the street — a papa tomato, a mama tomato and a little baby tomato. Baby tomato starts lagging behind. Papa tomato gets angry, goes over to Baby tomato and squishes him... and says 'Ketchup!'"

– Mia Wallace (actress Uma Thurman) in the 1994 movie "Pulp Fiction"

MEDITERRANEAN POTATO SALAD

INGREDIENTS

6 medium red potatoes, skin on, cubed

2 tbsp white wine vinegar

1 cup sour cream

½ cup mayonnaise

⅛ cup olive oil

2 tbsp minced fresh dill

1 tbsp capers, rinsed and drained

1 tsp dried oregano

½ tsp kosher salt

1 cup crumbled feta cheese

½ cup Kalamata olives, pitted and halved

Lisa: Potato salad. Red or white? Hot or cold? Mayo or vinegar?

Julie: Why? Are you taking a survey?

Lisa: Pay attention. Potato salad. How do you like it?

Julie: Well, duh, with potatoes.

Lisa: Argh. Forget you – I'm doing my own spin with dill, capers, feta and Kalamata olives.

Julie: But will it have spuds?

Lisa: #@$%!

DIRECTIONS

1) In a large pot, cover potatoes with cold water and bring to a boil over high heat. Cook potatoes until just tender, about 15 minutes. Drain potatoes and place in a large bowl. Sprinkle with white wine vinegar and let cool. 2) In a medium bowl, blend sour cream, mayonnaise, olive oil, dill, capers, oregano and salt. Stir in feta cheese. Gently fold mixture into potatoes. Chill at least 2 hours and add olives just before serving.

Serves 6

CHOPPED GREEK SALAD

INGREDIENTS

4 large tomatoes, seeded and chopped

1 English cucumber, peeled, seeded and chopped

1 large red bell pepper, chopped

1 large green pepper, chopped

2 tbsp minced fresh mint

1 tsp dried oregano

3 tbsp olive oil

2 tbsp red wine vinegar

¼ tsp kosher salt

¼ tsp freshly ground black pepper

¾ cup crumbled feta cheese

¼ cup Kalamata olives, pitted

Here are a few tips I've gleaned from long nights spent doing "research" in authentic Greek restaurants – a booze-o-ouzo hangover is epic and it's super-fun to yell Opa! for everything from a plate of flaming cheese to a Mouskouri medley. But here's something I learned the hard way, never ask, "Where's the lettuce?" A few raised eyebrows and tongue-clicks later, I was informed leafy greens are taboo in Greek salad. We left them out but I sure hope there's no rule against using fresh mint along with the sweet tomatoes, crisp cucumbers, tangy feta and Kalamata olives...

DIRECTIONS

1) In a large bowl, combine tomatoes, cucumbers, red and green peppers, mint and oregano. 2) In a small bowl, whisk oil, vinegar, salt and pepper. Pour over vegetables and toss to coat. Cover and let sit for 30 minutes, allowing flavors to blend. 3) Before serving, stir in feta and olives.

Serves 4-6

BITE ME BIT

"There are two kinds of people – Greeks, and everyone else who wish they was Greek."

– Gus Portokalos (actor Michael Constantine) in the 2002 movie "My Big Fat Greek Wedding"

JULIE'S TABBOULEH

INGREDIENTS

1½ cups medium-grind bulgur

1 cup canned chickpeas, rinsed and drained

3 tbsp olive oil

1 tsp ground cumin

1 cup crumbled feta cheese

3 large tomatoes, seeded and diced

1 English cucumber, peeled, seeded and diced

¼ cup oil-packed sun-dried tomatoes, drained and finely chopped

2 tbsp fresh lemon juice

2 tbsp chopped fresh flat-leaf parsley

2 tbsp chopped fresh mint

½ tsp kosher salt

¼ tsp freshly ground black pepper

I'm Julie and this is my tabbouleh. It rhymes with my name coolly. A classic Middle Eastern salad I love truly. Adding sun-dried tomatoes and feta makes it newly. Unruly!

DIRECTIONS

1) In a small saucepan, bring 3 cups of lightly salted water to a boil. Place the bulgur in a heatproof bowl and cover with boiling water. Let stand at room temperature for 30 minutes. If there is any remaining water, drain bulgur in a fine-mesh sieve, pushing out excess liquid. 2) In a large mixing bowl, combine bulgur, chickpeas, olive oil and cumin. Stir in feta, tomatoes, cucumber, sun-dried tomatoes, lemon juice, parsley, mint, salt and pepper. Let sit for 10 minutes for flavors to combine. Serve at room temperature.

Serves 6-8

BITE ME BIT

"Julie, Julie, Julie, do ya love me?
Julie, Julie, Julie, do ya care?
Julie, Julie, are ya thinking of me?
Julie, Julie will ya still be there?"

– 1970 Bobby Sherman song
"Julie, Do Ya Love Me"

ISRAELI COUSCOUS SALAD with ROASTED VEGETABLES

INGREDIENTS

Roasted Vegetables

2 cups peeled and cubed butternut squash

2 large red bell peppers, diced

2 small zucchini, diced

1½ cups canned chickpeas, rinsed and drained

2 tbsp olive oil

1 tbsp balsamic vinegar

1 large garlic clove, minced

1 tsp dried oregano

½ tsp kosher salt

¼ tsp freshly ground black pepper

1 sprig fresh rosemary

Couscous

1 tbsp butter

1¾ cups Israeli couscous

1 tsp lemon zest

3 cups chicken broth

¾ cup crumbled feta cheese

¼ cup chopped fresh mint

2 tbsp olive oil

2 tbsp balsamic vinegar

I read the papers every day. I know what's what in the Middle East. But let me tell you this, Jimmy Carter, Shimon Peres and King Abdullah – you want lasting peace in the region? Forget your summits, negotiators, and Nobel Prizes. We know what could bring these feuding Biblical brothers to the table. Couscous. Israeli couscous. Its chewy goodness, nutty taste – combined with the sweetness of its roasted vegetables, fragrant mint, crumbled feta – make this salad a perfect mate for either chicken or fish. Now, when do we fly to Stockholm and collect our award?

DIRECTIONS

1) For the roasted vegetables, preheat oven to 450°F. Coat a large baking sheet with non-stick cooking spray. 2) In a large bowl, combine squash, red peppers, zucchini and drained chickpeas. Toss with 2 tbsp olive oil, 1 tbsp vinegar, garlic, oregano, salt and pepper. Spread vegetable mixture on prepared baking sheet and lay rosemary sprig in the center. Roast for 30-35 minutes or until the vegetables are tender and browned, stirring every 10 minutes. Remove rosemary and set vegetables aside. 3) For the couscous, in a large saucepan, melt butter over medium-high heat. Add couscous and lemon zest and sauté for 2 minutes. Add broth and bring to a boil. Reduce heat to medium-low, cooking uncovered until couscous is tender, 10-12 minutes. Strain excess liquid and set aside. 4) In a large bowl, stir together roasted vegetables, cooked couscous, feta, mint and remaining 2 tbsp olive oil and 2 tbsp balsamic vinegar. Serve at room temperature or cover and refrigerate for 2 to 8 hours.

Serves 6-8

INGREDIENTS

3 medium zucchini, cubed

2 medium red bell peppers, cubed

1 medium yellow pepper, cubed

1 medium eggplant, peeled and cubed

2 tbsp olive oil

½ tsp kosher salt

¼ tsp freshly ground black pepper

¾ lb package fusilli pasta

¾ cup shredded semi-soft Asiago cheese

3 tbsp olive oil

2 tbsp white wine vinegar

2 tbsp minced fresh oregano

2 tbsp chopped rehydrated sun-dried tomatoes

SHAZAM! VEGETABLE PASTA SALAD with ASIAGO CHEESE

DIRECTIONS

1) Preheat oven to 425°F. Line a baking sheet with aluminum foil and coat with non-stick cooking spray. 2) In a medium bowl, toss zucchini, red peppers, yellow peppers, eggplant, olive oil, salt and pepper. Transfer to prepared baking sheet. Roast in oven for 20-25 minutes, stirring occasionally until lightly browned. Remove from oven and cool slightly. 3) For the pasta, in a large pot, bring lightly salted water to a boil. Cook fusilli until tender, about 12 minutes. Drain and place in a large bowl. Add roasted vegetables, Asiago cheese, olive oil, white wine vinegar, oregano and sun-dried tomatoes. Toss well to coat. Serve at room temperature or refrigerate to chill.

Serves 6

CREAMY PESTO PASTA SALAD

INGREDIENTS

1 lb fusilli pasta

1 tbsp kosher salt

1 tbsp olive oil

Basil Pesto

2 cups fresh basil leaves, firmly packed

1 large garlic clove

½ cup pine nuts

1 tsp kosher salt

¼ tsp freshly ground black pepper

½ cup olive oil

1 cup freshly grated Parmesan cheese

¼ cup mayonnaise

1 tbsp fresh lemon juice

Basil is known as the "King of Herbs." But garlic, the so-called "Stinking Rose," is a lowly clove. Who'd ever think the two would get along so well? My Cuisinart, that's who.

DIRECTIONS

1) For the pasta, bring a large pot of water to a boil. Add salt and pasta, cooking until pasta is tender. Drain well and toss with olive oil. Cool to room temperature while preparing the pesto. 2) For the pesto, wash the basil, discard the stems and dry thoroughly. Set aside. 3) Place the garlic, pine nuts, salt and pepper in a food processor. Process 10 seconds to chop garlic. Add basil leaves and pulse 4-5 times to shred basil. Scrape down the sides of the bowl. With the machine running, slowly pour in the olive oil in a steady stream until the mixture is smooth, about 20 seconds. Add the Parmesan, mayonnaise and lemon juice, processing just until incorporated. 4) Transfer pesto to a large serving bowl and toss with cooled pasta. Serve with additional Parmesan if desired.

Serves 8

BITE ME BIT

Eli: I always wanted to be a Tenenbaum.

Royal: Me too, me too.

– from the 2001 movie "The Royal Tenenbaums"

BITE ME BIT

In Ancient Greece, basil was linked to profanity and insanity. We know a few folks who should lay off the @#$%ing herb.

CAPRESE ORZO SALAD

INGREDIENTS

2 cups cherry tomatoes, halved

2 cups pearl (bite-sized balls) bocconcini cheese

¼ cup olive oil

¼ cup chopped fresh basil

1 small garlic clove, minced

1½ tsp kosher salt

¼ tsp freshly ground black pepper

1½ cups orzo

2 tbsp olive oil

We can read our Dad like a book. A bright smile says he won his tennis game. Crossed arms tell us he's starving. Thumb and index finger spread an inch apart, we know he's quizzing the waiter about the firmness of the Caprese salad's tomatoes. We get it – the Italian classic isn't salvageable with mealy, tasteless tomatoes – and that's why this orzo pasta salad hits all the high notes by using year-round juicy and flavorful cherry tomatoes, melt-in-your-mouth bocconcini and slivers of chopped sweet basil. One bite and our Dad started tapping his toe – that's his food-lovers' happy-dance.

DIRECTIONS

1) In a medium bowl, gently stir together tomatoes, bocconcini, olive oil, basil, garlic, salt and pepper. Let stand at room temperature for 1 hour, allowing flavors to blend. 2) For the orzo, in a medium pot, bring water to a boil over high heat. Add the pasta and cook until tender. Drain well and place in a large bowl, allowing to cool for 20 minutes. 3) Add remaining 2 tbsp olive oil and tomato mixture to orzo, tossing to coat.

Serves 6

Respect
me

**Vegetables You'll Still
Love the Next Day**

CRISPY BAKED ZUCCHINI CHIPS

INGREDIENTS

¼ cup milk

¾ cup freshly grated Parmesan cheese

½ cup breadcrumbs

½ tsp kosher salt

⅛ tsp freshly ground black pepper

4 large zucchini, sliced into ¼-inch thick rounds

Do you always fall for the "bad boy" greaser? Y'know, the slick bar fly who draws you in and keeps you coming back for more? Don't get duped again — it's time for a healthy relationship with the "nice guy," the oven chip.

DIRECTIONS

1) Preheat oven to 425°F. Line a baking sheet with aluminum foil and coat with non-stick cooking spray. 2) For the chips, pour milk in a small bowl. In a medium bowl, combine Parmesan, breadcrumbs, salt and pepper. Working one at a time, dip zucchini rounds in milk and then coat in the Parmesan mixture. 3) Lay crusted slices on prepared baking sheet and bake for 20 minutes. Flip zucchini rounds and continue to bake another 10 minutes. Sprinkle with kosher salt and serve.

Serves 4-6

BITE ME BIT

Solange:...Why can't nice guys be more like you?

James Bond: Because then they'd be bad.

– from the 2006 movie 'Casino Royale'

CLEVER CARAMELIZED CAULIFLOWER

INGREDIENTS

1 large head cauliflower, about 3 lbs

1 tbsp sugar

½ tsp kosher salt

¼ tsp freshly ground black pepper

¼ tsp ground cinnamon

⅛ tsp paprika

⅛ tsp ground cumin

⅛ tsp cayenne pepper

3 tbsp melted butter

I feel for Mark Twain. At the mention of cauliflower food writers inevitably blast the literary icon for his slandering the veggie as "nothing but cabbage with a college education." Surely he didn't mean to disparage the snowy white heads. When roasted, cauliflower is transformed into an elegant, sweet and tender side dish – a truly brilliant veggie with a PhD in Gastronomy.

DIRECTIONS

1) Preheat oven to 475°F. 2) Break apart the cauliflower into large florets and cut off the thicker stems. Place cauliflower in a single layer in a roasting pan or on a baking sheet. 3) In a small bowl, stir together sugar, salt, pepper, cinnamon, paprika, cumin and cayenne pepper. 4) Drizzle melted butter over cauliflower and sprinkle with the combined spices until evenly coated. Place in oven and bake 18-20 minutes stirring halfway through cooking. Remove from oven when cauliflower is tender-crisp and lightly browned around the edges. Serve immediately.

Serves 6-8

OASTED-RAY EGETABLES-VAY with PECANS and PARMESAN

INGREDIENTS

2 lbs sweet potatoes, peeled and cubed

1 lb carrots, peeled and cubed

1 lb parsnips, peeled and cubed

3 tbsp olive oil

1 tsp kosher salt

¼ tsp freshly ground black pepper

Pecan Parmesan Topping

1 cup chopped pecans

⅓ cup freshly grated Parmesan cheese

¼ cup finely chopped fresh flat-leaf parsley

1 tbsp fresh lemon juice

1 tbsp lemon zest

1 tbsp olive oil

An encoded message for those of you who need to camouflage egetables-vay:

Es-yay. Ese-thay are-way egetables-vay. Ook-lay under-way e-thay uttery-bay ecans-pay and-way ich-ray armesan-pay. Ut-bay on't-day orry-way. O-nay one-way ill-way ever-way ink-thay ese-thay eet-sway oasted-ray egetables-vay are-way actually-way ealthy-hay…ey-thay aste-tay oo-tay ood-gay!

DIRECTIONS

1) Preheat oven to 425°F. Line a large baking sheet with aluminum foil. 2) In a large bowl, toss sweet potatoes, carrots and parsnips with olive oil. Transfer to baking sheet and sprinkle with salt and pepper. Roast vegetables, stirring often, for 1 hour or until tender. Transfer to a serving plate. 3) For the topping, in a small bowl, combine pecans, Parmesan, parsley, lemon juice, lemon zest and olive oil. Sprinkle over vegetables before serving.

Serves 6

SWEET BALSAMIC ROASTED CARROTS

INGREDIENTS

2 lbs carrots, peeled and cut into 2-inch sticks resembling French fries

2 tbsp butter

2 tbsp packed brown sugar

1 tsp balsamic vinegar

½ tsp kosher salt

¼ tsp freshly ground black pepper

DIRECTIONS

1) Preheat oven to 450°F. Line a baking sheet with aluminum foil and coat with non-stick cooking spray. 2) In a small saucepan, melt butter over medium heat. Add the brown sugar and vinegar, stirring to combine just until the sugar melts. Remove from heat. 3) In a medium bowl, toss cut carrots with brown sugar glaze, salt and pepper. Place on baking sheet in a single layer. 4) Bake 15-20 minutes, until carrots are starting to brown on the bottom. Stir carrots and return to oven for 5-10 minutes until carrots are caramelized and tender.

Serves 6

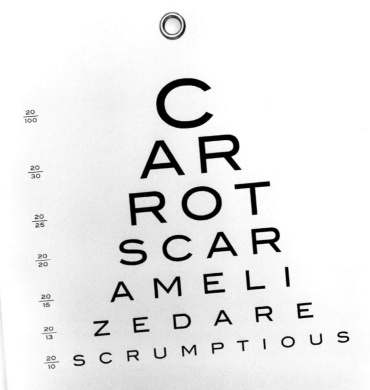

PRALINE-TOPPED SWEET POTATO CASSEROLE

INGREDIENTS

5 medium sweet potatoes, peeled and quartered

½ cup packed brown sugar

1½ tsp vanilla extract

2 large egg whites

½ cup evaporated milk

Streusel Topping

1 cup flour

⅔ cup packed brown sugar

½ cup chopped pecans, toasted

¼ cup melted margarine

½ tsp ground cinnamon

2 tsp cinnamon-sugar, for topping

Eureka! We've discovered the 32nd flavor! A scoop of this irresistible side dish – pillowy mashed sweet potatoes buried under a crunchy streusel topping – and you'll see why it belongs alongside Rocky Road and Mint Chocolate Chip. Enjoy the sweet satisfaction without the ice cream headache, but come Thanksgiving, look for our creation (Pilgrim Praline? Yummy Yam?) in the freezer case.

DIRECTIONS

1) Preheat oven to 350°F. Coat an 11x7-inch baking dish with non-stick cooking spray. 2) Place quartered sweet potatoes in a large pot and cover with cold water. Bring to a boil over high heat. Reduce heat, simmering for 15-20 minutes or until very tender. Drain well, place potatoes in a large bowl and mash. 3) For the streusel topping, in a small bowl, combine flour, brown sugar, pecans, margarine and cinnamon. 4) Stir 1 cup of streusel into mashed sweet potatoes. Add brown sugar, vanilla, egg whites and evaporated milk, stirring to combine. Spoon into prepared baking dish, sprinkle with remaining topping and cinnamon-sugar. Bake uncovered for 45 minutes.

Serves 8

BITE ME BIT

"There's something about the ice cream truck that makes kids lose it. And they can hear that s**t from ten blocks away. They don't hear their mothers calling but they hear that mother-f***ing ice cream truck."

– Eddie Murphy in the 1983 movie "Delirious"

BITE ME BIT

"If you don't eat yer meat, you can't have any pudding. How can you have any pudding if you don't eat yer meat?"

– from the Pink Floyd song "Another Brick in the Wall, Part II"

ATOMIC #79 (4 letters) CARROT PUDDING with BROWN SUGAR DRIZZLE

INGREDIENTS

Carrot Pudding

½ cup butter, softened

½ cup packed brown sugar

1 large egg

1 tbsp orange juice

1 tsp vanilla extract

1¼ cups flour

1 tsp baking powder

½ tsp baking soda

½ tsp kosher salt

½ tsp ground cinnamon

2½ cups coarsely grated carrots (5-6 carrots)

Brown Sugar Sauce

1 cup packed brown sugar

1½ tbsp cornstarch

¼ tsp kosher salt

1 cup water

2 tbsp butter

1 tsp vanilla extract

New York Times crosswords are my religion and editor Will Shortz is my deity. My day isn't complete without his puzzle, and a meal isn't whole until I've eaten a dessert-like side dish alongside a main course of chicken, meat or fish. Here are a few clues that reminded me that the proof is in the ____(7).

1. It's said Howard Hughes measured every one he ate. (6)
2. Heroin manufactured illicitly in Mexico. (10)
3. To overwhelm with brilliance. (6)
4. Cannelle, fr. (8)
5. Color skin turns after a spray-on tan (6)

DIRECTIONS

1) For the carrot pudding, preheat oven to 350°F. Coat an 8-inch round or square baking dish with non-stick cooking spray. 2) In an electric mixer, cream butter with brown sugar on medium-high speed until light and fluffy. Add the egg, orange juice and vanilla. Combine until well mixed. 3) In a medium bowl, sift the flour, baking powder, baking soda, salt and cinnamon together. Add flour mixture and grated carrots to butter-sugar mixture. Mix just until flour disappears making sure not to overmix the batter. Transfer to prepared baking dish. Bake 32-35 minutes or until golden around the edges. 4) For the brown sugar sauce, in a medium saucepan, whisk brown sugar, cornstarch and salt. Whisk in water and bring to a boil over high heat. Lower heat to medium, whisking constantly until sauce is smooth and has thickened slightly, 4-6 minutes. Remove from heat and whisk in butter and vanilla. Serve drizzled over pieces of carrot pudding.

Serves 6-8

Dear Auntie Em —

I was following this yellow brick road forever.
While Toto nibbled on my shoes, I was ravenous.
At first, this dim scarecrow flung a squash
at me. I'm like, ding-dong, I can't eat
it like that! Kept walking and met up with
a tin man who tossed me some melted
margarine, told me to oil him and then I
could have the leftovers. NO THANKS! Muddled
on until we bumped into some fraidy cat
who was busy tossing salt over his shoulder.
What a wuss! Anyway, dragged them all
along until we got to this place called
Munchkinland. So welcoming! Lollipop Guild
took all the ingredients, poured in some sugar
and spice, and cheerfully whipped up a
delectable butternut squash casserole topped
with crumbled vanilla wafers.

Over the rainbow rocks! Not coming home.

XOXO, Dorothy

INGREDIENTS

6 cups peeled and cubed
butternut squash

1 cup milk

½ cup sugar

3 tbsp melted margarine

2 tbsp flour

1 tsp vanilla extract

½ tsp ground cinnamon

¼ tsp kosher salt

2 large eggs, lightly beaten

Vanilla Wafer Topping

4 cups coarsely crushed
vanilla wafers

¾ cup packed brown sugar

⅓ cup melted margarine

SWEET SQUASH and VANILLA WAFER CASSEROLE, OH MY!

DIRECTIONS

1) Preheat oven to 425°F. Coat a 13x9-inch baking dish with non-stick cooking spray. **2)** In a large pot, cover butternut squash with cold water. Bring to a boil over high heat, reduce heat to medium and continue to boil until soft, about 15 minutes. Drain well. **3)** Place squash in a large bowl and mash until smooth. Add milk, sugar, margarine, flour, vanilla, cinnamon, salt and eggs. Stir well to combine. Transfer mixture to prepared baking dish and bake 45 minutes. **4)** For the topping, in a medium bowl, combine crushed wafers, brown sugar and margarine. Sprinkle over baked casserole and return to oven for 5 minutes until lightly browned.

Serves 8

SOUTHWESTERN SWEET POTATO FRIES

INGREDIENTS

2 large egg whites

2 tbsp olive oil

1 lime, juiced

1 tsp sugar

1 tsp ground cumin

½ tsp chili powder

½ tsp kosher salt

¼ tsp freshly ground black pepper

2 lbs (about 4) sweet potatoes, peeled and cut lengthwise into ½-inch thick strips

Creamy Lemon Dip

½ cup mayonnaise

2 tsp fresh lemon juice

1 tsp lemon zest

1 tsp chopped fresh thyme

¼ tsp kosher salt

Welcome Small Fry!

It is with great joy that Lisa and Julie announce the birth of their healthy little fry. Weighing in at a light 2 pounds, she was born perfectly crisp on the outside, creamy on the inside. This Tex-Mex tuber is welcomed with open mouths by proud grandparents Mr. and Mrs. Y. Gold and Dr. and Mrs. I. Russet.

DIRECTIONS

1) Preheat oven to 425°F. Line a large baking sheet with parchment paper. 2) In a large bowl, whisk egg whites until frothy. Whisk in olive oil, lime juice, sugar, cumin, chili powder, salt and pepper. Add potatoes, tossing to coat. Spread potatoes in a single layer on prepared baking sheet and roast them in the oven for 20 minutes or until golden on the bottom. Turn the potatoes over and continue to bake for an additional 15 minutes or until golden brown all over. 3) For the dip, in a small bowl, whisk mayonnaise, lemon juice, lemon zest, thyme and salt. Serve with baked fries.

Serves 4

DOUBLE-STUFFED BAKED POTATOES

INGREDIENTS

6 large baking potatoes

2 cups sour cream

½ cup shredded cheddar cheese

¼ cup butter, softened

½ tsp kosher salt

¼ tsp freshly ground black pepper

¼ cup freshly grated Parmesan cheese

We challenge any dastardly critic of the poor, maligned tuber to refuse this decadent spud. Baked to perfection, its ivory insides have been scooped out, mashed with butter, cheese and sour cream and baked until golden brown beauties emerge.

DIRECTIONS

1) Preheat oven to 400°F. 2) Scrub each potato and pat dry. Use a fork to pierce each potato in several places. Bake the potatoes directly on the oven rack for 50-60 minutes or until tender and easily pierced with the tip of a knife. 3) Remove from oven and cut the potatoes in half lengthwise. Using a small spoon carefully (don't go too deep or you'll rip the skins) scoop out the flesh from inside the potatoes and place in a medium bowl. 4) Line a baking sheet with aluminum foil. Arrange potato shells on baking sheet and return to oven until they are slightly crisp, about 10 minutes. Meanwhile, using a potato masher or fork, mash potato flesh and stir in sour cream, cheddar cheese, butter, salt and pepper.
5) Spoon potato mixture back into the potato shells mounding them high and sprinkling each potato with Parmesan cheese. Bake for 15 minutes.

Serves 8-10

BITE ME BIT

In 1987, due to pressure from anti-smoking groups, Mr. Potato Head's signature pipe was yanked from his mouth and running shoes were stuck on his feet. In his next incarnation, he'll be carrying a yoga mat.

STEAKHOME CREAMED SPINACH

INGREDIENTS

4 (10oz/283g) packages frozen chopped spinach

2 (6oz/170g) containers Kraft Philadelphia Whipped Cream Cheese

¼ cup melted butter

½ tsp kosher salt

¼ tsp freshly ground black pepper

2 tbsp freshly grated Parmesan cheese

Among the mahogany walls and dirty martinis, something great is happening in swanky steakhouses across the nation...carnivores are eating spinach. A simple side dish that seems healthy next to fried hash browns and marbled rib-eyes, the overly creamy restaurant version is still too flaccid and watery for our taste. Using whipped cream cheese, our easy, silky smooth spinach brings home all the taste of the upscale steakhouse without the $15 side-dish robbery and the velvet banquettes.

DIRECTIONS

1) Preheat oven to 350°F. Coat an 11x7-inch baking dish with non-stick cooking spray. 2) Defrost spinach according to package directions. Drain very well, squeezing spinach to ensure all excess liquid is removed. 3) In a food processor, place cream cheese, melted butter, salt, pepper and spinach together. Process for 10 seconds. Using a rubber spatula scrape down the sides of the bowl and do 3-4 quick pulses to combine. 4) Transfer to prepared baking dish, sprinkle top with Parmesan and bake uncovered for 20 minutes.

Serves 8

BITE ME BIT

"Did you ever see the customers in health-food stores? They are pale, skinny people who look half dead. In a steakhouse you see robust, ruddy people. They're dying, of course, but they look terrific."

– Bill Cosby, comedian

SHOWDOWN CHILI with CORNBREAD MUFFINS

INGREDIENTS

Vegetarian Chili

1 tbsp olive oil

1 medium red onion, chopped

1 tbsp chili powder

1 tsp dried oregano

1 tsp ground cumin

½ tsp kosher salt

½ tsp freshly ground black pepper

2 large red bell peppers, chopped

2 cups sliced white mushrooms

1 medium carrot, peeled and chopped

1 large garlic clove, minced

½ cup canned chopped green chili peppers, drained

1 (28oz/796ml) can diced tomatoes, with juice

2 cups canned black beans, rinsed and drained

1¾ cups canned chickpeas, rinsed and drained

1½ cups canned red kidney beans, rinsed and drained

1 cup mild salsa

1 cup vegetable broth

½ cup couscous

1 tbsp cocoa powder, sifted

1 tsp packed brown sugar

¼ tsp cayenne pepper

1 cup frozen corn kernels, thawed

Shredded Monterey Jack or cheddar cheese, for topping

11:59am, Main Street

His clickin' spurs announce him before he throws open the saloon doors.

"I'm hungry as a buzzard. Don't want no eggs or mutton. Got that, woman?" he bellows as he fingers his six-shooter.

"First, I ain't your woman and second, I'm standin' right here," she replies. "Don't gotta' yell. Think you comin' in here, smellin' of gunpowder, scares me? Now just sit down."

She slides a bowl of her bean-filled-vegetable-packed chili down the bar. Next, she tosses him a few of her tasty, moist, cornbread muffins.

"I. Said. No. Meat," he growls after eatin' a big spoonful. At that, he reaches for his holster, but he ain't no match for her quick draw – she points her Colt at him.

"Tastes. Meaty. Just. Vegetables," she hisses before pulling the trigger. "Dumber than a bag o' bricks."

DIRECTIONS

THE CHILI

1) In a large soup pot, heat olive oil over medium heat. Add onions and season with chili powder, oregano, cumin, salt and pepper. Cook until onion is tender, about 5 minutes. Add red peppers, mushrooms, carrots, minced garlic and chopped green chili peppers. Cook another 5 minutes, stirring occasionally. Stir in diced tomatoes, black beans, chickpeas, kidney beans, salsa, vegetable broth, couscous, cocoa powder, brown sugar and cayenne pepper.
2) Bring to a boil over high heat. Reduce heat to low, cover and simmer gently covered for 40 minutes, stirring occasionally. Add corn and serve in bowls, topped with shredded cheese.

Mini Cornbread Muffins

½ cup frozen corn kernels, thawed

1 cup flour

¾ cup yellow cornmeal

1 tbsp baking powder

1 tsp kosher salt

pinch cayenne pepper

½ cup melted butter

½ cup sugar

¼ cup honey

1 large egg

½ tsp vanilla extract

1 cup buttermilk

¼ cup roasted red peppers, patted dry and finely diced

THE MUFFINS

1) Preheat oven to 400°F. Coat 2 mini-muffin tins with non-stick cooking spray. 2) Place thawed corn kernels on a plate. Pat dry and set aside. 3) In a large bowl, combine flour, cornmeal, baking powder, salt and cayenne pepper. 4) In a small bowl, whisk together melted butter, sugar, honey, egg, vanilla and buttermilk. 5) Add butter mixture, roasted red peppers and corn kernels to dry ingredients. Stir gently to combine, just until flour disappears. Spoon batter into prepared muffin cups, filling to the top. Bake for 10 minutes. Cool for 5 minutes before removing from tin to a wire rack. Serve alongside chili.

Yield: 30-35 mini muffins

BITE ME BIT

"Chili represents your three stages of matter: solid, liquid and eventually gas."

– Dan Conner (actor John Goodman) on the television series "Roseanne"

BOUNTIFUL CORN PUDDING

INGREDIENTS

1¼ cups yellow cornmeal

4 cups whole milk

½ tsp kosher salt

⅓ cup butter

2 cups fresh corn kernels
(3-4 ears)

2 tsp sugar

½ tsp kosher salt

⅛ tsp cayenne pepper

3 large egg yolks

3 large egg whites

¼ tsp cream of tartar

Sing to the tune of "Three Blind Mice"*

**Fresh-shucked corn, fresh-shucked corn,
I love to say shuck, I love to say shuck**

**It is like saying a few words at once
So naughty yet nice a curser's delight
Did you ever hear such a wonderful sound
As shuck, shuck, shuck, shuck, shuck, shuck**

*for extra fun, sing it in rounds

DIRECTIONS

1) Preheat oven to 375°F. Coat an 8-inch square baking dish with non-stick cooking spray. 2) Separate egg yolks into a small bowl and egg whites into the bowl of an electric mixer. Set both aside. 3) In a large saucepan, whisk cornmeal, milk and salt over medium heat. Bring mixture to a boil, whisking constantly until mixture begins to thicken, about 3 minutes. Reduce heat to low, stir frequently and cook 5 minutes until mixture is very thick. Remove from heat and transfer to a large bowl. Cool to room temperature, about 20 minutes. 4) Meanwhile, in a large skillet, melt butter over medium heat. Add corn kernels, sugar, salt and cayenne pepper, sautéing for 5 minutes. Transfer to food processor and puree until kernels are chopped, about 10 seconds. 5) Once cornmeal mixture has cooled, stir in pureed corn kernels and egg yolks until well combined. 6) Using an electric mixer with the whisk attachment, beat the egg whites and cream of tartar on high speed until stiff peaks form. Doing half at a time, gently fold egg whites into cornmeal mixture. Spread batter into prepared dish and bake 30-35 minutes until pudding is puffed and top is golden. Serve immediately.

Serves 6-8

MASTERFUL MUSHROOM and FETA BREAD PUDDING

INGREDIENTS

3 tbsp chopped fresh
flat-leaf parsley

1 tbsp chopped fresh oregano

1 tsp chopped fresh thyme

1 tsp lemon zest

1 large garlic clove, minced

1 tbsp olive oil

8 cups thinly sliced assorted
mushrooms (cremini, shiitake,
button, portobello)

1 cup chopped celery

½ tsp kosher salt

¼ tsp freshly ground
black pepper

1 cup chopped roasted
red peppers

4 large eggs, lightly beaten

2½ cups milk

1½ cups crumbled feta cheese

1½ egg breads (challahs),
crusts removed and cut into
1-inch cubes, about 10 cups

½ cup crumbled feta cheese,
for topping

Ladies and Gentlemen, the taking of photos inside the museum is strictly prohibited. Please, follow me...here on your left, is a work of true genius. Breathtaking, isn't it? Notice how the brilliant green herbs mingle with the sautéed mushrooms and the ruby red peppers are interwoven throughout. Such style and technique. Admire the genius of contrasting sweet egg bread and tangy feta...the balance...perfection. Now, moving on, let us examine the apples painted by a Frenchman named Cézanne. Not as inspiring, wouldn't you agree?

DIRECTIONS

1) Preheat oven to 350°F. Coat a 13x9-inch baking dish with non-stick cooking spray. 2) In a small bowl, combine parsley, oregano, thyme, lemon zest and garlic. Set aside. 3) In a large skillet, heat oil over medium heat. Add mushrooms, celery, salt and pepper. Sauté until soft and liquid has evaporated, about 12 minutes. Add half the parsley mixture and all the roasted red peppers stirring over medium heat for 2 minutes. Remove from heat. 4) In a large bowl, combine remaining parsley mixture, eggs, milk and 1½ cups feta, stirring well to combine. Add mushroom mixture and bread cubes, stirring gently. 5) Transfer to prepared baking dish and sprinkle with ½ cup feta cheese. Bake uncovered 40-45 minutes, until set and top is golden.

Serves 8

BITE ME BIT

"O great creator of being. Grant us one more hour to perform our art and perfect our lives."

– Jim Morrison, musician

CHEESY, CHEESY, CHEESY BROCCOLI SOUFFLÉ

INGREDIENTS

1 tbsp freshly grated Parmesan cheese

2½ cups broccoli florets (1 large head of broccoli)

¼ cup butter

¼ cup flour

1½ cups whole milk

1 tsp kosher salt

½ tsp Dijon mustard

1 cup shredded cheddar cheese

6 large egg yolks

6 large egg whites

½ tsp cream of tartar

"The Brady Bunch" taught me a lot – pork chops go with applesauce and freckles can be bleached with lemon juice. But it was Alice tiptoeing as her soufflé baked that really stuck with me. Seems I was duped – loud noises don't level a soufflé, but repeatedly opening the oven does. So leave the door shut and let this airy, savory soufflé soar. One whiff of the melted cheesy goodness and like Marcia, you too will be saying, "Oh! My nose!"

DIRECTIONS

1) Preheat oven to 325°F. Coat the bottom (not the sides) of a 2-quart soufflé dish with non-stick cooking spray. Sprinkle Parmesan cheese on the bottom of the dish and shake to coat. Set aside. 2) Bring a large pot of water to a boil over high heat and add broccoli, turn heat to low and cook 2-3 minutes until tender but not mushy. Drain well and chop florets into smaller pieces. Set aside. 3) In a medium saucepan, melt the butter over medium heat. Add flour, whisking constantly until smooth, 1 minute. Slowly pour in milk and continue whisking constantly to prevent lumps from forming. Add salt and Dijon mustard, continuing to stir until mixture thickens, about 2 minutes. Remove from heat and stir in cheese and broccoli. 4) In a small bowl, lightly whisk egg yolks. While constantly whisking, add a small amount of the warm cheese mixture to the yolks. Once combined, add the rest of the yolks to the remaining cheese mixture, whisking briskly to mix. Transfer to a large bowl and set aside to cool slightly. 5) Using an electric mixer, beat the egg whites and cream of tartar on high speed until stiff peaks form. Lightly fold half of the egg whites into the cheese sauce. Gently fold in the remaining egg whites taking care not to overmix. Carefully pour batter into prepared soufflé dish. Bake 50-55 minutes until puffy and golden brown. Remove from oven and serve immediately.

Serves 6-8

PARMESAN-CRUSTED ASPARAGUS

INGREDIENTS

¾ cup mayonnaise

2 tbsp Dijon mustard

2 tsp fresh lemon juice

1 tsp kosher salt

1½ cups panko (Japanese breadcrumbs)

¾ cup freshly grated Parmesan cheese

2 large bunches of asparagus

2 tbsp olive oil

I wouldn't be surprised if one day I was strolling down the supermarket snack aisle and found a box of crispy asparagus tucked in with the Bugles and Cheetos. That's right, asparagus. Coated in a cheesy breadcrumb mixture and baked to a golden crisp, these addictive spears are a family favorite. So put away the party mix – just assemble this ideal company-is-coming side dish in advance and pop it in the oven 15 minutes before dinner.

DIRECTIONS

1) Preheat oven to 450°F. Coat a large baking sheet with non-stick cooking spray. 2) In a large bowl, whisk mayonnaise, Dijon mustard, lemon juice and salt. 3) On a large plate, combine panko and Parmesan. 4) Stalk by stalk, dip asparagus in mayonnaise mixture, followed by the panko mixture. Place crusted asparagus on the prepared baking sheet and sprinkle the stalks with olive oil. 5) At this point you can place the tray in the refrigerator for a few hours before baking. To cook, bake 14-16 minutes, turning the asparagus halfway through cooking. Sprinkle with coarse salt before serving.

Serves 4

MINTED SWEET PEA PURÉE

INGREDIENTS

4 cups frozen peas

½ cup Kraft Philadelphia Whipped Cream Cheese

¼ cup butter, room temperature

2 tbsp chopped fresh mint

1 tsp kosher salt

When we take spoon after spoon of this delicious purée we are reminded of King John II of England. It's reported that the pea-obsessed monarch died after eating seven bowls of the little green legumes. The lesson we carry with us is to stop at six.

DIRECTIONS

1) In a medium saucepan bring salted water to a boil over high heat. Add frozen peas, reduce heat to low and simmer for 5 minutes until tender. Drain well. Transfer peas to a food processor. Add cream cheese, butter, mint and salt. Purée until smooth, 15-20 seconds. Remove from processor and serve warm.

Serves 6-8

BITE ME BIT

"I have scarcely closed my eyes all night. Heaven only knows what was in the bed, but I was lying on something hard, so that I am black and blue all over my body. It's horrible!"

– from Hans Christian Andersen's "The Princess and the Pea"

BALSAMIC GRILLED VEGETABLE STACKS

INGREDIENTS

Marinade

⅓ cup balsamic vinegar

⅓ cup olive oil

1 small garlic clove, minced

1 tsp Dijon mustard

1 tsp kosher salt

¼ tsp freshly ground black pepper

Vegetables

2 large red bell peppers, quartered lengthwise and seeded

2 large yellow peppers, quartered lengthwise and seeded

2 large zucchini cut into ⅓-inch diagonal slices, total of 12

6 medium portobello mushrooms (approx. 3-inch diameter), peeled, gills gently scooped out with small spoon

6 rosemary sprigs (4 inches in length), leaves removed from the bottom half

Julie: Word association.

Husband: Lose-lose?

Julie: Grilled.

Husband: New York?

Julie: Marinated in oil and vinegar.

Husband: Veal chop?

Julie: Quit it. Edible part of plants.

Husband: Vegetables.

Julie: Barbeque.

Husband: Salami?

Julie: Argh. Peppers, zucchini and portobellos.

Husband: All yours?

Julie: Promise?

DIRECTIONS

1) For the marinade, in a large bowl, whisk balsamic vinegar, olive oil, garlic, Dijon mustard, salt and pepper. Add red peppers, yellow peppers and zucchini slices, tossing well to coat. Marinate at room temperature for 15 minutes. Add mushrooms, tossing gently and marinate another 15 minutes. 2) Lightly coat grill with non-stick cooking spray and heat to medium-high heat. Remove vegetables from marinade and keep marinade to brush on vegetables while grilling. 3) Working in batches, grill the vegetables until tender and lightly charred, about 8-10 minutes for the peppers and 7 minutes for the mushrooms and zucchini. Brush with marinade once or twice during cooking. 4) Remove from grill. When you are almost ready to serve the stacks, place the mushrooms upside down on a flat surface. Next, layer with a slice of red pepper, zucchini, yellow pepper and another slice of zucchini. Poke the rosemary sprig through the middle of each stack with the leaves at the top.

Serves 6

FALAFEL VEGGIE BURGERS

INGREDIENTS

1 tbsp olive oil

1 small yellow onion, chopped

1 large carrot, peeled and chopped

3½ cups canned chickpeas, rinsed and drained well

1 cup canned sliced mushrooms, rinsed and drained well

1 tbsp fresh lime juice

¼ cup chopped fresh flat-leaf parsley

1 tbsp ground cumin

1 tbsp tahini

½ tsp kosher salt

¼ tsp freshly ground black pepper

5 slices white bread, crust removed and put in food processor to make coarse crumbs

Creamy Tahini Sauce

½ cup mayonnaise

½ cup sour cream

2 tbsp fresh lemon juice

1 tbsp olive oil

1 tbsp tahini

½ tsp kosher salt

¼ tsp freshly ground black pepper

2 tbsp finely chopped fresh mint

2 tbsp finely chopped fresh flat-leaf parsley

8 pita pockets

2 cups shredded iceberg lettuce

Way back when, hauling limestone sure built up an appetite. Yup, falafel is THE original veggie burger, a classic meatless meal traced back to ancient Egyptian times. Don't worry – no heavy lifting required today – grab a McFried falafel, or, better yet, go back to your oasis and bake up your own hearty taste straight off King Tut's table.

DIRECTIONS

1) Preheat oven to 350°F. Line a baking sheet with aluminum foil and coat with non-stick cooking spray. 2) In a medium skillet, heat olive oil over medium-low heat. Add onion and cook until softened, about 6 minutes. Remove from heat and allow to cool slightly. 3) In a food processor, combine cooked onions, carrots, chickpeas, mushrooms, lime juice, parsley, cumin, tahini, salt and pepper. Process until smooth, stopping to scrape down the sides of the bowl. Transfer to a large bowl and add breadcrumbs, mixing until all ingredients are thoroughly combined. 4) Form 8 burgers from the mixture and place on prepared baking sheet. Bake 30 minutes, flipping halfway through. 5) For the sauce, in a medium bowl, vigorously whisk mayonnaise, sour cream, lemon juice, olive oil, tahini, salt and pepper. Stir in chopped mint and parsley. 6) To serve, tuck veggie burger in a pita pocket along with a few tablespoons of sauce and about ¼ cup shredded lettuce.

Serves 8

BITE ME BIT

"...and then I would take the other hand with the falafel thing and I'd just put it on your ***** but you'd have to do it really light, just kind of a tease business..."

– Bill O'Reilly, as quoted in a sexual harassment suit filed against him by a Fox News producer in 2004

Crave me

Satisfying Pasta, Rice and Grains

CARAMELIZED ONION and GOAT CHEESE PASTA

INGREDIENTS

Caramelized Onions

1 tbsp olive oil

1 tbsp butter

2 medium white onions, halved and thinly sliced

1 tsp sugar

½ tsp kosher salt

¼ cup balsamic vinegar

¾ lb penne pasta

1 tbsp olive oil

1 large garlic clove, minced

¾ cup dry white wine

5 plum tomatoes, seeded and chopped

4 cups fresh baby spinach, stemmed and thinly sliced

2 tbsp finely diced sun-dried tomatoes

1 tbsp chopped fresh basil

½ tsp kosher salt

¼ tsp freshly ground black pepper

⅓ cup freshly grated Parmesan cheese

½ cup soft fresh goat cheese, crumbled

Onions are a little like high school gym coaches. They have a reputation for being harsh, but warm them up a little and, boy, can they be sweet. In this case, 20 minutes of heat transforms the pungent bulb into a deep brown, sugary marmalade. Pair it with tangy goat cheese and you've got a rewarding pasta.

DIRECTIONS

1) For the onions, in a large skillet, melt oil and butter over medium heat. Stir in onions, sugar and salt. Sauté 15-20 minutes, until onions are a dark golden brown. Stir in balsamic vinegar and cook until liquid has evaporated, about 1½ minutes. Remove from heat and set aside. **2)** In a large pot of boiling, salted water cook pasta until just done. Drain well and set aside. **3)** In a large skillet, heat olive oil over medium heat. Add garlic and sauté 30 seconds, until fragrant. Turn heat to high, stir in white wine and reduce for about 3 minutes. Reduce heat to medium, add cooked pasta, caramelized onions, chopped tomatoes, spinach, sun-dried tomatoes, basil, salt and pepper, cooking for 1-2 minutes.
4) Remove from heat and stir in Parmesan cheese. Transfer to serving platter and crumble in goat cheese. Serve immediately.

Serves 6

LUSTFUL CREAMY CHICKEN FETTUCCINE

INGREDIENTS

Grilled Chicken

4 boneless, skinless chicken breast halves

2 tbsp olive oil

1 large garlic clove, minced

2 tbsp fresh lemon juice

½ tsp dried basil

½ tsp dried oregano

½ tsp kosher salt

¼ tsp freshly ground black pepper

1 lb fettuccine

Tomato Cream Sauce

2 tbsp olive oil

1 medium yellow onion, diced

2 small garlic cloves, minced

2 (19oz/540ml) cans Italian seasoned stewed tomatoes, pureed

⅛ tsp crushed red pepper flakes

1 cup heavy cream

1 cup freshly grated Parmesan cheese

½ tsp kosher salt

½ tsp freshly ground black pepper

Dear Alfredo –

I don't know quite how to tell you this, but we're done. You bore me. Yes, I used to crave you, but now, you make me weary. My new love can both stand alone and be a big hit around the table… might not be as rich as you, but certainly spicier, smoother, more irresistible and fulfilling.

Arrivederci, Alfie. Xoxo

DIRECTIONS

1) Place chicken breasts in a large resealable plastic bag. Add olive oil, garlic, lemon juice, basil, oregano, salt and pepper. Shake to combine, allowing to sit at room temperature for 30 minutes before grilling. 2) Preheat grill to medium and lightly oil grates. Grill chicken breasts, uncovered, 6-8 minutes per side or until the chicken is cooked through. Remove from grill and allow to sit 5 minutes before slicing. Cut into bite-size pieces and set aside. 3) In a large pot of boiling, salted water cook fettuccine according to package directions. Drain well and keep warm. 4) For the sauce, in a large saucepan, heat olive oil over medium heat. Add onion and cook, stirring until softened, about 3 minutes. Add garlic, stirring for 30 seconds. Stir in pureed tomatoes and red chili flakes, continuing to cook over medium heat for 10 minutes. Turn heat to low and add cream, stirring 2-3 minutes. Remove from heat and stir in Parmesan cheese, salt and pepper. 5) To serve, toss cooked fettuccine and sliced chicken into tomato cream sauce. Serve immediately.

Serves 8

BITE ME BIT

"The hottest love has the coldest end."

– Socrates, philosopher

MAESTRO'S PASTA alla NORMA

INGREDIENTS

1 large eggplant (about 1 lb), peeled, sliced into ¼-inch thick rounds

2 tbsp olive oil

½ tsp kosher salt

¼ tsp freshly ground black pepper

Sicilian Sauce

2 tbsp olive oil

1 small red onion, chopped

2 large garlic cloves, minced

⅛ tsp crushed red pepper flakes

2 cups chicken broth

2 cups plum tomatoes, cored and cut into 1-inch chunks

1 tbsp balsamic vinegar

½ tsp kosher salt

¼ tsp freshly ground black pepper

1 tbsp chopped fresh basil

½ cup crumbled ricotta salata or soft ricotta

¾ lb fusilli or penne pasta

This classic Sicilian sauce has been hitting the right note since 1831, the year it was named for Bellini's opera. Music to your palate, the sweet roasted eggplant is combined with a spicy tomato sauce and tangy ricotta salata, giving rise to a full-bodied aria.

DIRECTIONS

1) Preheat oven to 450°F. Line a baking sheet with aluminum foil and coat with non-stick cooking spray. 2) Place eggplant slices in a single layer on prepared baking sheet, drizzle with olive oil and season with salt and pepper. Bake for 10 minutes, turn the slices over and bake an additional 10 minutes, until soft and golden. Once cool enough to handle, cut into 1-inch pieces. Set aside. 3) For the sauce, in a large skillet, heat olive oil over medium heat. Add onion and cook, stirring frequently until softened, about 3 minutes. Add garlic and crushed red pepper flakes, continuously stirring for 1 minute, until garlic becomes fragrant. Add chicken broth and bring to a boil over high heat. Reduce heat to low and simmer for 3 minutes. Add tomatoes and continue to simmer on low for 15 minutes, until the tomatoes have softened. Add eggplant pieces, balsamic vinegar, salt and pepper. Stir well to combine. Remove from heat and add fresh basil and ricotta salata. 4) For the pasta, bring a large pot of lightly salted water to a boil over high heat. Add pasta and cook until tender. Drain well and return to pot. Toss hot pasta with sauce and serve immediately.

Serves 6

SMOOTH SPINACH and RICOTTA PASTA

INGREDIENTS

1 lb fusilli pasta

1 tbsp olive oil

8 cups baby spinach leaves, stemmed and cut into ½-inch strips

½ tsp kosher salt

¼ tsp freshly ground black pepper

1½ cups ricotta cheese

1 cup half-and-half

½ cup reserved pasta water

1 cup freshly grated Parmesan cheese

2 tbsp finely sliced fresh basil leaves

True-blue Pastafarians, we ignored all the Carbaphobian warnings and continued to buy bulk-size boxes. No one was going to scare us away from the luscious white noodles – long and short, hollow and swirled. This is our nirvana, Mon...let's all delight in this creamy dish of tender pasta paired with subtle ricotta cheese, mellow baby spinach and sharp, tangy Parmesan.

DIRECTIONS

1) Bring a large pot of lightly salted water to a boil over high heat. Stir in pasta and cook until tender. Reserve ½ cup pasta cooking water; drain pasta well. 2) In a large skillet, heat olive oil over medium heat. Add spinach, salt and pepper. Cook until spinach just begins to wilt, about 1-2 minutes. Stir in ricotta cheese, half-and-half and the reserved pasta water. Simmer on low heat for 5 minutes. Add cooked pasta and Parmesan cheese, stirring until well blended. Garnish with basil and serve immediately.

Serves 6-8

BITE ME BIT

"Pattycake, pattycake, Pasta Man. Gimme pasta power as fast as you can."

– Mario and Luigi in the television show "The Super Mario Bros. Super Show!"

PIQUANT PASTA PUTTANESCA

INGREDIENTS

2 tbsp olive oil

1 medium red onion, finely chopped

2 large garlic cloves, minced

½ cup black olives, pitted and halved

1 tbsp capers, rinsed and drained

½ tsp dried oregano

¼ tsp kosher salt

⅛ tsp crushed red pepper flakes

1 (28oz/796ml) can diced tomatoes

¼ cup dry red wine

¾ lb fettuccine pasta

¼ cup freshly grated Parmesan cheese

2 tbsp finely chopped fresh flat-leaf parsley

Quick and easy, spicy and fragrant, robust and satisfying, it's no wonder this Neapolitano dish is also known as "whore's spaghetti." Myth has it that prostitutes would use this aromatic sauce to lure men into their bordellos, so, unless you're looking for unexpected visitors, keep your windows closed.

DIRECTIONS

1) For the sauce, heat olive oil in a medium skillet over medium heat. Add onion and cook 3-4 minutes until softened, stirring occasionally. Add garlic and sauté until fragrant, about 1 minute. Add olives, capers, oregano, salt, crushed red pepper flakes and continue to sauté for 2 minutes. Add diced tomatoes and red wine, bringing to a boil, reduce heat to medium-low and simmer uncovered for 10 minutes, stirring occasionally. 2) For the pasta, bring a large pot of lightly salted water to a boil over high heat. Add pasta and cook until tender. Drain well and return to pot. Toss hot pasta with puttanesca sauce and Parmesan cheese. Top each serving with fresh parsley.

Serves 6

SOFT RICOTTA GNOCCHI in TOMATO SAUCE

INGREDIENTS

Gnocchi Dough

4 cups ricotta cheese

3 large eggs

1 cup freshly grated
Parmesan cheese

1 tsp kosher salt

¼ tsp freshly ground
black pepper

4 cups flour

Tomato Sauce

2 tbsp olive oil

1 large carrot, peeled
and chopped

1 small red onion, chopped

2 large garlic cloves, minced

2 (28oz/796ml) cans diced
tomatoes, with liquid

2 tbsp tomato paste

⅛ tsp crushed red pepper flakes

2 tsp sugar

½ tsp kosher salt

½ tsp freshly ground
black pepper

These small dumplings are harder to pronounce – NOK-ee? NYO-ke? NEE-okee? – than to make from scratch. Using basic ingredients such as ricotta, eggs, flour and Parmesan cheese we've created the lightest, most tender-textured gnocchi. Or, is that NYAW-kee?

DIRECTIONS

1) Dust 2 baking sheets with flour. Set aside. 2) For the dough, in a large bowl, using your hands or a wooden spoon, combine ricotta, eggs, Parmesan, salt and pepper. Add flour 1 cup at a time to form a soft dough. Transfer the dough to a lightly floured work surface and knead gently for 2 minutes. 3) Divide the dough into 6 pieces and roll each into a ball. Roll out each ball into ½-inch thick ropes. Cut each rope into 1-inch slices and gently place on prepared baking sheets. If not cooking right away, cover and place in refrigerator until ready to use. 4) For the sauce, in a large saucepan, heat oil over medium heat. Add carrot and onion, stirring for 3-5 minutes or until tender. Stir in minced garlic and cook until fragrant, about 1 minute. Add diced tomatoes, tomato paste and crushed red pepper flakes, bringing to a boil over high heat. Reduce heat to low and simmer uncovered for 15-20 minutes. Remove from heat and use a hand held or countertop blender to process until smooth. Season with sugar, salt and pepper. 5) To cook gnocchi, bring a large pot of lightly salted water to a boil over high heat. Drop pieces into boiling water and cook until gnocchi rise to the surface, about 2-3 minutes. Remove gnocchi using a slotted spoon and place in a serving bowl. Top with tomato sauce and serve.

Serves 8-10, yielding approximately 120 gnocchi

STRIKING THREE-CHEESE POLENTA LASAGNA

INGREDIENTS

1 cup shredded Fontina cheese

1 cup ricotta cheese

⅓ cup freshly grated Parmesan cheese

1 large egg

2 tsp chopped fresh basil

½ tsp kosher salt

Polenta

2 cups water

1½ cups whole milk

1 tsp kosher salt

1 cup yellow cornmeal

½ cup freshly grated Parmesan cheese

1 tbsp butter

Tomato Sauce

2 tbsp olive oil

1 small white onion, chopped

2 small garlic cloves, minced

1 (28oz/796ml) can whole Italian style tomatoes, undrained, crushed by hand

1 tsp sugar

1 tsp kosher salt

¼ tsp freshly ground black pepper

1 tbsp chopped fresh basil

Ready for a curveball? This lasagna is noodle-free. The same basic principle of lasagna construction applies, but, in place of pasta, polenta hugs the cheesy layers of Fontina, ricotta and Parmesan cheese. A unique and most delicious surprise, you won't need steroids to throw this towards the plate.

DIRECTIONS

1) Preheat oven to 350°F. Coat a 13x9-inch baking dish with non-stick cooking spray. As well, coat an 8x8-inch square baking dish with non-stick cooking spray. Set both aside. 2) In a medium bowl, stir together Fontina, ricotta, Parmesan, egg, basil and salt. Set aside. 3) For the polenta, in a large saucepan, bring water, milk and salt to a boil over high heat. Slowly whisk in cornmeal and reduce heat to low and simmer, stirring often with a wooden spoon until mixture is very thick, 5-7 minutes. Remove from heat and stir in Parmesan and butter. Immediately transfer to the 13x9-inch baking dish, spreading evenly to coat the bottom. Let polenta set for 10 minutes. Slice into 12 pieces and then slice each piece lengthwise to make thinner, lasagna-like noodles, to total 24 slices. 4) To assemble, lay 8 polenta slices on the bottom of the 8x8-inch baking dish. Top with half of the Fontina-ricotta mixture, followed by another 8 polenta slices. Spread remaining cheese mixture over polenta and finish with final 8 slices. Bake uncovered for 30 minutes, or until lightly browned and heated through. Let sit 5 minutes before cutting, serving each piece topped with tomato basil sauce. 5) For the tomato sauce, while polenta bakes, heat olive oil in a medium saucepan over medium heat. Add onion and sauté until tender, about 5 minutes. Add garlic, stirring for 30 seconds. Stir in crushed tomatoes, sugar, salt and pepper. Bring to a boil over high heat, reduce heat to low and simmer uncovered 15-20 minutes. Remove from heat and stir in basil. Yield: 2¼ cups sauce.

Serves 6-8

FANTASTIC 4 MUSHROOM and CHEESE LASAGNA

INGREDIENTS

Mushroom Sauce

1 (1.1oz/30g) package dried porcini mushrooms

1 tbsp olive oil

¼ cup diced shallots

2 cups sliced button mushrooms

2 cups sliced shiitake mushrooms

2 large portobello mushrooms, stemmed, gills scraped with a small spoon, sliced

1 tsp dried oregano

1 cup crumbled feta cheese

¼ cup rehydrated sun-dried tomatoes, sliced into thin strips

¼ cup flour

½ tsp kosher salt

1 cup milk

1 cup evaporated milk

Cheese Filling

2½ cups ricotta cheese

1 cup shredded mozzarella cheese

½ cup milk

¼ cup freshly grated Parmesan cheese

1 large egg, lightly beaten

¼ tsp kosher salt

¼ tsp freshly ground black pepper

12 oven-ready lasagna noodles

½ cup shredded mozzarella cheese, for topping

How do you make vegetarian lasagna meaty? Start with 4 types of savory and substantial mushrooms, add in intensely robust sun-dried tomatoes and layer mild-to-sharp cheese throughout. One bite of this incredibly aromatic lasagna and you'll discover the stretch of the cheese and the might of the mushroom foursome. Look out Dr. Doom... this is a powerful quartet.

DIRECTIONS

1) Preheat oven to 375°F. Coat a 13x9-inch baking dish with non-stick cooking spray. 2) For the sauce, place dried porcini mushrooms in a small bowl and cover with 1 cup of hot water. Let sit for 20 minutes or until softened. Remove mushrooms from liquid, rinse and pat dry. Chop mushrooms, discarding any hard stems. 3) In a large skillet, heat oil over medium heat. Add shallots and sauté for 3 minutes. Add porcini, button, shiitake, portobello mushrooms and oregano. Sauté until tender, stirring frequently for about 8 minutes. Remove from heat and stir in feta and sun-dried tomatoes. Set aside. 4) Place flour and salt in a saucepan over medium-high heat. Gradually add milk and evaporated milk, whisking constantly for 5 minutes or until thickened. Remove from heat and stir into mushroom mixture. 5) For the cheese filling, in a medium bowl, combine ricotta, mozzarella, milk, Parmesan, egg, salt and pepper. 6) To assemble the lasagna, in the prepared baking dish, spread a thin layer of the mushroom sauce and top it with 4 noodles. Spread ⅓ of remaining sauce and top with ½ of the cheese mixture. Top with 4 more noodles, half of the remaining mushroom sauce and all the remaining cheese filling. Finish with 4 noodles topped with the rest of the mushroom sauce. Sprinkle ½ cup mozzarella cheese over the top, cover with aluminum foil and bake for 30 minutes. Remove foil and continue to bake for 10 minutes.

Serves 8

BITE ME BIT

Did you know that "go hang a salami" and "I'm a lasagna hog," read the same spelled backwards?

BOLOGNESE-SMOTHERED PARMESAN POLENTA

INGREDIENTS

Polenta

5 cups water

1 tsp kosher salt

1 cup yellow cornmeal

¼ cup freshly grated
Parmesan cheese

Bolognese Sauce

1 lb lean ground beef

¼ cup milk

3½ cups chopped mushrooms
(you can use a variety of button,
shiitake, cremini)

1 large carrot, peeled
and finely chopped

1 small red onion, finely chopped

2 large garlic cloves, minced

1 tsp dried basil

1 tsp dried oregano

½ tsp kosher salt

¼ tsp freshly ground
black pepper

4 cups tomato sauce

½ cup dry red wine

1 piece of Parmesan rind,
2-3 inches long (the rind is
the outside edge on a chunk
of fresh Parmesan)

½ cup freshly grated Parmesan
cheese, for serving

On our insatiable Italian honeymoon my husband ate 18 bowls of pasta Bolognese in 17 days. An impressive feat until you consider that I ate 22 servings of polenta during that same gloriously gluttonous time. I did my new spouse proud. Now, many meals later, our newlywed passions are reunited with a rich and robust Bolognese sauce poured over cheesy polenta. Mangiamo.

DIRECTIONS

POLENTA

1) Coat an 11x7-inch baking dish with non-stick cooking spray. In a large pot, bring 5 cups of water and 1 teaspoon of salt to a boil over high heat. Reduce heat to low and slowly add the cornmeal, stirring constantly with a wooden spoon, about 10 minutes. The mixture should be thick and smooth. 2) Remove from heat, stir in ¼ cup Parmesan cheese and spoon into prepared baking dish. Set aside.

BOLOGNESE SAUCE

1) For the sauce, in a large skillet, sauté ground beef over medium-high heat, breaking it up as it cooks. Cook for 5 minutes, or until it is no longer pink. Drain in colander and return beef to skillet. 2) Add milk to skillet and cook over medium heat for 3 minutes, until milk is absorbed. Add mushrooms, carrot, onion, garlic, basil, oregano, salt and pepper. Cook over medium-low heat for 8 minutes, until the onion is softened. 3) Add tomato sauce, red wine and Parmesan rind to the meat mixture. Bring to a boil, reduce heat to low and simmer partially covered for 30 minutes. Remove from heat and discard Parmesan rind. 4) For serving, slice polenta into 6-8 servings and spoon Bolognese sauce over each portion. Finish with freshly grated Parmesan cheese.

Serves 6-8

ENTICING DEEP-DISH MEAT LASAGNA

INGREDIENTS

Meat Sauce

2 lbs lean ground beef

1 (28oz/796ml) can diced tomatoes

1 cup tomato paste

3 tbsp packed brown sugar

1 tbsp chopped fresh basil

1½ tsp kosher salt

1 tsp dried oregano

Cheese Filling

2 large eggs, lightly beaten

4 cups ricotta cheese

¾ cup freshly grated Parmesan cheese

1 tbsp chopped fresh basil

1 tsp kosher salt

12 oven-ready lasagna noodles

3 cups shredded mozzarella cheese, divided in half

¼ cup freshly grated Parmesan cheese, for topping

At first, I thought it was my melodious singing, the floral garland atop my flowing hair and the fact that I was only wearing a sheet that was luring construction workers, dogs and letter carriers to my front door. But no, sad to say, it was this lasagna, and, what's worse, it's Lisa's recipe. Guess I can stop my lyre lessons now.

DIRECTIONS

1) Preheat oven to 375°F. Coat a 13x9-inch baking dish with non-stick cooking spray. 2) For the sauce, in a large skillet, brown beef over medium-high heat. Drain and return to pan, adding diced tomatoes with their juice, tomato paste, brown sugar, basil, salt and oregano. Bring to a boil and then turn down to low, simmering for 30 minutes. 3) For the cheese filling, in a medium bowl, whisk eggs, ricotta, Parmesan, basil and salt. 4) To assemble, spread 1 cup of meat sauce in the prepared dish. Top with 4 noodles, ½ of the ricotta mixture, 1½ cups mozzarella and 1 cup meat sauce. Top with 4 more noodles, remaining ricotta and remaining mozzarella. Place 4 remaining noodles on top, cover with remaining meat sauce and sprinkle with Parmesan cheese. Bake uncovered for 35 minutes.

Serves 8

BITE ME BIT

"To attract men, I wear a perfume called 'New Car Interior.'"

– Rita Rudner, comedian

Spending endless hours in the kitchen takes a toll – feet throb, sweat trickles, hair frizzes and sometimes, in the middle of peeling the 30th potato, exhaustion kicks in.

Seeking company and inspiration, I turned on the television. Newscasts were depressing, soap operas distracting and game shows enraging...c'mon dude...Rice-A-Roni is so not $12.99/box. Off went the boob tube.

It was then that I figured out how to keep going. Music. The other taste that stirs the soul. Let me share with you the most uplifting mix of cooking music, tunes guaranteed to shake you, wake you and elate you...

Lip Synch
Tunes to Cook to

SONG LIST

Tired of Being Alone Al Green
Mama Told Me Not to Come Tom Jones
Can't Take My Eyes Off of You Lauryn Hill
Changes Seu Jorge
Adventures In Solitude The New Pornographers
Big Brother Stevie Wonder
Hard Sun Eddie Vedder
A Little Less Conversation Elvis Presley
Let's Get It On Marvin Gaye
Rafters Moby
Heaven Yusuf Islam
The Lady is a Tramp Frank Sinatra
Light My Fire Erma Franklin
I Want You Back (Z-trip remix) Jackson 5
Sing Annie Lennox
I Will The Beatles

BOTTOMLESS BOWL CHICKEN LASAGNA

INGREDIENTS

1 tbsp olive oil

6 boneless, skinless chicken breast halves, cut into ¾-inch cubes

2 large carrots, peeled and shredded

1½ cups sliced mushrooms

1 small yellow onion, diced

3 cups chicken broth

1 (28oz/796ml) can diced tomatoes

1 cup tomato sauce

1 tsp dried oregano

½ tsp dried basil

¼ tsp kosher salt

⅛ tsp freshly ground black pepper

6 oven-ready lasagna noodles, broken

1½ tsp cornstarch

1 cup ricotta cheese, for topping

½ cup shredded mozzarella cheese, for topping

¼ cup freshly grated Parmesan cheese, for topping

Lisa sometimes calls me Garfield for my lazy, lasagna-loving ways. When cravings strike, and I don't have the time or patience for layering, this cheese-topped pasta delivers quick-fix happiness in a bowl of tender noodles, succulent chicken and sweet vegetables.

DIRECTIONS

1) Heat the olive oil in a large soup pot over medium-high heat. Sauté chicken for 4 minutes until lightly browned. Stir in carrots, mushrooms and onions, cooking an additional 4-5 minutes. 2) Add broth, diced tomatoes with juice, tomato sauce, oregano, basil, salt and pepper. Bring to a boil over high heat. Reduce heat to medium-low and cook covered for 5 minutes. Turn heat to high and return to a boil. Add lasagna noodles and simmer over low heat for 20 minutes or until tender. 3) In a small bowl, combine cornstarch and a ladle of liquid from the soup pot. Mix to combine and stir into pot, thickening the broth. 4) Spoon the stew into bowls and top each serving with ricotta, mozzarella and Parmesan.

Serves 6

COCONUT LIME STICKY RICE

INGREDIENTS

1½ cups jasmine rice

1½ cups coconut milk, well shaken

1½ cups water

1 tbsp fresh lime juice

1 tsp lime zest

1 tsp sugar

1 tsp kosher salt

Okay, the song was really irritating, but Harry Nilsson was right. If you put the lime in the coconut then you do feel better. Less annoying, we hope, our tropical rice dish mixes a plain long grain with creamy coconut milk and tart lime juice, creating a swinging side dish that works great alongside Thai, Indian and Caribbean flavors.

DIRECTIONS

In a medium saucepan, combine rice, coconut milk, water, lime juice, lime zest, sugar and salt. Bring to a boil over high heat. Cover and reduce heat to low, simmering for 20 minutes. Remove from heat and let stand covered for 5 minutes. Fluff gently with fork.

Serves 6

BITE ME BIT

"I have a wild bunch of coconuts."

– Benny Hill, comedian

HEL...

DRAMATIC RED BEET RISOTTO

INGREDIENTS

1¼ lbs beets, trimmed, rinsed and peeled

1 tbsp olive oil

5-6 cups chicken broth

2 tbsp butter

2 tbsp olive oil

1 medium red onion, finely chopped

2 cups Arborio or Carnaroli rice

¾ cup dry white wine

¾ cup freshly grated Parmesan cheese

2 tbsp butter

¼ tsp kosher salt

¼ tsp freshly ground black pepper

DIRECTIONS

1) Preheat oven to 450°F. **2)** Place whole, peeled beets on a large piece of aluminum foil. Drizzle with 1 tbsp olive oil and tightly wrap beets into a foil packet. Place packet on a baking sheet and roast until tender, about 45-55 minutes. Remove from oven and let cool. **3)** When the beets are cool enough to handle, cut them into ¼-inch cubes and set aside to cool. **4)** In a medium saucepan, warm chicken broth over low heat. Keep at a bare simmer, covered. **5)** In a large saucepan, melt 2 tbsp butter and 2 tbsp olive oil over medium-low heat. Add onion, stirring occasionally until softened but not browned, 8-10 minutes. Increase heat to medium-high and stir rice into onions, stirring constantly for 1 minute. Pour in the white wine, stirring until most of the liquid is absorbed, about 1 minute. Reduce heat to low and ladle in ½ cup of the hot broth, stirring until the broth is almost completely absorbed. Continue adding ½ cup of broth at a time, stirring constantly and letting each addition be almost completely absorbed before adding the next. Continue this process for 20 minutes. The risotto is ready when the rice is mostly tender but with a hint of texture to it. At this point, stir in the roasted beets, Parmesan cheese, butter, salt and pepper. Blend well and remove from heat, letting it stand 3-4 minutes before serving.

Serves 8-10

SPECIAL FRIED RICE

INGREDIENTS

Sauce

3 tbsp soy sauce

2 tbsp oyster sauce

2 tbsp ketchup

2 tbsp packed brown sugar

1 tsp sesame oil

¼ tsp grated fresh ginger

Dash of hot pepper sauce, optional

Vegetable Rice

2 tsp vegetable oil

2 large eggs, lightly whisked

1 tbsp peanut oil

1 small white onion, diced

1 medium carrot, peeled and diced

1 medium red bell pepper, diced

1 small garlic clove, minced

1 cup frozen green peas

4 cups cooked long grain white rice, chilled

Fried rice is the yin and yang of Chinese cooking – flexible AND firm. On the one hand you're free to improvise – feel like adding some broccoli or chicken? Go right ahead. On the other hand there is a science to achieving the perfect fried rice, a rule we always adhere to: cold rice. When stir-fried, warm rice will result in a mushy mountain, whereas hardened, day-old grains will remain separated. Must be an ancient Chinese secret, but this one-dish meal is successfully laid back and regimented all at once.

DIRECTIONS

1) For the sauce, in a small bowl, whisk soy sauce, oyster sauce, ketchup, brown sugar, sesame oil, ginger and hot sauce (if using). Set aside. 2) Over medium heat, heat vegetable oil in a deep skillet or wok. Pour eggs into the skillet and cook without stirring for 30 seconds. Break egg into smaller pieces, cooking 1 minute more. Transfer to a small plate. 3) Using the same skillet, heat the peanut oil over medium-high heat. Add onion and cook until just softened, 1-2 minutes, stirring often. Add carrots and red peppers, continuing to cook for 2 minutes. Stir in garlic and frozen peas and cook until garlic is fragrant, about 1 minute. Add cooked rice, reserved egg and soy sauce mixture to the vegetables, stirring well to combine and cooking for 1 minute to heat through.

Serves 6-8

SUPER-SAUCY PEANUT BUTTER NOODLES

INGREDIENTS

Peanut Sauce

½ cup smooth peanut butter

½ cup hoisin sauce

¼ cup fresh lime juice

2 tbsp soy sauce

2 tbsp packed brown sugar

1 (14oz/400g) package fresh udon noodles

2 cups cold cooked shrimp, chopped

1 cup diced extra firm tofu

¾ cup thinly sliced red bell pepper

¾ cup snow peas, trimmed and cut on the diagonal

¼ cup chopped honey roasted peanuts

¼ cup chopped fresh flat-leaf parsley

2 tbsp sesame seeds, toasted

It's so unfair. Lisa never gets called the saucy sister. Everyone thinks she's the sweet one but that's just because she doesn't get caught rolling her eyes or crossing her arms. Well, fine, all you gullible ones out there. I'll be the saucy one. That way I get to hoard this addictively sweet and salty peanut-hoisin sauce.
So. There.

DIRECTIONS

1) For the sauce, in a small saucepan, whisk peanut butter, hoisin, lime juice, soy sauce and brown sugar. Bring to a boil over medium heat, stirring often. Remove from heat and set aside to cool. 2) Place noodles in a large heatproof bowl and cover with boiling water. Let stand for 3 minutes and gently loosen noodles. Drain well. 3) In a large bowl, toss noodles with peanut sauce, shrimp, tofu, red peppers and snow peas. Garnish with peanuts, parsley and sesame seeds. Serve at room temperature or chilled.

Serves 6

BITE ME BIT

"You are a saucy little thing, aren't you?"

— Simon Cowell, judge on "American Idol"

TOFU PAD THAI with SWEET CHILI SAUCE

INGREDIENTS

1 (1 lb/454g) package wide rice stick noodles

4 tsp vegetable oil, divided in half

1 (12oz/350g) package extra firm tofu, cut into ½-inch cubes

2 large eggs

3 large egg whites

2 cups fresh bean sprouts

½ cup minced fresh flat-leaf parsley

Sweet Chili Sauce

1¼ cup Heinz chili sauce

½ cup packed brown sugar

4 tbsp water

2 tbsp fish sauce

1 tbsp fresh lime juice

2 tsp grated fresh ginger

⅔ cup coarsely chopped dry roast peanuts, for topping

Lime wedges, for serving

If this cookbook thing doesn't work out, we've always got Bangkok. We'll open a street stall of our own and take the others by storm with our unsurpassed version of their national dish. Sure, our competition will use similar ingredients, but our vibrant Pad Thai will be adored for its spot-on sauce-to-noodle ratio, golden-cooked tofu and still-crispy bean sprouts. So delicious, we'll have longer lines than the women offering "soapies."

DIRECTIONS

1) Cook noodles in boiling water for 5 minutes. Drain and rinse under cold water. 2) In a large skillet, heat 2 tsp oil over medium-high heat. Cook tofu for 5-7 minutes, until browned. Remove from pan. 3) Whisk 2 eggs and 3 egg whites. In the skillet, heat remaining 2 tsp oil over medium-high heat. Add eggs and cook for 1 minute, stirring constantly. Set aside. 4) For the sauce, in a medium bowl, combine chili sauce, brown sugar, water, fish sauce, lime juice and ginger. Add sauce and drained noodles to skillet with egg mixture in it. Cook for 2 minutes over medium-high heat. Stir in tofu, bean sprouts and parsley, cooking an additional 3-5 minutes. Serve sprinkled with peanuts and garnished with lime wedges.

Serves 6-8

Gobble me

You'll Flip for the Bird

BITE ME BIT

Cowardly Lion: ...What puts the "ape" in apricot? What have they got that I ain't got?

Dorothy, Scarecrow, & Tinman: Courage!

– from the 1939 movie "The Wizard of Oz"

APRICOT AMARETTO CHICKEN

INGREDIENTS

6 boneless, skinless chicken breast halves

½ cup flour

2 large eggs

1½ cups panko (Japanese breadcrumbs)

2 tsp lemon zest

1 tsp kosher salt

½ tsp freshly ground black pepper

Apricot Amaretto Sauce

1 tbsp cornstarch

2 tbsp water

1½ cups chicken broth

¾ cup apricot jam

1 tbsp soy sauce

1 tbsp amaretto liqueur

2 cups canned apricots, drained and sliced

Warning: If you are a U.S. Marine, turn the page immediately.

They're certainly a loyal, heroic and fearless bunch but did you know that many in the Corps consider apricots the enemy? Yes, according to superstition, this velvety-skinned, golden fruit is a jinx – the mere mention of its name, let alone eating one, has the power to unleash a can of whoopass. But our experience with this smooth and sweet fruit has been more delicious than malicious, especially when it's mixed into an amaretto sauce that smothers this crunchy-coated chicken.

DIRECTIONS

1) Preheat oven to 400°F. Line a baking sheet with aluminum foil and coat with non-stick cooking spray. 2) Place chicken breasts between 2 sheets of wax paper and pound to even thickness, about ½-inch thick. 3) Place flour in a small bowl. In another bowl, lightly whisk eggs. In a third bowl, mix panko crumbs with lemon zest, salt and pepper. 4) Dust chicken breasts with flour, shaking off any excess. Dip into egg, then coat in panko mixture, patting to adhere. Place on prepared baking sheet. Bake 20-25 minutes, turning once halfway through. 5) For the sauce, in a small bowl, mix together cornstarch and water. In a medium saucepan, combine chicken broth, apricot jam and soy sauce. Bring to a boil over medium-high heat. Add cornstarch mixture, reduce heat to medium and stir continually for 4-5 minutes, or until slightly thickened. Remove from heat and mix in amaretto liqueur and sliced apricots. 6) To serve, cut each chicken breast into 3 pieces and pour sauce over the top. Serve immediately to ensure chicken coating remains crisp.

Serves 6

OVEN-FRIED CHICKEN with BUTTERMILK GRAVY

INGREDIENTS

Marinade

1½ cups buttermilk

2 tbsp Dijon mustard

1 large garlic clove, minced

1 tbsp olive oil

1 tsp lemon zest

½ tsp kosher salt

¼ tsp freshly ground black pepper

6 boneless, skinless chicken breast halves

2½ cups coarsely crushed corn flakes

1 cup freshly grated Parmesan cheese

Buttermilk Gravy

2 tbsp butter

3 tbsp flour

2 cups chicken broth

¼ cup buttermilk

¼ tsp kosher salt

I know. The term "oven-fried" is a contradiction. But we've found a most satisfying compromise, a happy medium to the traditionally fat-laden chicken. You can still have your down-home meal, creamy mashed potatoes and buttery corn to boot, just forget the fryer. Enjoy your juicy, crackling chicken smothered in creamy buttermilk gravy without punishing your arteries. See? Give-and-Take, Live-and-Bake.

DIRECTIONS

1) In a large shallow dish, whisk buttermilk, Dijon mustard, garlic, olive oil, lemon zest, salt and pepper. Add chicken breasts to marinade, cover and refrigerate at least 1 hour or preferably overnight. 2) Preheat oven to 375°F. Line a baking sheet with aluminum foil and coat with non-stick cooking spray. 3) In a medium bowl, combine corn flake crumbs and Parmesan. Remove chicken from marinade (discard used marinade) and coat each breast well in the corn flake mixture. Arrange on prepared baking sheet and bake 20-25 minutes, until cooked through and coating is golden. 4) For the gravy, in a medium saucepan, melt butter over low heat. Whisk in the flour until well blended. Gradually add the chicken broth, stirring constantly over medium heat. Bring the mixture to a boil and stir for 3-5 minutes or until thickened to a gravy-like consistency. Remove from the heat and stir in the buttermilk and salt. 5) To serve, slice cooked chicken breasts in half and pour gravy over the top.

Serves 6

MOM'S LEMON CHICKEN

INGREDIENTS

Marinade

¾ cup fresh lemon juice

¼ cup olive oil

¼ cup dry white wine

6 boneless, skinless chicken breast halves

½ cup flour

1 tbsp lemon zest

1 tsp kosher salt

½ tsp freshly ground black pepper

4 tbsp olive oil, divided in half

¼ cup packed brown sugar

½ cup chicken broth

¼ cup fresh lemon juice

6 lemon slices

1 tbsp toasted sesame seeds, for topping

I'm like Pavlov's dog. The whir of the electric juicer instantly triggers my salivary glands. Even as I write about it I drool a bit at the thoughts of the great things – fresh OJ, lemon meringue pie, veal piccata – that can come from its sweet hum. However, the best (slurp), um, tastiest (swallow) thing to come from the juicer is our Mom's lemon chicken. Marinated in white wine and lemon juice (gulp), the chicken is topped with brown sugar and lemon slices and then (glug) baked in a citrus broth mixture.

DIRECTIONS

1) Combine lemon juice, olive oil, white wine and chicken breasts in a large glass bowl. Cover and refrigerate at least 4 hours, but preferably overnight. 2) Preheat oven to 350°F. Coat a 13x9-inch baking dish with non-stick cooking spray. 3) In a medium bowl, combine flour, lemon zest, salt and pepper. Remove chicken from marinade (discard remaining marinade) and lightly coat in flour mixture, shaking off excess. 4) In a large skillet, heat 2 tbsp of the olive oil over medium heat. Add half the chicken breasts and cook until browned, about 3 minutes per side. Transfer browned chicken to the prepared baking dish and repeat with remaining 2 tbsp oil and chicken, adding to baking dish in a single layer. 5) Sprinkle brown sugar over chicken breasts. Pour chicken broth and lemon juice around chicken. Top each breast with a lemon slice and bake for 20 minutes. Garnish with toasted sesame seeds.

Serves 6

BITE ME BIT

"I believe if life gives you lemons, make lemonade...then find someone that life gave vodka to and have a party."

– Ron White, comedian

GREENHOUSE HERB CHICKEN

INGREDIENTS

2 large egg whites

1 cup breadcrumbs

½ tsp dried oregano

½ tsp dried basil

½ tsp kosher salt

¼ tsp freshly ground black pepper

6 boneless, skinless chicken breast halves

3 tbsp olive oil

Herb Sauce

1 tbsp olive oil

¼ cup finely sliced green onions

1 tbsp dried oregano

1 large garlic clove, minced

1 tbsp dried thyme

2 tbsp finely chopped fresh flat-leaf parsley

½ cup balsamic vinegar

3 cups chicken broth

4 tbsp tomato paste

We recycle. We walk more than drive. But, we're willing to deforest Mother Nature's herb garden for the sake of this aromatic chicken. Don't start picketing us – this earthy, savory sauce of oregano, thyme and parsley is our favorite renewable resource.

DIRECTIONS

1) Place egg whites in a small dish. On a large plate, combine breadcrumbs, oregano, basil, salt and pepper. 2) Dip each chicken breast in egg whites, then coat in breadcrumb mixture, patting well to adhere. 3) In a large skillet, heat 3 tbsp olive oil over medium-high heat. Brown chicken breasts, about 2 minutes per side or until golden. Remove from pan and set aside. 4) After wiping the skillet clean, heat 1 tbsp olive oil over medium heat. Add green onions, oregano, garlic, thyme and parsley. Sauté for 1 minute, stirring constantly. Add balsamic vinegar and cook for 2 minutes. Add chicken stock and tomato paste, bring to a boil and then reduce heat to low, simmering uncovered for 2 minutes. Return chicken breasts to skillet, simmering covered for 20 minutes.

Serves 6

BITE ME BIT

"Opie, you haven't finished your milk. We can't put it back in the cow, you know."

– Aunt Bee (actress Frances Bavier) in the television series "The Andy Griffith Show"

BODACIOUS HERB and GOAT CHEESE CHICKEN BREASTS

INGREDIENTS

Creamy Filling

1 cup cream cheese, softened

½ cup goat cheese, softened

3 fresh basil leaves, finely chopped

1 tsp minced fresh thyme

1 tsp fresh lemon juice

¼ tsp kosher salt

¼ tsp freshly ground black pepper

6 boneless, skinless chicken breast halves

6 slices white bread, crusts removed

2 tbsp melted butter

1 cup mayonnaise

2 tbsp Dijon mustard

1 tbsp fresh lemon juice

¼ tsp kosher salt

Move over, Jenna Jameson. These perfectly plump, beautifully formed, creamy-filled mounds are the new stars of food porn. Thanks to a crispy exterior of homemade breadcrumbs and a rich interior of herbs and cheese, these tantalizing, outrageously juicy and flavorful chicken breasts are nothing short of, well, we'll let you guess.

DIRECTIONS

1) Preheat oven to 425°F. Coat a 13x9-inch baking dish with non-stick cooking spray. 2) For the filling, in a small bowl, mash together cream cheese, goat cheese, basil, thyme, lemon juice, salt and pepper until combined. Divide mixture into 6 equal portions and form into the shape of a small tube. Set aside. 3) Place chicken between two sheets of wax paper and pound to even thickness, about ¼-inch thick. Pat the chicken dry, lay the smooth side of the chicken breast down and place a portion of the cheese mixture at the wider end of each piece. Roll the chicken up, starting at the end where the cheese was placed. Place in prepared baking dish seam side down. Set aside. 4) For the breadcrumb coating, in a food processor, pulse bread until fine crumbs. In a small dish, combine breadcrumbs with melted butter, tossing with a fork. 5) In a small bowl, whisk mayonnaise, Dijon mustard, lemon juice and salt. Brush each rolled chicken breast with the mayonnaise mixture and press the breadcrumbs on to coat. Bake 30-33 minutes, until golden. Slice on the bias to serve.

Serves 6

BALSAMIC CHICKEN with SWEET PEPPERS

INGREDIENTS

¼ cup flour

2 large egg whites

¼ cup breadcrumbs

¼ cup freshly grated
Parmesan cheese

2 tbsp olive oil

6 boneless, skinless
chicken breast halves

Balsamic Sauce

2 tsp olive oil

2 large red bell peppers,
sliced into strips

2 large green peppers,
sliced into strips

½ cup raisins

½ cup balsamic vinegar

3 tbsp sugar

½ tsp kosher salt

¼ tsp freshly ground
black pepper

½ cup toasted slivered
almonds, for topping

I made a really expensive blunder – peppers were sliced, plump raisins measured out and chicken sautéed to a golden crisp. But, oops, no cheap balsamic vinegar. Luckily, I discovered a small bottle of the dark beauty tucked away in the pantry and proceeded to use the entire 4 ounces to create the fragrant, syrupy sauce.

Here are the lessons I learned:

1. Always check for all ingredients before starting,
2. Reduced balsamic vinegar has the same rich taste whether it comes from a $50 vial or a $3.15 jug,
3. Licking all the plates clean does not bring with it absolution of guilt.

DIRECTIONS

1) Preheat oven to 375°F. Line a baking sheet with aluminum foil and coat with non-stick cooking spray. 2) Place flour in a shallow dish. Put egg whites in a separate bowl. Combine the breadcrumbs and Parmesan in a third dish. Dust chicken with flour, shaking off any excess. Dip in egg whites and then coat in the breadcrumb mixture. 3) In a large skillet, heat olive oil over high heat. Sauté the chicken for 2 minutes per side or until golden brown. Place chicken on prepared baking sheet and finish cooking in the oven for 18-20 minutes. 4) For the sauce, in a large skillet, heat olive oil over medium heat. Add red and green peppers and sauté for 8 minutes. Add raisins and stir for 1 minute. Add the balsamic vinegar, sugar, salt and pepper, mixing 1-2 minutes, coating the peppers. 5) To serve, slice chicken and top with balsamic sauce and toasted almonds.

Serves 6

BITE ME BIT

"I could have sexual chemistry with vinegar."

– Jessica Alba, actress

CHICKEN PARMESAN, REVAMPED!

INGREDIENTS

½ cup flour

2 large eggs, lightly beaten

1 cup panko (Japanese breadcrumbs)

1 cup freshly grated Parmesan cheese

6 boneless, skinless chicken breast halves

3 tbsp olive oil

2 cups chicken broth

1 cup tomato sauce

½ cup shredded mozzarella cheese

½ cup freshly grated Parmesan cheese

She won't organize your junk drawer or suggest a new eye shadow but Lisa is a makeover maven. She has transformed Chicken Parmesan from a traditionally greasy, leathery mess into a healthful, tender success. Cheesy and moist, this super-quick version (less than 15 minutes) will leave you plenty of time to alphabetize the take-out menus.

DIRECTIONS

1) Place flour in a small bowl. In another bowl, lightly beat eggs. In a third bowl, combine panko and Parmesan cheese. 2) Place chicken between two sheets of wax paper and pound to even thickness, about ½-inch thick. Lightly coat chicken in flour mixture, shaking off excess. Dip into beaten eggs and then transfer to panko mixture, patting the crumbs on both sides. 3) In a large skillet, heat oil over medium-high heat. Add chicken and sauté until lightly browned, about 3 minutes per side. Reduce heat to low. Add chicken broth to pan, spread 3 tbsp tomato sauce on each chicken breast and sprinkle with mozzarella and Parmesan. 4) Cover skillet and simmer until chicken is cooked through, about 6 minutes.

Serves 6

PECAN-CRUSTED LIME CHICKEN

INGREDIENTS

½ cup flour

½ tsp kosher salt

¼ tsp freshly ground black pepper

6 tbsp Dijon mustard

¼ cup melted margarine

2 limes, juiced

1 lime, zested

2 large eggs, lightly beaten

2 cups chopped pecans

2 cups breadcrumbs

6 boneless, skinless chicken breast halves

This recipe is to cooking what "Smoke on the Water" is to my kids' learning guitar. No matter your skill level, it'll always turn out good. But the similarities don't end there – both have 4 simple steps and both are confidence boosters that'll have you showing off for company. Now that you've nailed this classic, it's time to move onto some new creations.

DIRECTIONS

Note: Once coated, this chicken should be refrigerated for 2 hours or more. When you are ready to bake it, preheat the oven to 350°F.

1) Line a baking sheet with aluminum foil and coat with non-stick cooking spray. **2)** In a medium bowl, combine flour, salt and pepper. In a large bowl, whisk Dijon mustard, margarine, lime juice, lime zest and eggs. On a large plate, combine pecans and breadcrumbs. **3)** Working one chicken breast at a time, lightly coat chicken in flour (shake off excess), dip in mustard mixture and finally coat in the pecan mixture. **4)** Place pecan-crusted chicken on prepared baking sheet and cover with wax paper. Chill in refrigerator for 2 hours or more. Bake for 30 minutes and serve with lime wedges.

Serves 6

BITE ME BIT

"What's the matter, Colonel Sanders? Chicken?"

– President Skroob (actor Mel Brooks) in the 1987 movie "Spaceballs"

CRUNCHY TORTILLA CHICKEN with AVOCADO DIP

INGREDIENTS

6 boneless, skinless chicken breast halves

1½ cups sour cream

2 tbsp packed brown sugar

2 tsp chili powder

1 tsp chopped fresh thyme

1 tsp kosher salt

½ tsp freshly ground black pepper

½ tsp garlic powder

2½ cups panko (Japanese breadcrumbs)

2 cups crushed tortilla chips

1 cup shredded cheddar cheese

½ cup (or ¼ cup depending how much spice you like) jarred jalapeno peppers, dried off and chopped

Avocado Dip

½ cup mayonnaise

½ cup sour cream

2 ripe avocados, peeled and pit removed

2 tbsp fresh lime juice

¼ tsp ground cumin

¼ tsp cayenne pepper

½ tsp kosher salt

¼ tsp freshly ground black pepper

Chicken, here. Word is, my south-of-the-border kin are havin' way more fun...the fiestas, the spices... while all I get is limp breading and a dunk in the deep fryer. What did you say? I get to be el pollo loco too? Tell me more. Marinated in sour cream, chili powder and brown sugar? Fabuloso. Rolled in crushed tortillas, cheddar and spicy jalapenos? ¡Caliente! Me...juicy, crunchy tortilla crust and dipped in creamy avocado? ¡Ay, caramba!

DIRECTIONS

1) For the chicken, place chicken breasts between 2 sheets of wax paper and pound to even thickness, about ½-inch thick. 2) In a large bowl, combine sour cream, brown sugar, chili powder, thyme, salt, pepper and garlic powder. Add chicken and toss to coat, cover and let marinate in the refrigerator for 2 hours. 3) Preheat oven to 425°F. Line a baking sheet with aluminum foil and coat with non-stick cooking spray. 4) In a large bowl, combine panko, tortilla crumbs, cheddar and chopped jalapenos. Remove chicken from marinade and coat each piece with panko mixture, pressing down so coating sticks well to each piece. Place on prepared baking sheet and bake 20-23 minutes, until golden and cooked through. 5) For the avocado dip, place mayonnaise, sour cream, avocado, lime juice, cumin, cayenne pepper, salt and pepper in a food processor. Blend until smooth, about 30 seconds. Serve alongside chicken but if you're not eating it immediately, place avocado pit in the bowl to keep the dip from turning brown. Cover and refrigerate until ready to use. This dip yields 2 cups.

Serves 6

YEE HAW...TEX-MEX CHICKEN TORTILLA CASSEROLE

INGREDIENTS

6 boneless, skinless chicken breast halves, thinly sliced

2 limes, juiced

2 tsp ground cumin

1 tsp chili powder

½ tsp dried oregano

Rice and Bean Filling

2 cups cooked white rice

2 cups canned black beans, rinsed and drained

½ cup canned chopped green chilies

1 large red bell pepper, diced

1 tbsp fresh lime juice

1 tsp ground cumin

2 cups tomato sauce

2 cups salsa

1 tsp ground cumin

1 tsp chili powder

12 (6-inch) tortillas

2 cups shredded Monterey Jack or cheddar cheese, divided in half

1 cup sour cream, divided in half

This here heap of melted cheese, beans, spices, tortillas and salsa is good for the belly, good for the soul. Now better eat it right quick before the Sheriff comes over the hill, blasts us all to kingdom come and steals our grub.

DIRECTIONS

1) Preheat oven to 375°F. Coat a 13x9-inch baking dish with non-stick cooking spray. **2)** In a large bowl, combine sliced chicken breast, juice of 2 limes, cumin, chili powder and oregano. **3)** Coat a large skillet with non-stick cooking spray. Over medium heat, sauté chicken until cooked through, about 6-8 minutes. Transfer to a medium bowl and stir in cooked rice, black beans, green chili peppers, red bell peppers, lime juice and cumin. Stir well to combine. **4)** In a separate bowl, combine tomato sauce, salsa, cumin and chili powder. **5)** To assemble the casserole, spread 1 cup of tomato sauce mixture on the bottom of the prepared baking dish. Place 6 tortillas over the sauce, overlapping if necessary. Spoon another cup of sauce over tortillas, followed by ½ of the chicken mixture, 1 cup of cheese and ½ cup of sour cream. Arrange another layer of tortillas, then 1 cup of sauce, remaining chicken, remaining cheese and sour cream. Top with remaining sauce. Cover with foil and bake 30-35 minutes.

Serves 8

BITE ME BIT

"One tequila, two tequila, three tequila, floor."

— George Carlin, comedian

FEEL-GOOD CHICKEN CURRY

INGREDIENTS

2 tbsp mild curry powder

1 tsp garam masala

1 tsp ground cumin powder

1 tsp chili powder

3 tbsp butter

1 medium yellow onion, diced

2 large garlic cloves, minced

2 tsp grated fresh ginger

½ tsp kosher salt

1 tbsp tomato paste

4 boneless, skinless chicken breast halves, thinly sliced

½ cup chicken broth

1 (19oz/540ml) can diced tomatoes, pulsed 2 times in a food processor

1¾ cups canned chickpeas, rinsed and drained

1 cup frozen green peas

¼ cup heavy cream

1 cup chopped roasted cashews, for topping

1 cup plain yogurt, for topping

Some crazy dudes climb straight up mountains to get a natural high. Others jump off the backs of them in search of the same buzz. But we have a much lazier answer, we just grab a bowl of curry. Yes, curry. Studies link curry consumption and the release of endorphins – dig in for your hassle-free Himalayan high.

DIRECTIONS

1) In a large skillet, over medium-high heat, toast curry powder, garam masala, cumin and chili powder until spices become fragrant, 30-60 seconds. Remove from skillet to a plate and set aside. 2) In the same skillet, melt butter over medium heat. Add onion and cook until tender and golden, 7-8 minutes. Add garlic, ginger, salt, tomato paste and reserved toasted spices, stirring to combine. Increase heat to high, add sliced chicken and stir to coat with spice mixture. Add chicken broth, processed tomatoes and bring to a boil. Reduce heat to a gentle simmer and let chicken cook and sauce thicken slightly, about 10 minutes. Add chickpeas, frozen peas and cream, cooking on medium heat for 3-5 minutes until heated through. 3) Season with salt to taste. Serve over rice, garnished with chopped roasted cashews and yogurt.

Serves 4-6

MAGICAL MOROCCAN GRILLED CHICKEN

INGREDIENTS

3 tbsp olive oil

2 tsp ground cumin

1 tsp dried oregano

½ tsp ground ginger

½ tsp kosher salt

¼ tsp freshly ground black pepper

1 large garlic clove, minced

6 boneless, skinless chicken breast halves

Honeyed-Citrus Sauce

¾ cup orange juice, pulp-free

¼ cup honey

1 tbsp fresh lemon juice

½ tsp ground cinnamon

½ tsp kosher salt

3 tbsp butter

½ cup toasted slivered almonds, for topping

Inspired by the spices of North African cuisine, this grilled chicken is going to make you want to crack out your beaded bra-sarong-set and gyrate like a Marrakech mama. Now, in between doing figure eights with your hips, put some couscous and grilled eggplant on the plate to round out this exotic chicken.

DIRECTIONS

1) In a large bowl, combine olive oil, cumin, oregano, ginger, salt, pepper and garlic. **2)** Place chicken between two sheets of wax paper and pound to even thickness, about ¼-inch thick. Add to olive oil mixture and refrigerate for 10-15 minutes while the grill heats to medium-high. Brush and oil the grill grate. **3)** Arrange the chicken flat on the grill and cook until firm to the touch, about 2-3 minutes per side. Remove from grill and keep warm. **4)** In a small saucepan, bring orange juice, honey, lemon juice, cinnamon and salt to a boil. Reduce heat and simmer for 8-10 minutes. Remove from heat and stir in 3 tbsp butter. **5)** Drizzle sauce over grilled chicken and top with toasted almonds.

Serves 6

BITE ME BIT

"Sticking feathers up your butt does not make you a chicken."

– from the 1996 Chuck Palahniuk novel "Fight Club"

LEMON and DILL GRILLED CHICKEN

INGREDIENTS

Marinade

2 shallots, cut in half

¾ cup fresh lemon juice

3 tbsp lemon zest

¼ cup Dijon mustard

¼ cup olive oil

1 tsp dried oregano

1 tsp kosher salt

1 tsp freshly ground black pepper

10 sprigs fresh dill, washed and uncut

6 boneless, skinless chicken breast halves

2 limes, for serving

Lisa never minds when her husband springs the "guess-who's-coming-to-dinner" question on her. She'll just whip up confit, coulis or some other French word that's not in my culinary vocab. Me, on the other hand, I like to have a dependable, delicious and easy "old faithful" in my repertoire – here it is, a simple yet hugely flavorful grilled chicken that has been marinated in a zesty lemon, dill and Dijon mixture.

DIRECTIONS

1) In a large bowl, whisk shallots, lemon juice, lemon zest, Dijon mustard, olive oil, oregano, salt and pepper. Pour into a glass 13x9-inch baking dish. 2) Place chicken between two sheets of wax paper and pound to even thickness, about ½-inch thick. Add to marinade, scattering dill sprigs on top. Refrigerate 2-8 hours, turning once. 3) Preheat grill to medium-high. Brush and oil the grill grate. Discard marinade and dill, grilling chicken breasts 5-6 minutes per side or until cooked through. Squeeze some lime juice over the cooked chicken and serve with a wedge of lime.

Serves 6

SMOKIN' BBQ CHICKEN

INGREDIENTS

Marinade

½ cup fresh lemon juice

2 tbsp vegetable oil

1 tsp dried oregano

8 boneless, skinless chicken breast halves

BBQ Sauce

1½ cups ketchup

1½ cups honey

1 tbsp vegetable oil

1 tbsp soy sauce

1 tbsp fresh lemon juice

1 tsp Worcestershire sauce

1 tsp sugar

½ tsp freshly ground black pepper

½ tsp paprika

Ever wonder why there's no Orange Light District? Red, the color of passion, stokes the appetite. If you're looking for something to ignite your desire and those pay-per-view movies featuring firemen are getting a little stale, this juicy grilled chicken, slathered in a full-bodied, ruby-red BBQ sauce, will satisfy any hunger. Okay, almost any hunger.

DIRECTIONS

1) In a large glass bowl, combine lemon juice, vegetable oil, oregano and chicken breasts. Cover and let marinate in the refrigerator for at least 1 hour. 2) For the sauce, in a large bowl, whisk ketchup, honey, oil, soy sauce, lemon juice, Worcestershire sauce, sugar, pepper and paprika. Set aside 1 cup of sauce in a small bowl for basting and keep remaining sauce for serving with the cooked chicken. 3) Preheat grill to medium heat. Remove chicken from marinade (discard used marinade) and cook uncovered on grill for 6-8 minutes per side, or until cooked through. In the last few minutes of cooking, brush chicken with 1 cup reserved barbeque sauce on both sides.

Serves 8

BITE ME BIT

"Pornography and cooking shows have created two new spectator sports."

– Mason Cooley, academic

GRILLED 照り焼き (teriyaki) CHICKEN

INGREDIENTS

Teriyaki Sauce

¾ cup mirin

1 cup soy sauce

⅓ cup sugar

2 tbsp rice vinegar

1 tsp sesame oil

1 tsp grated fresh ginger

2 tbsp cornstarch

2 tbsp water

6 boneless, skinless chicken breast halves

1 tsp olive oil

2 large red bell peppers, cubed

1 large yellow pepper, cubed

Our mission is to make your life easier. Why then are we telling you how to make teriyaki sauce from scratch versus buying it? You'll never achieve the lustrous teri (sheen) when you yaki (grill) with preservative-laden bottled versions. Our perfectly balanced, 簡単な (easy) and 楽しい (delicious) sauce is a tasty payoff for 10 minutes' work.

DIRECTIONS

1) For the sauce, in a medium saucepan, bring mirin to a boil over medium heat. Reduce to low and simmer for 8 minutes. Add soy sauce, sugar, rice vinegar, sesame oil and ginger, whisking to combine. 2) In a small bowl, stir together cornstarch and water. Add to saucepan, turn heat to high and continue to whisk until slightly thickened, about 5 minutes. Remove from heat and let cool. 3) Place chicken in a bowl and toss with ½ cup teriyaki sauce. Allow to marinate in the refrigerator at least 30 minutes. 4) Heat grill to medium-high and oil the grill grate. Remove chicken from marinade (discard used marinade) and grill 6-8 minutes per side or until cooked through. Allow chicken to sit a few minutes before slicing on the bias. 5) In a large skillet, heat olive oil over high heat. Add peppers and stir fry for 3 minutes. Add sliced chicken and ½ cup teriyaki sauce, heating through. Store leftover teriyaki sauce in the refrigerator for up to 1 week.

Serves 6

BITE ME BIT

どうもありがとうミスターロボット (Dōmo arigatō misutō Robotto)
また会う日まで (Mata au hi made)
どうもありがとうミスターロボット (Dōmo arigatō misutā Robotto)
秘密を知りたい (Himitsu wo shiritai)

– from the 1983 Styx song "Mr. Roboto"

CRUNCHY CHICKEN WINGS with SWEET and SAVORY DIPPING SAUCES

INGREDIENTS

Chicken Wings

3 lbs chicken wings, split, wing-tip removed
¾ cup buttermilk
1 large egg
¾ cup yellow cornmeal
¾ cup flour
1 tsp kosher salt
1 tsp chili powder
1 tsp ground cumin
¼ tsp freshly ground black pepper

Sweet Dipping Sauce

1 cup apricot jam
¼ cup cider vinegar
2 tbsp packed brown sugar
1 tsp Dijon mustard
¼ tsp grated fresh ginger

Tangy Blue Cheese Dipping Sauce

1 cup crumbled blue cheese
½ cup buttermilk
½ cup sour cream
¼ cup mayonnaise
1 tbsp white wine vinegar
½ tsp sugar
½ tsp kosher salt
¼ tsp freshly ground black pepper

A few Dating 101 tips: less is more, let him pay, don't eat chicken wings, respect his mother. Well, I'm not so sure. My husband said that I sealed the deal at $4.99 Wing Night, where I rolled my sleeves high and devoured a basketful. I'm still charming him with these cornmeal-crusted wings baked to a grease-free golden crisp and dunked in a sweet apricot or tangy blue cheese dipping sauce.

DIRECTIONS

1) Place wings in a glass 13x9-inch baking dish. In a medium bowl, whisk buttermilk and egg. Pour over wings and marinate in refrigerator for at least 3 hours, up to 24 hours. 2) For the wings, preheat oven to 400°F. Line a baking sheet with aluminum foil and coat with non-stick cooking spray. 3) In a large bowl, combine cornmeal, flour, salt, chili powder, cumin and pepper. Remove wings from marinade (discard used marinade) and working a few at a time, coat in cornmeal mixture. Place on prepared baking sheet. 4) Bake 40-45 minutes, turning once halfway through baking. 5) For the sweet dipping sauce, in a small saucepan, combine jam, vinegar, brown sugar, Dijon mustard and ginger. Heat over medium heat until sugar has dissolved and ingredients are combined. Cool before serving. 6) For the blue cheese dipping sauce, in a medium bowl, use a fork to mash together blue cheese and buttermilk until it looks like cottage cheese. Add sour cream, mayonnaise, vinegar, sugar, salt and pepper, stirring well to combine.

Serves 4-6 (or 2 very hungry wing lovers)

CHICKEN and VEGETABLE LO MEIN

INGREDIENTS

1 (14oz/400g) package fresh lo mein, chow mein or other Chinese noodles

1 cup chicken broth

⅓ cup soy sauce

3 tbsp oyster sauce

2 tbsp hoisin sauce

2 tbsp mirin

1 tbsp cornstarch

1 tbsp peanut oil

3 cups chopped bok choy

2 large red bell peppers, chopped

1½ cups chopped celery

3 cups deli roasted chicken breast, shredded or cubed

A plea to Irish rockers U2. Just once, don't you think you could sing it my way? Try it. "Where the Sheeps Have Lo Mein." Catchy and delicious. Our saucy Chinese noodles, with veggies and chicken abounding, are a guaranteed #1 hit and will curb any craving for the take-out carton. So, for your next tune, Bono, how do you like "Someday, buddy, Someday?"

DIRECTIONS

1) Fill a large saucepan with water and bring to a boil. Once boiled, reduce heat to low and add fresh noodles. Stir to loosen the noodles and cook for about 2 minutes. Drain and set aside. 2) In a medium bowl, whisk broth, soy sauce, oyster sauce and hoisin sauce. In a small bowl, dissolve the cornstarch in the mirin. Add cornstarch mixture to broth mixture whisking well to combine. Set aside. 3) In a wok or a large skillet, heat peanut oil over high heat. Add bok choy, red peppers and celery. Stir fry for 2-3 minutes until the vegetables have softened slightly. Add chicken, softened noodles and broth mixture. Cook, stirring for 2 minutes, until sauce is thickened.

Serves 6

CHINESE ORANGE ALMOND CHICKEN

INGREDIENTS

6 boneless, skinless chicken breast halves

1 large egg

½ cup milk

½ cup flour

¼ tsp kosher salt

2 cups panko (Japanese breadcrumbs)

2 cups sliced almonds

2 tbsp butter

Orange Sauce

¼ cup sugar

1 tbsp flour

1 tbsp cornstarch

¼ tsp kosher salt

¾ cup orange juice

¼ cup water

2 tbsp fresh lemon juice

2 tsp butter

1 tsp orange zest

1 tsp lemon zest

Craving Chinese food? Instead of scouring the menu for the #32 Almond Chicken, save yourself the calories and chemicals and go for our goo-free version. Not only is it easy to make but it's also free of MSG, salt-mine-sodium and the deep-fryer glaze.

DIRECTIONS

1) Preheat oven to 350°F. Line a baking sheet with aluminum foil and coat with non-stick cooking spray. 2) Place chicken between 2 sheets of wax paper and pound to even thickness, about ½-inch thick. 3) In a small bowl, whisk egg, milk, flour and salt. In a shallow dish, combine panko and almonds. 4) Dip chicken breasts in egg mixture and then coat in panko-almonds, pressing gently to adhere. 5) In a large skillet, melt 2 tbsp butter over medium heat. Add coated chicken breast, cooking 3 minutes per side or until lightly browned on both sides. Remove from skillet and place on prepared baking sheet. Bake 20 minutes. 6) For the sauce, in a medium saucepan, whisk sugar, flour, cornstarch and salt. Add orange juice, water and lemon juice, whisking well to combine. Place over high heat and bring to a boil. Reduce heat to low, stirring constantly for 2-3 minutes or until sauce thickens. Remove from heat and add 2 tsp butter, orange zest and lemon zest. Stir well to combine. 7) To serve, diagonally slice each chicken breast into 4 pieces and drizzle with warm orange sauce.

Serves 6

ASIAN CHICKEN LETTUCE BUNDLES

INGREDIENTS

Sauce

½ cup sushi vinegar

½ cup soy sauce

3 tbsp oyster sauce

1 tbsp sesame oil

2 tbsp cornstarch

Chicken

3 boneless, skinless chicken breast halves

¼ cup dry white wine

3 tbsp cornstarch

2 large egg whites

½ tsp kosher salt

1 tbsp vegetable oil

1 large garlic clove, minced

1 cup water chestnuts, rinsed and chopped

2 medium red bell peppers, finely chopped

2 medium carrots, peeled and julienned

2 (1.1oz/30g) packages dried portobello mushrooms, rehydrated in boiling water for 20 minutes, rinsed well, patted dry and chopped

Topping

½ cup sliced almonds

2 (3oz/85g) packages ramen noodles, crushed

Iceberg lettuce leaves

6 tbsp hoisin sauce

Chew with your mouth closed. Don't put your feet on the table. That's pretty much the extent of my rules governing dining etiquette. When it comes to eating I like to take my cue from the Indian culture, hands-on. Fiddling with my food since childhood, these moo-shu-like lettuce wraps are another great excuse to hold dinner in the palm of my hand. Now I just have to remember: napkin, not sleeve.

DIRECTIONS

1) For the sauce, in a medium bowl, whisk sushi vinegar, soy sauce, oyster sauce, sesame oil and cornstarch. Set aside. 2) For the chicken, in a food processor, pulse chicken breasts until finely chopped. Place in a medium bowl and set aside. In a small bowl, stir together white wine, cornstarch, egg whites and salt. Pour over chopped chicken and marinate for 10 minutes. 3) Fill a large saucepan with water and bring to a boil over high heat. Pour chicken and marinade into boiling water and stir constantly to break up lumps. Cook 4-5 minutes or until chicken is no longer pink. Drain chicken mixture into a strainer. Set aside. 4) In a large skillet, heat vegetable oil over medium-high heat. Add garlic, water chestnuts, red peppers, carrots and mushrooms, stirring until softened. Add chicken mixture and continue cooking for another 3 minutes. Add reserved sauce to skillet, turn heat to high and stir until sauce has thickened, about 3 minutes. 5) For the topping, in a small skillet, brown almonds and noodles over medium heat until golden. 6) To serve, divide chicken mixture among lettuce leaves topping each with 1 tbsp of hoisin sauce and sprinkle with almonds.

Serves 4-6

SWEET 'n' STICKY WINGS

INGREDIENTS

3 lbs chicken wings, split, wing-tip removed

1 cup honey

½ cup soy sauce

½ cup packed brown sugar

¼ cup ketchup

2 tbsp Heinz chili sauce

½ tsp garlic powder

½ tsp grated fresh ginger

WINGDING [NOUN]: A NOISY, EXCITING CELEBRATION OR PARTY.

And, if we might amend that definition, it involves intensely gooey, honey-soy chicken wings. They are best shared with those who do not ask where they can find moist towelettes.

DIRECTIONS

1) Coat a 13x9-inch baking dish with non-stick cooking spray. Place the wings in the dish and set aside. 2) In a small saucepan, combine honey, soy sauce, brown sugar, ketchup, chili sauce, garlic powder and ginger. Bring to a boil over medium-high heat. Once boiling, pour honey mixture over chicken wings. Cover and marinate in refrigerator for a few hours or overnight. 3) Preheat oven to 375°F. 4) Remove wings from refrigerator and cover with aluminum foil. Bake in marinade for 55 minutes, stirring occasionally. Remove foil cover and bake wings for an additional 15 minutes or until sauce is thickened.

Serves 6

BITE ME BIT

Competitive eater Joey "Jaws" Chestnut set a new record at the 2008 Wing Bowl XVI when he ate 241 chicken wings in 30 minutes.

TURKEY BURGERS with MANGO MAYO

INGREDIENTS

Turkey Burgers

¼ cup mango chutney, pureed smooth

¼ cup sour cream

¼ cup finely diced celery

¼ cup panko (Japanese breadcrumbs)

2 tsp Dijon mustard

1 tsp fresh lemon juice

½ tsp kosher salt

1 lb ground turkey breast

1 tbsp olive oil

Mango Mayonnaise

½ cup diced mango

¼ cup mayonnaise

1 tsp fresh lime juice

1 tsp sugar

4 hamburger buns

Before Oprah had anything to say about the subject, turkey burgers elicited as much excitement from carnivores as a Richard Simmons workout. Even more delectable and flexible than its beefy cousin, the turkey burger once again proves what we knew all along – Oprah's always right.

DIRECTIONS

1) For the burgers, in a large bowl, whisk chutney, sour cream, celery, panko, Dijon mustard, lemon juice and salt. Add ground turkey, mix well and shape into 4 patties. Place on a plate, cover and refrigerate for 2 hours to firm up slightly before cooking. 2) Preheat barbeque to medium-high heat and lightly oil the grill. Brush the burgers with 1 tbsp olive oil, place on grill and cook 8-9 minutes per side, until meat is thoroughly cooked through. The internal temperature of the turkey burger should be between 160°F-165°F. 3) For the mango mayonnaise topping, place mango, mayonnaise, lime juice and sugar in a food processor or blender. Process until smooth. Place turkey burger on a hamburger bun and top with mango mayonnaise.

Serves 4

BITE ME BIT

"Allow myself to introduce…myself. I'm Richie Cunningham and this is my wife Oprah."

– Austin Powers (actor Mike Myers) in the 1997 movie "Austin Powers: International Man of Mystery"

BANG-ON ROASTED TURKEY BREAST

INGREDIENTS

2 large garlic cloves, minced

¼ cup honey

2 tbsp olive oil

2 tbsp Dijon mustard

2 tbsp soy sauce

1 tbsp balsamic vinegar

1 tbsp finely chopped fresh basil

½ tsp freshly ground black pepper

3½ lb boneless turkey breast

1 cup chicken broth, divided in half

Sentence starters that make us cringe:

1. "Anywhoo…"
2. "But I digress…"
3. "Do I have a story…"

No, please don't ramble on. For two girls who like to cut to the chase, this quick, oven-roasted turkey breast is ideal. Forget the dark meat and the wings – the breast, beautifully browned, moist and juicy, is both succulent and succinct.

DIRECTIONS

1) For the marinade, in a small bowl, mix together garlic, honey, olive oil, Dijon mustard, soy sauce, vinegar, basil and pepper. Set aside. 2) Rinse turkey breast and pat dry. Place in a shallow roasting pan and coat turkey breast in the marinade. Cover and refrigerate at least 4 hours, turning occasionally. 3) Preheat oven to 325°F. 4) Bring turkey to room temperature before roasting. Add ½ cup of chicken broth to the bottom of the pan and cover the turkey with aluminum foil. Roast for 1½ hours, basting with the pan juices once or twice during cooking. Remove the foil and raise the oven temperature to 450°F. Add the remaining ½ cup of chicken broth to the pan and continue to roast for 20 minutes or until an instant-read thermometer, inserted into the thickest part of the breast, registers 175°F. 5) Remove from the oven and allow turkey to stand for 10 minutes before carving. In a small saucepan over high heat, warm any remaining pan juices and serve with turkey slices.

Serves 6-8

LICKITY SPLIT TURKEY, STUFFING and CRANBERRY SAUCE

INGREDIENTS

Turkey Marinade

1 (1.38oz/39g) envelope onion soup mix

2 cups apricot jam

1 cup French salad dressing

1 tbsp honey mustard

1 tbsp paprika

1 tsp garlic powder

1 tsp celery salt

1 tsp freshly ground black pepper

16-18 lb whole turkey

1 turkey-size (19"x23") oven bag

1 tbsp flour

Stuffing

2 egg breads (challahs), crusts removed and cut into 1-inch cubes (approximately 14 cups total)

¼ cup butter

1 medium white onion, finely chopped

4 large celery stalks, finely chopped

1 tbsp chopped fresh sage

1 tbsp chopped fresh thyme

4 cups chicken broth

1 tbsp soy sauce

4 large eggs

People often groan at the thought of eating leftover turkey for a week...we look forward to it. Our turkey, roasted in an oven bag, not only cooks in half the time of traditional recipes but also has twice the moistness and flavor. The gravy is smooth and rich, the stuffing is sweet and savory and the cranberry sauce is perfection – finally a feast we can be thankful for year-round.

DIRECTIONS

THE TURKEY

1) Keep only bottom rack in oven. Preheat oven to 350°F. 2) In a medium bowl, combine envelope of onion soup mix, jam, French dressing, honey mustard, paprika, garlic powder, celery salt and pepper. Mix well and set aside. 3) Make sure the turkey cavity is empty. Rinse and pat the turkey dry. Sprinkle the bottom of the oven bag with flour and shake around the bag to prevent the bag from bursting during cooking. Place the oven bag in a large roasting pan with sides at least 2-inches high. Place the turkey in the bag and pour onion soup mixture over the turkey, making sure the entire turkey is covered with sauce. Seal the bag with the twist tie provided in the package. Cut 6 slits (each ½-inch long) in the top of the bag to allow the steam to escape. NOTE: You do not turn or baste the turkey during cooking. 4) Place the turkey in the oven until an instant-read thermometer inserted into the thickest part of the thigh reaches 180°F and the breast of the turkey at the thickest point reaches an internal temperature of 170°F. Don't be surprised if the turkey takes under 2 hours as the bag dramatically speeds up cooking time...go by the thermometer dial, not the time in the oven. 5) When the turkey is done, slit the bag

1½ cups half-and-half

2 tbsp chopped fresh
flat-leaf parsley

1 tsp kosher salt

½ tsp freshly ground
black pepper

1 cup dried cranberries
or dried cherries

¼ cup melted butter, for topping

Sweet Cranberry Sauce

3 cups fresh or frozen
cranberries

1 cup orange juice or
cranberry juice

½ cup sugar

½ cup packed brown sugar

½ cup dried cherries

and lift out the turkey placing it on a large cutting board. Allow the turkey to rest for 20 minutes before carving. **6)** For the gravy, take the sauce that remains in the roasting pan and strain it into a large saucepan. Allow it to sit for a few minutes and then skim off any fat that has come to the surface. Over high heat, reduce sauce to desired consistency. Taste for salt and pepper and pour over sliced turkey.

Serves 10-12

THE STUFFING

1) Preheat oven to 325°F. Arrange bread cubes in a single layer on 2 baking sheets. Bake 30 minutes or until golden, swapping tray positions and rotating halfway through baking. Set aside to cool. **2)** Coat a 13x9-inch baking dish with non-stick cooking spray. Set aside. **3)** In a large skillet, melt butter over medium heat. Add onions and celery. Sauté 10 minutes or until golden. Stir in sage, thyme, chicken broth and soy sauce, simmering for 10 minutes or until vegetables are tender. Allow to cool for 5 minutes. **4)** In a large bowl, whisk eggs, half-and-half, parsley, salt and pepper. Stir in onion-celery mixture. Add bread cubes and cranberries, gently tossing to coat, ensuring all bread is soft and moist. Transfer to prepared baking dish. Drizzle with melted butter and bake for 45-50 minutes, until top is golden.

Serves 8-10

SWEET CRANBERRY SAUCE

1) Rinse and drain cranberries. In a large saucepan, combine cranberries, orange juice, sugar, brown sugar and dried cherries. Bring to a boil over high heat. Reduce heat to medium and simmer uncovered until cranberries pop open and sauce thickens, about 10 minutes. Spoon off any foam that has formed and cool to room temperature before serving.

Yield: 2 cups cranberry sauce

Catch me

Hooked on Fish

HALIBUT, TOMATOES and THYME in WHITE WINE

INGREDIENTS

Halibut

2 tbsp olive oil

6 (6oz) halibut fillets, skin removed

¼ tsp kosher salt

¼ tsp freshly ground black pepper

Wine and Tomato Broth

1 tbsp olive oil

1 large shallot, thinly sliced

1 large garlic clove, minced

½ cup dry white wine

1 (28oz/796ml) can diced tomatoes, drained well

2 cups chicken broth

1¾ cups canned white kidney (cannellini) beans, rinsed and drained

½ tsp minced fresh thyme

½ tsp kosher salt

¼ tsp freshly ground black pepper

TOP 10 REASONS TO MAKE THIS:

10. To show up Captain High Liner, the bearded dude who breads everything.
9. Nobody will say, "Mmm...tastes like chicken."
8. Your mother-in-law is allergic to fish.
7. Thyme is an herb. Now that Simon & Garfunkel song makes even less sense.
6. With a glass of milk, you cover all your food groups.
5. Can drop "Order Pleuronectiformes" (n. flatfish) into the convo.
4. Less "experimental" than blowfish.
3. If ever you meet someone fluent in Mennonite Low German, you'll be able to communicate: Halibut = en Seefesch.
2. So easy to make. Like shooting fish in a barrel.
1. You get to eat and drink your dinner at the same time.

DIRECTIONS

1) In a large skillet, heat olive oil over high heat. Season fish with salt and pepper. Add fish to pan, browning 2 minutes per side until golden. Remove from pan and set aside. 2) Wipe skillet clean and add olive oil over medium-low heat. Add the shallots and garlic, stirring continuously for 1 minute. Add the white wine and increase the heat to medium-high, cooking for 1 minute. Stir in the drained diced tomatoes, chicken broth, beans, thyme, salt and pepper. Bring to a boil and then reduce heat to low, simmering for 10 minutes. Add fish to pan, cover and let simmer another 10 minutes or until cooked through.

Serves 6

WALNUT-CRUSTED HALIBUT with LEMON WINE SAUCE

INGREDIENTS

6 (6-8oz) halibut fillets, skin removed

½ tsp kosher salt

¼ tsp freshly ground black pepper

Walnut Crust

1½ cups panko (Japanese breadcrumbs)

1 cup chopped walnuts

½ cup freshly grated Parmesan cheese

2 tbsp melted butter

1 tbsp horseradish

1 tbsp Dijon mustard

1 tbsp chopped fresh flat-leaf parsley

1 tbsp chopped fresh dill

1 tsp lemon zest

1 tbsp olive oil

Lemon Wine Sauce

1 tsp olive oil

2 tbsp finely chopped shallots

1 cup dry white wine

2 tbsp fresh lemon juice

2 tbsp butter

2 tbsp chopped fresh dill

Kosher salt and freshly ground black pepper to taste

PISCES FEBRUARY 19 – MARCH 20

You've been feeling pretty blah and boring lately. Don't fret because today's your day to dive in. Take the bait and get ready for a thrilling experience – becoming part of the "in" crowd, happily mingling amongst bold, rich and nutty sorts. Surprisingly, you'll get on especially well with the cheesy, crusty and whiny ones too.

DIRECTIONS

1) Preheat oven to 425°F. Line a baking sheet with aluminum foil and coat with non-stick cooking spray. 2) Pat the fish dry with paper towel and season with salt and pepper. Place on prepared baking sheet ½ inch apart. 3) For the crust, in a medium bowl, combine panko, walnuts and Parmesan. Mix in melted butter, horseradish, Dijon mustard, parsley, dill and lemon zest to form a crumbly mixture. Divide panko mixture evenly atop fish and press gently to adhere. Drizzle 1 tbsp olive oil on top of fish. Bake until cooked through, 12-15 minutes. 4) For the sauce, in a medium saucepan, heat 1 tsp olive oil over medium heat. Add shallots and stir for 2 minutes, until slightly softened. Turn heat to high and add white wine and lemon juice. Boil until liquid is reduced, about 6-8 minutes. Reduce heat to low and stir in 2 tbsp butter until melted. Remove from heat and add fresh dill. Season with salt and pepper to taste. Serve over crusted halibut.

Serves 6

BITE ME BIT

"Fish, to taste right, must swim three times – in water, in butter and in wine."

– Polish proverb

SWEET and SOUR HALIBUT

I love a good bet. You'll eat a spoonful of cinnamon for $10? Count me in. A swig of suicide hot sauce for $15? Money well spent. But here's the one thing I'd never bet against...this halibut. It's the 21, the Royal Flush, baby. Perfectly sweet and sour flavors and guaranteed rave reviews from company make this an ace fish dish.

INGREDIENTS

Halibut

8 (6-8oz) halibut fillets, skin removed

¼ cup dry white wine

1 tsp kosher salt

Sweet and Sour Sauce

1 cup ketchup

¾ cup rice vinegar

¾ cup sugar

¼ cup soy sauce

¼ cup dry white wine

1 tbsp sesame oil

3 large red bell peppers, diced

2 large celery stalks, diced

1 small yellow onion, diced

2 cups seeded and diced tomatoes

2 cups frozen green peas

5 tbsp water

3 tbsp cornstarch

DIRECTIONS

1) Preheat oven to 450°F. Line a baking sheet with aluminum foil and coat with non-stick cooking spray. 2) Place fish on prepared baking sheet, sprinkle with ¼ cup white wine and salt. Bake for 10-12 minutes or until fish flakes easily. Set aside. 3) For the sauce, in a large bowl, whisk ketchup, rice vinegar, sugar, soy, wine and sesame oil. Set aside. 4) Place red peppers, celery and onion in a large skillet over medium heat. Cover and let the vegetables sweat to soften, about 6 minutes. Uncover and add tomatoes and peas, stirring gently to combine. Add ketchup mixture and cook uncovered for 5 minutes. 5) To thicken the sauce, in a small bowl, dissolve cornstarch in water. Add to sauce and cook over medium heat for 3 minutes or until slightly thickened. Pour sauce over fish and serve.

Serves 8

BITE ME BIT

"I'd be willing to bet you, if I was a betting man, that I have never bet on baseball."

– Pete Rose, baseball player

MISO GLAZED COD

INGREDIENTS

Miso Marinade

¾ cup sake

¾ cup mirin

1 cup white miso paste

2 tbsp soy sauce

½ cup packed brown sugar

6 (6oz) cod fillets
(can also use halibut
or sea bass)

Made famous by celebrity chefs Nobuyuki "Nobu" Matsuhisa and Wolfgang Puck, the pairing of miso and cod is, well, like peanut butter and jelly...they belong together. Though super-simple to make, remember to plan ahead because the longer the fish marinates, the better.

DIRECTIONS

1) For the marinade, combine sake and mirin in a medium saucepan over high heat. Boil for 30 seconds. Turn heat to low and add miso paste and soy sauce, stirring until the paste is completely dissolved. Add brown sugar and turn the heat back to high, stirring continuously until sugar has dissolved. Remove from heat and cool to room temperature. 2) Pat the cod fillets dry with paper towels. Place fish in a large resealable plastic bag and pour in the marinade. Refrigerate 12-24 hours, turning fish occasionally. 3) Preheat oven to 450°F. Line a baking sheet with aluminum foil and coat with non-stick cooking spray. 4) Remove fish from marinade, lightly wiping off any excess marinade clinging to the fillets. Place cod on prepared baking sheet and bake 6-7 minutes. Finish fish under the broiler, 2-3 minutes, to get a glaze on top.

Serves 6

BITE ME BIT

"...Ok, let's go to John Travolta. He wrote down 'miso,' a type of Italian soup. What was your wager? You wrote down 'horny,' 'miso horny.'"

– Alex Trebek (played by actor Will Ferrell) in a 1997 episode of "Saturday Night Live"

SURPRISE! COD WRAPPED in RICE PAPER

INGREDIENTS

1½ tsp chopped fresh basil

¾ tsp kosher salt

½ tsp freshly ground black pepper

6 rice paper sheets

6 (6-8oz) cod fillets, 1-inch thick

Sauce

1 tsp olive oil

2 shallots, finely chopped

1 large garlic clove, minced

6 tbsp soy sauce

¼ cup rice wine vinegar

1½ tsp sugar

⅛ tsp crushed red pepper flakes

2 tbsp olive oil

I'm a sucker for anything that arrives gift-wrapped. One time Lisa really threw me when she delivered a fine little bundle to my doorstep. At first I thought it was a new iPod, but then she unveiled a perfect parcel of cod wrapped in Vietnamese rice paper. I never could imagine – a present where you get to eat the gift AND the wrapping paper.

DIRECTIONS

1) Preheat oven to 450°F. 2) In a small bowl, mix basil, salt and pepper. Set aside. 3) For the rice paper, fill a pie dish with warm water. Carefully submerge 1 piece of rice paper in water for 20 seconds, remove, lay on a dish towel and place 1 cod fillet in the center of the softened wrapper. Repeat with remaining 5 rice paper rounds and cod. Divide basil mixture among fillets. Fold the ends of the rice paper around the cod and enclose securely. Set aside. 4) For the sauce, in a small sauté pan, warm 1 tsp olive oil over low heat. Add shallots and garlic. Sauté until softened. Add soy sauce, rice wine vinegar, sugar and red pepper flakes, stirring for 1 minute. Remove from heat and set aside. 5) In a large ovenproof skillet, heat 2 tbsp olive oil over high heat. Add cod parcels and sear on both sides, 2 minutes per side. Place skillet in preheated oven for 5 minutes to finish cooking. Spoon sauce over each piece and serve.

Serves 6

BITE ME BIT

"Advice is cheap, Ms. Molloy. It's the things that come gift-wrapped that count."

– Horace Vandergelder (actor Walter Matthau) in the 1969 movie "Hello, Dolly!"

LIP-SMACKING CRISPY COD SANDWICH

INGREDIENTS

Cornmeal Crusted Cod

½ cup yellow cornmeal

½ tsp kosher salt

¼ tsp freshly ground black pepper

¼ cup milk

6 (6oz) cod fillets

Tartar Sauce

1 cup mayonnaise

¼ cup finely chopped dill pickle

1 tbsp fresh lemon juice

2 tsp Dijon mustard

Pinch of cayenne pepper

6 hamburger buns

Shredded iceberg lettuce

Sing to the tune of "My Bonnie Lies over the Ocean"

Today is the best day of his life,
Today is the day he eats fish,
My hubby will surely be drooling,
When he takes a big bi-ite of this.

Fish fillet, fish fillet,
Oh pile the tartar on high, -igh, -igh,
Fish fillet, fish fillet,
Baked crispy and easy as pie.

DIRECTIONS

1) Preheat oven to 450°F. Line a baking sheet with aluminum foil and coat with non-stick cooking spray. 2) In a medium bowl, combine cornmeal, salt and pepper. Pour the milk into a separate bowl. 3) Working with one fillet at a time, dip the fish in milk and then dredge in the cornmeal mixture, completely coating the fish. Place on prepared baking sheet and bake for 7 minutes. Flip fillets and bake an additional 6 minutes, until golden. 4) For the tartar sauce, in a small bowl, whisk mayonnaise, pickle, lemon juice, Dijon mustard and cayenne pepper. 5) To serve, put crusted fish in buns and top with tartar sauce and shredded lettuce.

Serves 6

CRUNCHY BAKED SEA BASS

INGREDIENTS

30 Ritz crackers, crushed into coarse crumbs

2 tbsp chopped fresh dill, divided in half

⅓ cup mayonnaise

1 large garlic clove, minced

2 tbsp fresh lemon juice

2 tsp lemon zest

4 (8oz) sea bass fillets, skin removed

¼ tsp kosher salt

¼ tsp freshly ground black pepper

What's caviar without toast points, lobster without melted butter, shrimp without cocktail sauce? Half of a perfect whole. So too is sea bass without a crisp cracker top. A firm and versatile whitefish, sea bass acts as the perfect base for lemon-garlic mayonnaise, refreshing dill and a rich buttery cracker topping.

DIRECTIONS

1) Put your oven rack in the mid-to-lower part of the oven to ensure that the crumb topping doesn't burn before the fish is cooked through. 2) Preheat oven to 450°F. Line a baking sheet with aluminum foil and coat with non-stick cooking spray. 3) In a medium bowl, combine cracker crumbs and 1 tbsp of dill. In another medium bowl, mix the remaining dill, mayonnaise, garlic, lemon juice and lemon zest. 4) Pat the fish dry with paper towel and season with salt and pepper. Place on prepared baking sheet, spread mayonnaise mixture over the fish and press the cracker crumbs on top. Bake 13-15 minutes, until the crumbs are golden and the fish is cooked through.

Serves 4

BITE ME BIT

Dr. Evil: When I ask for sharks with frickin' laser beams on their heads, I expect sharks with frickin' laser beams on their heads! What do we have?

Number Two: Sea Bass

– From the 1997 movie "Austin Powers: International Man of Mystery"

INGREDIENTS

1 tbsp olive oil

2 shallots, finely chopped

1 large garlic clove, minced

1 lb chopped fresh mushrooms (can use a variety of button, shiitake, cremini)

¼ cup chicken broth

¼ cup dry white wine

1 tbsp fresh flat-leaf parsley

2 tsp chopped fresh thyme

½ tsp kosher salt

¼ tsp freshly ground black pepper

1 cup panko (Japanese breadcrumbs)

4 (6oz) sole fillets, about ½-inch thick

MERRYMAKING MUSHROOM-CRUSTED SOLE

DIRECTIONS

1) Preheat oven to 425°F. Line a baking sheet with aluminum foil and coat with non-stick cooking spray. 2) In a large skillet, heat oil over medium heat. Add shallots and garlic, stirring until softened, about 4 minutes. 3) Add mushrooms and continue to cook until the liquid released from the mushrooms has evaporated. 4) Remove mushroom mixture from heat and add chicken broth, wine, parsley, thyme, salt, pepper and panko. Stir to combine; the mixture should stick together. 5) Pat fish dry with paper towel and place on prepared baking sheet. Top fillets with mushroom mixture, patting down to cover the whole piece. Bake 10-12 minutes, until topping becomes slightly crusty.

Serves 4

Pssst...

The Best Kitchen Secrets

SERVING REFRESHMENTS To make sure that you never experience premature evacuation, remember that a 750ml bottle of wine pours out 4 (approximately 6oz each) glasses worth. As well, you get 16 (1½ oz) shots out of a 750ml liquor bottle and 5 flutes out of a bottle of champagne.

BUYING FISH Look in the eyes (should be bright and clear), inspect the skin (taut skin should be blemish-free and gills should be bright red) and take a whiff (there shouldn't be any offensive smell – fresh means virtually no odor).

TOASTING NUTS Put the nuts in a small ungreased frying pan and place over medium heat for 4-6 minutes, stirring often, until golden brown. Alternatively, you can toast them by spreading them in a single layer on an ungreased baking sheet. Bake at 350°F, stirring or shaking often, for 5-10 minutes. Watch carefully in order not to burn them. Transfer to plate and cool.

SOFTENING BROWN SUGAR, MARSHMALLOWS AND CREAM CHEESE To soften rock-hard brown sugar or marshmallows, place a slice of white bread in the bag or container. As for cream cheese, if you need it at room temperature quickly, put the cream cheese package in a resealable plastic bag and submerge it in hot water for 5-10 minutes.

AVOIDING STICKY UTENSILS If you're worried about cling-ons such as honey, peanut butter or cheese, coat a measuring cup, spoon or cheese grater with non-stick cooking spray.

MAKING PERFECT CORN To husk corn, using a damp cloth, brush in a downward motion to remove corn silks. Bring a large pot of water to a boil. Add 1 tbsp sugar and ½ cup milk. Add corn, return to a boil. Remove pot from heat, cover, and let sit for 10-15 minutes.

HOW TO HARD-BOIL AN EGG Place eggs in a saucepan, cover with cold water and add a pinch of salt. Bring to a rapid boil over high heat. Once the water boils, remove saucepan from heat and cover. Let eggs stand covered for 12 minutes. Rinse under cold water and peel.

SIZZLING TILAPIA with SWEET MANGO SALSA

INGREDIENTS

Mango Salsa

2 mangoes, peeled and diced

1 cup diced red bell pepper

2 tbsp fresh lime juice

2 tbsp olive oil

1 tsp jalapeno pepper, seeds removed, finely minced

½ tsp kosher salt

¼ tsp freshly ground black pepper

Tilapia

4 (5-6oz) tilapia fillets

2 tsp chili powder

2 tsp ground cumin

1 tsp dried oregano

1 tsp kosher salt

2 tbsp olive oil

Lights, Camera…I know it can be hard to get enthusiastic about fish. A reputation as "healthy" certainly doesn't bring on the glitz and glam. But don't be blinded by the charm of chicken or the magnetism of meat. A mild fish like tilapia, rubbed in spices and sautéed, delivers exciting razzle-dazzle, and, topped with a sweet mango salsa… it's ShowTime!

DIRECTIONS

1) For the mango salsa, in a medium bowl, combine mango, red pepper, lime juice, olive oil, jalapeno pepper, salt and pepper. Gently fold together with a rubber spatula, letting the mixture sit at room temperature for at least 30 minutes. 2) Pat the fish dry with a paper towel. In a small bowl, mix together chili powder, cumin, oregano and salt. Rub both sides of each piece of tilapia with spice mixture. 3) In a large skillet, heat 2 tbsp olive oil over medium-high heat. Add half the fish to the skillet and sauté until lightly browned and cooked through, about 3 minutes per side. Transfer cooked fish to serving platter and using oil left in the pan repeat with the remaining tilapia. Place cooked tilapia on a platter and spoon mango salsa on each piece.

Serves 4

ASIAN TUNA BURGERS

INGREDIENTS

Tuna Burger

1½ lbs tuna steaks, finely chopped by hand

1 tbsp soy sauce

1 tbsp rice wine vinegar

1 large garlic clove, minced

2 tsp grated fresh ginger

½ tsp kosher salt

¼ tsp freshly ground black pepper

Wasabi Mayonnaise

6 tbsp mayonnaise

2 tsp soy sauce

2 tsp rice wine vinegar

1 tsp wasabi powder (or more if you want it spicier)

6 hamburger buns

2 cups shredded iceberg lettuce

3 large tomatoes, sliced

You don't care where the beef is and you don't want to talk turkey? Well, try this – topped with a spicy wasabi mayonnaise, this tuna burger will give you plenty of meat to chew on.

DIRECTIONS

1) Line a baking sheet with parchment paper. Set aside. 2) For the burgers, in a medium bowl, mix chopped tuna with soy sauce, rice wine vinegar, garlic, ginger, salt and pepper. Using wet hands to prevent sticking, divide the mixture into 6 equal portions, shaping into patties about 1-inch thick. Place on prepared baking sheet and refrigerate for 20 minutes before grilling. 3) For the sauce, in a small bowl, whisk mayonnaise, soy sauce, rice wine vinegar and wasabi powder. Cover and refrigerate at least 15 minutes, allowing flavors to blend. 4) Coat grill rack with oil and heat to medium. Grill tuna burgers, about 3 minutes per side for medium doneness. Remove from grill and let stand 5 minutes. Place on bun and top with wasabi mayonnaise, shredded lettuce and sliced tomato.

Serves 6

BITE ME BIT

"What if you mix the mayonnaise in the can with the tuna fish? Or... hold it! Chuck! I got it! Take live tuna fish and feed 'em mayonnaise! Oh this is great. [speaks into tape recorder] Call Starkist!"

– Bill Blazejowski (actor Michael Keaton) in the 1982 movie "Night Shift"

GRILLED SWORDFISH with OLIVE RELISH

INGREDIENTS

4 (6-8oz) swordfish steaks

¼ cup olive oil

1 lemon, juiced

1 tbsp capers, drained and chopped

1 tbsp chopped fresh flat-leaf parsley

1 large garlic clove, minced

1 tsp lemon zest

½ tsp dried oregano

½ tsp kosher salt

¼ tsp freshly ground black pepper

Olive Relish

¼ cup green olives, pitted and chopped

¼ cup black olives, pitted and chopped

¼ cup olive oil

1 tbsp red wine vinegar

1 tbsp chopped fresh basil

1 tsp capers, drained and chopped

⅛ tsp freshly ground black pepper

Open secret. Free gift. Tight slacks. All oxymorons. If you'd add "meaty fish" to the list, think again. Mild and firm swordfish is both hearty and filling. Why else would it be sold as "steaks"? Move aside, beef. Straight off the grill, topped with an aromatic, bold relish of olives and capers – this swordfish is terribly good.

DIRECTIONS

1) For the swordfish, place the steaks in a large resealable plastic bag. In a medium bowl, whisk together olive oil, lemon juice, capers, parsley, garlic, lemon zest, oregano, salt and pepper. Pour over fish and place in refrigerator to marinate for at least 1 hour and up to 12 hours. Turn the bag occasionally so marinade covers the fish. 2) For the relish, in a small bowl, combine green olives, black olives, olive oil, red wine vinegar, basil, capers and pepper. Cover and refrigerate until ready to use. Allow to come to room temperature before serving on cooked fish. 3) Bring swordfish to room temperature. Preheat grill to medium-high and lightly oil grill grates. Remove fish from marinade and dry with paper towel. Place on grill and cook 3-4 minutes per side or until cooked through and flakes easily. Top cooked swordfish with heaping spoonful of olive relish.

Serves 4

BITE ME BIT

"There isn't any symbolism. The sea is the sea. The old man is an old man. The boy is a boy and the fish is a fish."

– Ernest Hemingway, American author commenting on his 1952 classic "The Old Man and the Sea"

SWEET CITRUS and SPICED SALMON

INGREDIENTS

Marinade

¾ cup pineapple juice

6 tbsp fresh lemon juice

6 (6oz) salmon fillets, skin removed

Topping

½ cup packed brown sugar

2 tsp lemon zest

2 tsp chili powder

1 tsp ground cumin

½ tsp kosher salt

¼ tsp ground cinnamon

We are gathered here today to pay our respects to old-style salmon. It has had a long run, having lived in such diverse places as Michelin-rated restaurants and tin cans. Sharp and pungent, dear salmon was the kind of fish that lingered in the home and, even with the help of a mint-chaser, repeatedly roosted on the palate. Well, the funky days are behind us, but salmon lives on, survived by these mild, delicate and beautifully flavored fillets. We will always keep the Omega-3s in our hearts. And let us say, Amen.

DIRECTIONS

1) In a large resealable plastic bag, combine pineapple juice, lemon juice and salmon. Refrigerate for 1 hour, turning occasionally. 2) Preheat oven to 400°F. Coat an 11x7-inch baking dish with non-stick cooking spray. 3) For the topping, in a small bowl, combine brown sugar, lemon zest, chili powder, cumin, salt and cinnamon. Remove salmon from refrigerator and dispose of marinade. Place fillets in prepared baking dish and rub brown sugar mixture over salmon. Bake 12 minutes or until fish is flaky.

Serves 6

CHILLED SALMON with LEMON DILL SAUCE

INGREDIENTS

1½ cups dry white wine

1½ cups water

1 lemon, sliced

2 sprigs fresh dill

1 dried bay leaf

½ tbsp whole black peppercorns

1 tsp kosher salt

½ tsp freshly ground black pepper

6 (6oz) salmon fillets, skin removed

Lemon Dill Sauce

1 cup mayonnaise

¼ cup buttermilk

1 tbsp chopped fresh dill

1 tbsp fresh lemon juice

1 tsp grainy mustard

½ tsp lemon zest

Say "Mrs. Smith's Fish Sauce Shop" five times fast... I can't do it twice. But rather than taking 10 minutes to untwist your tongue, you could pull together this super-easy poached fish dish. By the time you can utter "Fisherman Fritz fishes fresh fish, fresh fish does fisherman Fritz fish," the salmon will be perfectly chilled and ready to be smothered in the zesty dill sauce.

DIRECTIONS

1) In a large skillet, combine wine, water, lemon slices, dill sprigs, bay leaf and peppercorns. Bring to a boil over high heat.
2) Season salmon fillets with salt and pepper. Once the water has boiled, add salmon to skillet, cover and turn the heat off, letting the fish poach for 10 minutes or until flaky. Remove salmon from liquid and transfer to plate, refrigerating for at least 2 hours before serving. 3) For the sauce, in a medium bowl, whisk mayonnaise, buttermilk, chopped dill, lemon juice, mustard and lemon zest. Chill and serve with poached salmon.

Serves 6

BITE ME BIT

Cookbook author Bob Blumer has turned urban legend into reality – he developed a foolproof method for poaching salmon in the dishwasher that requires aluminum foil, a wash-dry cycle and lemon-scented detergent.

Meet me

A Bloody Good Time For Meat Lovers

ROAST BEEF with HERBED BREADCRUMB CRUST

INGREDIENTS

5 lb boneless beef top loin roast

1 tsp kosher salt

1 tsp freshly ground black pepper

1 tbsp vegetable oil

6 slices white bread with crust, pulsed in food processor into coarse crumbs

2 tbsp chopped fresh flat-leaf parsley

2 large garlic cloves, minced

1 large shallot, minced

1 tsp dried thyme

1 tsp dried rosemary

½ tsp kosher salt

¼ cup melted butter

½ cup Dijon mustard

1 tbsp dry white wine

Horseradish Sauce

1 cup sour cream

¼ cup white horseradish

2 tbsp Dijon mustard

1 tsp fresh lemon juice

½ tsp kosher salt

⅛ tsp cayenne pepper, optional

In the lore of Greek mythology, or in the lore of Wikipedia, the Delphic oracle was having a chat with Apollo and happened to mention that horseradish is worth its weight in gold. Maybe they had just wolfed down some gefilte fish together. Or maybe they were discussing how much it enhances this classic Sunday dish.

DIRECTIONS

1) Place oven rack on bottom level to prevent roast beef crust from burning. Preheat oven to 400°F. Line a baking sheet with aluminum foil. Place a roasting rack on the baking sheet and coat with non-stick cooking spray. 2) Trim the meat of visible fat and then pat dry with paper towel. Season with 1 tsp salt and 1 tsp pepper, rubbing on all sides. 3) In a large skillet, heat oil over medium-high heat. Brown the meat on all sides, about 3 minutes per side. Transfer meat to the prepared roasting rack. Set aside. 4) In a large bowl, combine breadcrumbs, parsley, garlic, shallots, thyme, rosemary, salt and melted butter. In a small bowl, combine ½ cup Dijon mustard and white wine. After brushing the roast with the Dijon mixture, lightly press the breadcrumb mixture to adhere. 5) Insert a meat thermometer into the thickest portion of the roast. Place in oven and for rare meat, thermometer should read 140°F, between 1 hour and 20 minutes and 1 hour and 30 minutes. Should the crust start to brown before cooking is finished, tent the roast with aluminum foil and continue cooking. 6) For the sauce, in a small bowl, combine sour cream, horseradish, Dijon mustard, lemon juice, salt and cayenne pepper. Refrigerate until ready to use. 7) After removing roast from oven let the meat rest for 10 minutes uncovered before slicing. Serve sliced roast with horseradish sauce on the side.

Serves 8-10

GRILLED NY STEAKS with RED WINE SAUCE

INGREDIENTS

Red Wine Sauce

1 tbsp butter

1 tbsp olive oil

¼ cup diced white onion

¼ cup peeled and chopped carrots

¼ cup chopped celery

1 tsp chopped fresh thyme

½ tsp freshly ground black pepper

1 cup dry red wine

3½ cups beef broth

1 tbsp tomato paste

½ tsp kosher salt

¼ tsp freshly ground black pepper

4 (10-12oz) prime New York strip steaks, 1½-inches thick

2 tbsp olive oil

2 tsp kosher salt

2 tsp freshly ground black pepper

Sing to the tune of "New York, New York"

Start lightin' the que, the beef is prime
I'm gonna gorge on it – NEW YORKS, NEW YORKS
These classic strip steaks, are timeless beauties
Right through the juicy core of them –
NEW YORKS, NEW YORKS

I wanna cut my meat with a fork, it's so tender
And perfectly cru-u-u-sted – top o' the grill

These forkfuls of mine, are made divine
When I add rich red wine sauce – to old New Yorks
If my lipids can take it, I'll make steak everyday
It's up to my ticker – NEW YORKS, NEW YORKS

DIRECTIONS

1) For the sauce, in a large skillet, melt butter and heat oil over medium heat. Add onion, carrots, celery, thyme and ½ tsp pepper. Stir and sauté for 5 minutes until vegetables are tender but not browned. Add the red wine, cooking for 5 minutes. Increase heat to medium-high, add beef broth and tomato paste, stirring occasionally, allowing the sauce to further reduce for 25 minutes or until reduced to 1 cup. Season with ½ tsp salt and ¼ tsp pepper. Set aside until steaks are prepared. **2)** For the steaks, remove them from the refrigerator 30 minutes before cooking to bring to room temperature. **3)** Preheat grill to high heat. Just prior to grilling, season steaks on both sides with olive oil, salt and pepper. Place on the hottest part of the grill to sear the outside and seal in the juices. Turn the steaks after 5 minutes and continue to cook another 5 minutes for a pink, medium center. Remove from grill and allow meat to rest for 5 minutes before slicing. Steaks will cook a few degrees more while resting. If you're unsure if steak is done, use a meat thermometer: 110°F (rare), 120°F (medium-rare), 125°F (medium), 130°F (medium-well), 140°F (well-done).

Serves 4-6

BITE ME BIT

"If we're not supposed to eat animals,
how come they're made out of meat?"

– Tom Snyder, TV talk show host

BEEF, MUSHROOM and PEPPER SHISH KEBABS

INGREDIENTS

Sweet Marinade

1½ cups ketchup

¾ cup Manischewitz wine
(sweet kosher wine)

6 tbsp packed brown sugar

1 tsp freshly ground black pepper

4 garlic cloves, peeled
and cut in half

1½ lbs sirloin steak,
cut into 1½-inch cubes

1 red bell pepper, seeded and
cut into 1½-inch pieces

1 yellow pepper, seeded and
cut into 1½-inch pieces

1 green pepper, seeded and
cut into 1½-inch pieces

½ lb button mushrooms, left
whole, stems trimmed

Forget tannins, lees and acidity. Try sniffing and swigging Manischewitz wine, our One and Only, the perfect blend of Concord grapes and corn syrup. Yes, corn syrup. Don't stick your noses in the air, you oenophiles out there — consider the magic this superior kosher wine can perform. Chunks of beef, crisp peppers and meaty mushrooms are marinated in a syrupy Manischewitz sauce and grilled to sweet-crusted, tender perfection.

DIRECTIONS

1) In a medium bowl, whisk ketchup, wine, brown sugar and pepper. Pour 1¼ cups marinade into a large resealable plastic bag and add garlic halves, beef cubes, red peppers, yellow peppers, green peppers and mushrooms to marinade. Seal bag, turn to coat and refrigerate at least 2 hours, up to 24 hours. Refrigerate remaining marinade to use for basting at the end of cooking. 2) Preheat barbeque to medium-high heat. 3) Remove meat and vegetables from plastic bag and discard marinade. Thread beef onto reusable metal skewers. Thread peppers and mushrooms on separate skewers from the beef to ensure even cooking. 4) Grill kebabs for 8-10 minutes, turning one-quarter rotation every 2-3 minutes or until the meat is cooked through and vegetables are tender-crisp. In the final 2 minutes of cooking time, baste all sides of beef and vegetable kebabs with reserved marinade. 5) Remove beef and vegetables from skewers and toss with extra marinade.

Serves 6

BRAISED BEEF SHORT RIBS

INGREDIENTS

6 lbs beef short ribs, bone-in, trimmed of excess fat

2 tsp kosher salt

2 tsp freshly ground black pepper

2 tbsp canola oil

2 medium yellow onions, chopped

2 medium carrots, peeled and chopped

2 medium celery stalks, chopped

4 large garlic cloves, minced

2 tbsp tomato paste

2 tbsp flour

3 cups dry, full-bodied red wine, such as Zinfandel

3 cups chicken broth

1 cup barbeque sauce

¼ cup sugar

2 sprigs fresh thyme

2 (3-inch long) strips orange zest, done with a vegetable peeler

2 dried bay leaves

1 tsp kosher salt

½ tsp freshly ground black pepper

In Act 5, Scene 5, Line 19, methinks Macbeth is soliloquizing about this recipe – yes, tomorrow, and tomorrow, and tomorrow. Or maybe it was Orphan Annie. In either case, it will always be a day away when you finally enjoy these fork-tender short ribs. What you'll need to do today is wait as the beef slowly cooks until it becomes succulent and falls from the bone. Worth every braising-hour, the ribs are then transferred to the refrigerator overnight, allowing the deep, rich flavors time to intensify.

DIRECTIONS

1) Preheat oven to 450°F. In a large roasting pan, arrange trimmed short ribs in a single layer. Season them on both sides with salt and pepper. Roast the ribs for 25 minutes. Turn them over using tongs and roast for another 20-25 minutes, until ribs are nicely browned. Transfer ribs to a large plate and set aside. 2) Reduce oven temperature to 300°F. 3) In a large, oven-safe pot, heat oil over medium-high heat. Add onions, carrots and celery to the pan and sauté, stirring often until vegetables are tender, about 10 minutes. Add garlic and sauté for 1 minute Stir in tomato paste and flour, cooking 1 minute. Add wine, chicken broth, barbeque sauce, sugar, thyme, orange zest, bay leaves, salt and pepper. Increase heat to high, bring to a boil and add short ribs, preferably in a single layer, along with any accumulated juices. Reduce heat to low, spoon some of the liquid over the ribs. Cover the pot and transfer to oven. 4) Braise for 2½ hours, turning the ribs with tongs every 45 minutes, skimming and discarding whatever fat may have risen to the surface. After cooking time, meat should be tender and pulling away from the bone. 5) Remove from oven

and allow ribs to cool in the liquid for 2 hours. **6)** Using a slotted spoon, transfer the meat that has fallen off the ribs into a storage container, shred the meat and refrigerate overnight. **7)** Strain the braising liquid through a fine-mesh sieve into a measuring cup, pressing gently on the solids to extract the liquid. Cover liquid and refrigerate overnight. Discard solids from sieve. **8)** The next day, remove the excess fat that has solidified at the top of the braising liquid. **9)** In a large heavy pot bring defatted liquid to a boil. Lower heat to medium-low and simmer for 15 minutes to reduce and thicken sauce. Add shredded meat from ribs and continue to simmer for 10-15 minutes, stirring occasionally, until heated through. Remove from heat and add salt and pepper to taste. Serve over mashed potatoes or creamy polenta.

Serves 6

BITE ME BIT

Jeffries: When am I going to see you again?
Lisa: Not for a long time...at least not until tomorrow night.

– from the 1954 movie "Rear Window"

H-CRUSTED BEEF TENDERLOIN

INGREDIENTS

3 lbs beef tenderloin, center cut

1 tsp kosher salt

½ tsp freshly ground black pepper

¼ cup Dijon mustard

2 tbsp seed mustard

¼ cup chopped fresh basil

¼ cup chopped fresh flat-leaf parsley

2 tbsp chopped fresh thyme

Lisa asked me, "What's with the h?" and I told her that I wanted to show my sensitive side. A certain kind of seasoning leaves people mumbling, unsure whether to say, "Herb," "erb" or "cannabis." So now there's no more tension. Just grab the basil, parsley and thyme because you're going to sculpt a crust on a lean, luscious cut of beef. And don't worry. You won't have to wrap it in – how do you say it? Fy-lo? Fee-lo?

DIRECTIONS

1) Preheat oven to 400°F. Line a baking sheet with aluminum foil and coat with non-stick cooking spray. 2) Place tenderloin on baking sheet and sprinkle with salt and pepper. Spread Dijon and seed mustard over the top and sides of the beef. 3) In a small bowl, combine basil, parsley and thyme and pat evenly over the beef. 4) Bake for 45 minutes for medium-rare, and a meat thermometer registers 145°F. Remove from oven and let stand 10 minutes before slicing.

Serves 8

BITE ME BIT

"You say 'erbs', and we say 'herbs', because there's a f***ing 'H' in it!"

— Eddie Izzard, comedian

BEEF BOURGUIGNON

INGREDIENTS

2 lbs stewing beef, cubed

½ tsp kosher salt

½ tsp freshly ground black pepper

2 tbsp vegetable oil

1 large yellow onion, cut into 1-inch cubes

1 large red onion, cut into 1-inch cubes

4 medium carrots, peeled, sliced thick on the bias

2 medium garlic cloves, minced

1 tsp finely chopped fresh rosemary

1 tsp finely chopped fresh thyme

½ tsp kosher salt

½ tsp freshly ground black pepper

¼ cup brandy or cognac

1 (750ml) bottle red wine, cabernet or pinot noir

2 cups beef broth

1 tbsp tomato paste

1 tbsp olive oil

1½ lbs cremini mushrooms, wiped clean, stems removed, left whole if not too large

3 tbsp butter, softened

3 tbsp flour

Crème anglaise. Foie gras. Bouillabaisse. Somehow everything sounds more complicated in French. Even the name of the French chef who helped make beef bourguignon famous, Auguste Escoffier, makes him sound very complicated. But don't be put off by the haute name. This retro classic dish isn't as EMBROUILLÉ as it sounds – it's rustic beef stew made robust with a bottle of full-bodied wine. So, in other words, chillez-vous.

DIRECTIONS

1) For a deeply flavored stew, you'll need to brown the beef. Dry beef cubes well with paper towel and toss with ½ tsp salt and ½ tsp pepper. In a large Dutch oven, heat vegetable oil over medium heat. Add beef and sauté until it is well browned on all sides but not burned. Add yellow onions, red onions and carrots, stirring until lightly browned, about 5 minutes. Add garlic, rosemary, thyme, salt and pepper, stirring for another minute. 2) Turn heat to high, add brandy and cook until only a thin glaze of liquid remains. Add red wine, beef broth and tomato paste, scraping up all brown bits that remain. Lower heat, cover and simmer gently for 2 hours or until the beef is tender. 3) When the beef is finished cooking, in a medium skillet, heat 1 tbsp olive oil over medium-high heat. Add mushrooms and brown well, 5-6 minutes. Stir into beef mixture. 4) In a small bowl, stir softened butter and flour into a paste. Add to beef and simmer over low heat until liquid becomes slightly thickened, about 10 minutes. Season to taste with salt and pepper. This stew is even better the following day as flavors have a chance to blend.

Serves 6-8

MAGNIFIQUE MEATLOAF with MUSHROOM GRAVY

INGREDIENTS

Meatloaf

2 tbsp olive oil

1 small white onion, diced

1 large garlic clove, minced

1 cup fresh breadcrumbs
(3 pieces of white bread,
crusts removed, pulsed in food
processor until crumbs)

2 large eggs

½ cup ketchup

1 tbsp soy sauce

2 tsp Worcestershire sauce

2 tsp Dijon mustard

1 tsp kosher salt

½ tsp freshly ground black pepper

½ tsp hot Asian chili sauce

2 lbs lean ground beef

Mushroom Gravy

2 tbsp olive oil

2 lbs mixed cremini and button
mushrooms, peeled and sliced

1 small white onion,
finely chopped

1 large garlic clove, minced

1 tbsp tomato paste

2 tbsp butter

¼ tsp kosher salt

¼ tsp freshly ground black pepper

2 tbsp flour

¼ cup dry red wine

2 cups beef broth

1 tbsp soy sauce

So I said to Lisa, embellishing this diner delight is pas de problème. Just give it a French name. La Plaque-Bleue Spéciale. But my blue ribbon-obsessed-sister outdid herself again, creating a tour de force – an elegant, moist, most flavorful meatloaf, topped with the perfect complement, a rich mushroom medley.

DIRECTIONS

1) For the meatloaf, preheat oven to 375°F. Cover the top of a metal cooling rack with aluminum foil and poke small holes all over foil to ensure drainage while the meatloaf cooks. Coat foil with non-stick cooking spray and place atop a large baking sheet. **2)** Heat oil in a small skillet over medium heat. Add onion and sauté 4-5 minutes until tender. Turn heat off and add minced garlic. Set aside to cool slightly. **3)** In a large bowl, mix breadcrumbs, eggs, ketchup, soy, Worcestershire, Dijon mustard, salt, pepper, chili sauce and onion mixture. Add ground beef, gently mixing just until combined. Transfer meat to foil-covered rack and shape into an oval about 2 inches high. Bake 60-65 minutes or until cooked through. Remove from oven and allow to sit 10 minutes before slicing. **4)** For the gravy, in a large skillet, heat oil over medium heat. Add sliced mushrooms and sauté for 3 minutes. Add onion, garlic, tomato paste, butter, salt and pepper, continuing to cook 2-3 minutes, until onions are tender. Sprinkle flour over mushrooms and toss to coat. Turn heat to high, add red wine, stirring until liquid has evaporated. Add beef broth and soy sauce, bringing to a boil. Reduce heat to low and simmer until gravy has thickened, about 5 minutes. Serve immediately with meatloaf.

Serves 6-8

RUSTIC MEATBALLS in MARINARA SAUCE

INGREDIENTS

Marinara Sauce

1 medium white onion, chopped

4 large garlic cloves, minced

3 tbsp olive oil

3 (28oz/796ml) cans diced tomatoes

½ cup dry red wine

1 tsp kosher salt

¼ tsp crushed red pepper flakes

¼ tsp freshly ground black pepper

¼ cup chopped fresh basil

3 tbsp sugar

Meatballs

3 large eggs, lightly beaten

2 cups soft breadcrumbs (5 pieces of white bread, crusts removed, pulsed in food processor until crumbs)

1 cup freshly grated Parmesan cheese

⅛ cup chopped fresh flat-leaf parsley

2 large garlic cloves, minced

1 tsp dried oregano

1 tsp kosher salt

½ tsp freshly ground black pepper

3 lbs lean ground beef

Rocco's Mama inspires us. She spends endless hours rolling meatballs in her son's restaurant basement, which made us wonder what it would take to persuade our own talented Mom to move from matzo balls to meatballs. Mom...you ok down there?

DIRECTIONS

1) For the sauce, in a large soup pot, combine onion, garlic and olive oil over medium-low heat and stir often until onion is tender, about 8 minutes. Add canned tomatoes, wine, salt, red pepper flakes and black pepper. Over high heat, bring to a boil. Reduce heat to low and simmer uncovered for 30 minutes. Remove from stove and using a hand held or countertop blender, puree sauce to desired consistency. Stir in basil and sugar. Cover and return to medium-low heat, cooking 5 minutes. Season with salt to taste. 2) For the meatballs, preheat oven to 375°F. Line 2 baking sheets with aluminum foil and coat with non-stick cooking spray. 3) In a large bowl, combine eggs, breadcrumbs, Parmesan, parsley, garlic, oregano, salt and pepper. Add ground beef, mixing to combine. 4) Shape meat mixture into approximately 50 meatballs and place on prepared baking sheets. Bake for 20 minutes total, turning the meatballs at the 10-minute mark. Remove from oven and place meatballs on paper towel to drain off any excess fat. Place meatballs in marinara sauce and serve with cooked pasta.

Serves 8-10

PA-ANA-A-KA-LA (Sunshine) PINEAPPLE MEATBALLS

INGREDIENTS

Meatballs

2 lbs lean ground beef

1 cup breadcrumbs

¾ cup milk

2 large eggs, lightly beaten

2 tsp kosher salt

½ tsp freshly ground black pepper

Sweet and Sour Pineapple Sauce

3 cups canned pineapple chunks, with syrup

1¾ cup Heinz chili sauce

1 cup cubed red bell pepper

½ cup soy sauce

½ cup cider vinegar

½ cup packed brown sugar

⅓ cup cornstarch

1 cup water

Can't you just hear Elvis strumming a uke? See Harry Truman sporting an Aloha shirt? Well, now you can taste some Polynesian paradise in these sweet and sour pineapple meatballs. Rock-a-hula Baby and get rolling on these supremely saucy, tender spheres best piled atop a Mauna-kea (white mountain) of rice.

PS. A special Mahalo Nui Loa to Susan Hall for sharing her recipe.

DIRECTIONS

1) For the meatballs, preheat oven to 500°F. Line a large baking sheet with aluminum foil and coat with non-stick cooking spray. 2) In a large bowl, mix the ground beef, breadcrumbs, milk, eggs, salt and pepper until combined. Add 2 handfuls of very cold water to the bowl and mix until combined. Shape the beef mixture into 1-inch meatballs. Place in a single layer on the prepared baking sheet and bake 12-15 minutes. Remove from oven and drain on paper towel. 3) For the sauce, in a large saucepan, combine pineapple chunks (with syrup), chili sauce, red peppers, soy sauce, vinegar and brown sugar. Place cornstarch in a small dish, stir in 1 cup of water until smooth and add to saucepan. Bring to a boil over medium heat, continuously stirring until sauce thickens. Gently stir meatballs into sauce, cooking until heated through.

Serves 8-10

BITE ME BIT

Grandpa Gustafson: I have been to Hawaii.

Mama Ragetti: Oh yeah? Which island?

Grandpa Gustafson: ComeonIwannalayya.

– from the 1995 movie "Grumpier Old Men"

HOISIN and GINGER BEEF STIR-FRY

INGREDIENTS

1½ lbs beef tenderloin, cut into thin, bite-size strips

¼ cup hoisin sauce

½ tsp grated fresh ginger

Vegetables

2 tbsp peanut oil

1 large garlic clove, minced

1 tsp grated fresh ginger

1½ cups sliced fresh mushrooms (shiitake, button or portobello)

1½ cups thinly sliced celery

1 large red bell pepper, sliced into thin strips

1½ cups snow peas, trimmed and cut on the diagonal

Asian Sauce

½ cup beef broth

¼ cup teriyaki glaze

¼ cup hoisin sauce

1 tbsp sesame oil

2 tbsp cornstarch

2 tbsp cold water

1 tbsp sesame seeds, toasted

1 tbsp thinly sliced fresh basil

Most stir-fry recipes commit the worst wok offenses: rubbery beef, not enough sauce and bland, mushy vegetables. Not ours. Get ready to stir-fry tenderloin until it's sweet and juicy. Get ready to be amazed by saucy, crisp vegetables. But most of all, get ready...do all the slicing and whisking before you even turn on the burner and you'll get a gold medal in the fast and furious sport of stir-frying.

DIRECTIONS

1) Place beef in a medium bowl and add ¼ cup hoisin sauce and ½ tsp fresh ginger. Set aside to marinate for at least 20 minutes. 2) Heat peanut oil in a large wok over high heat. Add garlic, 1 tsp ginger, mushrooms, celery and red pepper, stir-frying for 2 minutes. Add snow peas, continuously tossing vegetables for 1 minute. Remove from wok and set aside. 3) For the Asian sauce, in a medium bowl, whisk beef broth, teriyaki glaze, ¼ cup hoisin sauce and sesame oil. In a small dish, combine cornstarch and water until smooth. Add to broth mixture and whisk to combine. Set aside. 4) Reheat wok over high heat. Add beef and stir-fry until browned, about 3 minutes. Add sauce and continue to cook for 1 minute, allowing it to thicken slightly. Return vegetables to wok and toss to combine. Remove from heat and sprinkle with sesame seeds and fresh basil.

Serves 6

BEEF FAJITAS with SOUTHWESTERN RICE

INGREDIENTS

2 lbs sirloin strip steak

Marinade

⅓ cup fresh lime juice

¼ cup tequila

2 tbsp vegetable oil

1 large garlic clove, minced

1 tsp chili powder

1 tsp ground cumin

½ tsp dried oregano

½ tsp freshly ground black pepper

½ tsp kosher salt

1 tbsp vegetable oil

Vegetables

1 tbsp vegetable oil

1 large white onion, halved and thinly sliced

1 large red bell pepper, thinly sliced

1 large yellow pepper, thinly sliced

½ tsp kosher salt

Julie: Breaker, breaker. Got your ears on, Dough Girl?

Lisa: Yes, Julie.

Julie: No, not Julie. It's Pencil Head and say 10-4.

Lisa (sigh): Big 10-4, Pencil Head.

Julie: What's your 20?

Lisa: Where else? On the way home from the supermarket.

Julie: Peel your eyeballs for Kojak with a Kodak.

Lisa: What are you talking about?

Julie: Smokey Bear. City Kitty. Johnny Law. Black 'n' Whites.

Lisa: Yah, ok. I mean, copy.

Julie: What's the grub tonight at Home Base?

Lisa: Fajitas. Want some, Pencil Head?

Julie: Roger Dodger. Put the hammer down and let the motor toter. Catch you on the flip-flop, Dough Girl. Eights.

DIRECTIONS

1) Preheat oven to 325°F. 2) Trim visible fat from steaks and set aside. 3) In a large bowl, whisk lime juice, tequila, 2 tbsp vegetable oil, garlic, chili powder, cumin, oregano and pepper. Add steak to marinade, turning to coat well. Marinate covered and chill for at least 2 hours or overnight. 4) Drain marinade from the meat and discard. Pat steaks dry with paper towel and season with ½ tsp kosher salt. Cut the meat across the grain, diagonally, into thin, finger-length strips. In a large skillet, heat 1 tbsp oil over high heat. Add sliced steak and stir for 2-3 minutes until desired

Southwestern Rice

1 tbsp olive oil

1 small white onion, finely chopped

1 green pepper, diced

1 small garlic clove, minced

2 cups chicken broth

1 cup uncooked long grain rice

½ tsp ground cumin

½ tsp chili powder

1 cup canned black beans, rinsed and drained

1 cup bottled salsa

8 (8-inch) flour tortillas

½ cup sour cream

½ cup bottled salsa

doneness. Remove beef from skillet and set aside. **5)** Add remaining 1 tbsp vegetable oil to skillet over high heat. Add onion, red pepper and yellow pepper, sautéing just until they start to soften, about 4 minutes. Season mixture with ½ tsp salt. Add beef, stir to combine and remove from heat. **6)** Warm tortillas by sealing them in an aluminum foil packet. Place them in preheated oven for 10 minutes. Keep wrapped until ready to assemble. **7)** For the rice, in a large saucepan, heat olive oil over medium heat. Add onions, green peppers and garlic, sauté 3 minutes until vegetables have softened. Stir in chicken broth, rice, cumin and chili powder and bring to a boil. Reduce heat to low, cover and simmer for 15 minutes or until water is absorbed and rice is tender. Remove cover and stir in black beans and salsa. **8)** To serve, place a spoonful of rice on the bottom of each warmed tortilla. Top with meat mixture. Add a spoonful of sour cream and salsa. Fold 2 sides of the tortilla in and roll up into a cylinder.

Serves 6-8

SWELL VEAL PICCATA

INGREDIENTS

2 tsp olive oil

1 large shallot, minced

2 cups chicken broth

1½ lbs (about 6 pieces) veal cutlets, ¼-inch thick

½ tsp kosher salt

½ tsp freshly ground black pepper

½ cup flour

2 tbsp olive oil, divided in half

3 tbsp fresh lemon juice

2 tbsp chopped fresh flat-leaf parsley

2 tbsp butter

1 tbsp capers, drained

Son #1: Someone saw you messin' around in the schoolyard with a girl. Wait'll the guys find out...
Son #2: I'm gonna slug you, you rat fink.
Mother: Boys, stop the ruckus. I have 5 minutes to get Father's dinner on the table.
Son #1: Don't sweat it, Mom. Just make that super duper saucy veal.
Mother: We don't sweat in this house, son. We perspire. I'll wash your mouth out with soap. Boys, to your room.
Sons: Aw, gee, Mom.

Father arrives home and immediately sits down and cuts into the zesty, tender veal scaloppini.

Mother: Dear, I'm very worried about the Beaver.
Father: Why, dear, this isn't beaver. It's veal.

DIRECTIONS

1) In a medium saucepan, heat olive oil over medium heat. Add shallots, cooking 2 minutes or until they begin to soften. Add chicken broth and bring to a boil over high heat. Turn heat down to medium, simmering for 6 minutes or until the liquid is reduced by half. Set aside. 2) Pat the veal dry with paper towel. Sprinkle each piece with salt and pepper. Place the flour on a flat surface. 3) Working in 2 batches, heat 1 tbsp oil in a large skillet over high heat. Dredge the first batch of cutlets on 1 side in flour, shaking off excess. Place in skillet, flour side down. Cook 1½ minutes, flip and cook another minute or until veal is no longer pink. Transfer to a serving plate. Repeat the process with the remaining veal cutlets. Add to serving plate. 4) Add the reserved chicken broth mixture into the skillet you were using. Bring to a simmer over medium heat for 2 minutes, scraping up the browned bits from the bottom of the pan. Remove from heat and stir in lemon juice, parsley, butter and capers. Pour the sauce over the veal cutlets.

Serves 4

VEAL MARSALA

INGREDIENTS

½ cup flour

½ tsp kosher salt

¼ tsp freshly ground black pepper

1½ lbs veal scaloppini

2 tbsp butter, divided in half

2 tbsp olive oil, divided in half

Marsala Sauce

1 large shallot, minced

½ lb button mushrooms, sliced

½ lb shiitake mushrooms, stemmed and sliced

1 cup dry Marsala

1 cup chicken broth

1 cup beef broth

2 tbsp butter

NOTES FROM THE SOFA

"During our first session, she told me all about her sweet daughter, Marsala. This made me pause. An interesting name choice. Motivated by love for Marcello Mastroianni? Marcel Marceau? It left me wondering what she might be sublimating. I had to delve deeper into the recesses of her subconscious. It wasn't until our third session that it became abundantly clear I was heading in the very wrong direction as she raved about her tender son, a kid named Vitello."

DIRECTIONS

1) Combine flour, salt and pepper in a shallow dish. Pat veal dry with paper towel then dredge both sides of the veal in flour, shaking off excess. 2) In a large non-stick skillet, heat 1 tbsp butter and 1 tbsp olive oil over medium-high heat. Add half the veal, searing it quickly on both sides, about 1-1½ minutes per side to just cook through. Remove and place on a serving plate. Repeat with remaining butter, olive oil and veal. Remove veal from pan and set aside. 3) For the Marsala sauce, using the same skillet, add shallots and mushrooms. Cook over high heat, continually stirring until mushrooms begin to soften, about 3 minutes. Add the Marsala and cook for 3 minutes. Stir in chicken and beef broth and bring to a boil. Boil for 7-8 minutes, stirring often. Turn heat to low, stir in the butter. Return veal to the pan, turning once or twice to baste it in the sauce and re-warm.

Serves 4-6

GRILLED VEAL CHOPS

INGREDIENTS

Marinade

¼ cup olive oil

2 tbsp red wine vinegar

2 tbsp fresh lemon juice

1 tbsp Dijon mustard

1 tbsp chopped fresh thyme

1 tbsp chopped fresh rosemary

1 tsp lemon zest

½ tsp kosher salt

¼ tsp freshly ground
black pepper

4 (14-16oz) bone-in veal rib
chops, about 1½-inch thick

1 lemon, cut into 4 wedges

Lisa's been trying out her jokes on me: Did you hear the one about the cow and the lamb? I can't tell you the punch line. I'm too ashamed. But I guess I have to cut her some slack – it's her heifer humor for her butcher. "He thinks I'm hilarious," she claims, "and he calls me honey."

DIRECTIONS

1) In a small bowl, whisk oil, vinegar, lemon juice, Dijon mustard, thyme, rosemary, lemon zest, salt and pepper. Place the veal chops in a resealable plastic bag and pour in the marinade, turning to coat. Marinate in the refrigerator for 4-6 hours. 2) Preheat barbeque grill to medium-high heat. 3) Remove chops from marinade and grill for 6-8 minutes per side for medium-rare. Quickly sear all the edges and remove from grill. 4) Grill lemon wedges until lightly charred and tender. Serve each veal chop with a grilled lemon wedge.

Serves 4

BITE ME BIT

"All normal people love meat. If I went to a barbeque and there was no meat, I would say 'Yo Goober! Where's the meat?' I'm trying to impress people here, Lisa. You don't win friends with salad."

– Homer Simpson on the television series "The Simpsons"

THE TOTALLY TUBULAR BURGER

INGREDIENTS

Burgers

2 lbs lean ground beef

¼ cup barbeque sauce

¼ cup breadcrumbs

1 tbsp Dijon mustard

1 tbsp olive oil

1 large egg

1½ tsp kosher salt

½ tsp freshly ground black pepper

4 hamburger buns

Special Sauce

½ cup ketchup

½ cup mayonnaise

1½ tbsp sweet green relish

2 tsp Worcestershire sauce

¼ tsp kosher salt

¼ tsp freshly ground black pepper

The '80s were, like, so good to us – Lisa had like, TOTALLY excellent bangs and I had a killer perm. As for our parents, they were, like, totally mental for burgers and we were, like, um, take a chill pill. But we were, like, totally happy when they opened a wicked burger restaurant and bummed when it went the way of the DeLorean. Now, we're, like, totally walking on sunshine again with this awesome remake of the mile-high burger.

DIRECTIONS

1) Preheat grill to medium-high heat. 2) Place ground beef, barbeque sauce, breadcrumbs, Dijon mustard, olive oil, egg, salt and pepper in a large bowl. Mix all ingredients together using your hands, taking care not to handle the meat too much. Form the meat into 4 (8oz) patties. 3) Lightly oil the grilling surface and place the patties on the preheated grill. Cook for about 6-8 minutes per side, depending on desired doneness. Remove from grill. 4) For the special sauce, in a small bowl, whisk ketchup, mayonnaise, relish, Worcestershire sauce, salt and pepper. Spread onto the insides of the buns and top with burger.

Serves 4 very hungry carnivores

BITE ME BIT

"I love this burger so much, I want to sew my ass shut."

– Barney (actor Neil Patrick Harris) on the television series "How I Met Your Mother"

CRUSTED LAMB CHOPS with BALSAMIC REDUCTION

INGREDIENTS

Crusted Lamb Chops

3 tbsp finely chopped fresh flat-leaf parsley

2 tbsp finely chopped fresh mint

1 tbsp finely chopped fresh thyme

2 large garlic cloves, minced

½ tsp kosher salt

⅛ tsp cayenne pepper

1 tbsp olive oil

2 slices white bread, pulsed in food processor into coarse crumbs

2 tbsp mayonnaise

2 tbsp Dijon mustard

2 racks of lamb, 1½ lbs each (7-8 chops on each), trimmed

1 tsp kosher salt

1 tsp freshly ground black pepper

Balsamic Reduction

1 tbsp olive oil

1 shallot, minced

⅓ cup balsamic vinegar

¾ cup chicken broth

1 tbsp butter

LISA'S #1 COMMANDMENT: HONOR THY BUTCHER.

She gets a blow dry to go see him. She defers to "the one who wears the white apron," the gatekeeper to the most prized rack of lamb. For her, he selects the leanest, freshest pink meat. For her, he Frenches (don't be a pig...it means he trims the ribs clean of excess fat and meat) the rack, all of which enhance her meltingly tender, impressive and deceptively easy-to-make, oven-roasted lamb chops. Lisa's getting a pedicure right now – she must be going to buy some veal chops.

DIRECTIONS

1) Preheat oven to 450°F. Line a baking sheet with aluminum foil and coat with non-stick cooking spray. 2) Combine parsley, mint, thyme, garlic, salt and cayenne in a pie plate. Set aside. 3) In a large skillet, heat olive oil over medium heat. Add breadcrumbs, stir to lightly toast, 2-3 minutes. Remove from skillet and toss with parsley mixture. 4) In a small bowl, stir together mayonnaise and Dijon mustard. 5) Season both sides of the lamb racks with salt and pepper. Over high heat, heat the same large skillet used for the breadcrumbs. Meat-side down, place 1 rack in the skillet and brown until a crust has formed, about 2 minutes. Turn the rack with tongs and sear the bottom for another 2 minutes. Remove lamb from pan, wipe bottom of skillet and repeat with remaining rack. Transfer lamb to a plate to cool slightly. 6) Coat both top and bottom of both racks with mayonnaise mixture, spreading it over the meaty portions but not covering the bones. Roll the meat in reserved breadcrumb mixture, pressing the crumbs to adhere.

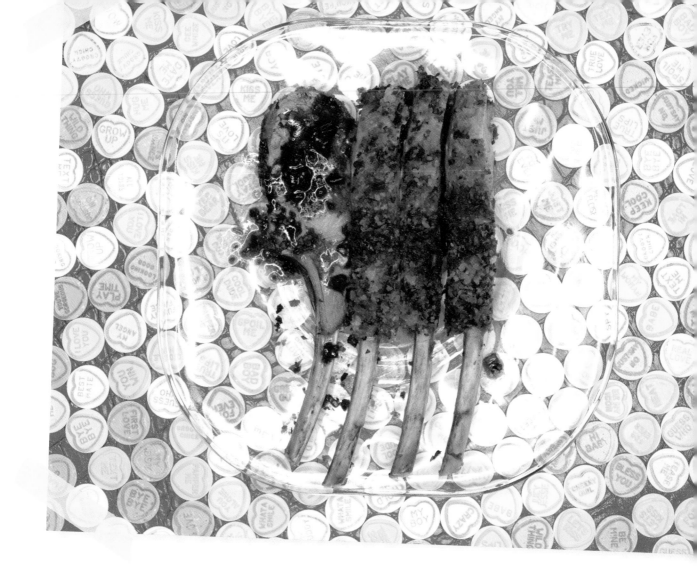

7) Place both racks on prepared baking sheet and roast for 20-25 minutes. Insert an instant read thermometer in the thickest part of the lamb, medium-rare will read 140°F. Allow lamb to sit 5-10 minutes before carving chops. Temperature will rise by 5 degrees as it sits. 8) For balsamic reduction, heat olive oil in a medium skillet over medium heat. Add shallots and cook 1 minute, until soft. Stir in balsamic vinegar, turn heat to high and cook 1 minute. Add chicken broth and bring to a boil. Lower heat to medium and reduce by half, 5-6 minutes. Remove from heat, stir in butter. To serve, spoon a small amount of sauce over carved lamb chops.

Serves 4-6

OSSO BUCO with GREMOLATA

INGREDIENTS

6 (8-10oz) veal shanks,
1½ inch thick, each tied with
kitchen string

½ cup flour

1 tsp kosher salt

1 tsp freshly ground
black pepper

¼ cup vegetable oil, divided

1 large red onion, finely chopped

3 medium carrots, peeled
and finely chopped

2 medium celery stalks,
finely chopped

4 large garlic cloves, minced

6 fresh sage leaves, chopped

1 sprig fresh rosemary, chopped

¼ cup chopped fresh
flat-leaf parsley

½ tsp kosher salt

½ tsp freshly ground
black pepper

¼ tsp crushed red pepper flakes

1 (28oz/796ml) can
diced tomatoes

1¼ cups dry white wine

4 cups chicken broth

Julie: Alex, I'll take "Fired Up!" for $800.

Alex: It means "bone with a hole."

Julie: What is...oh dear...I don't think I can say this on television...

Alex: Sorry, Julie. Lisa?

Lisa: What is "Osso Buco"?

Alex: Correct.

Lisa: Alex, I'll take "On Top" for $1,000.

Alex: Parsley, lemon zest, olive oil.

Julie: What is "slather it on me"?

Alex: Sorry, Julie. Lisa?

Lisa: What is "gremolata that garnishes succulent braised veal shanks"?

Alex: Correct. Now, for your final question. The category is "Culinary Traditions of Northern Italy" and the clue is "delicious to spoon."

Julie: Who is "Ralph Macchio"?

Alex: Unfortunately...no. Lisa?

Lisa: What is "savory marrow"?

Alex: Correct. You win. Julie, good luck with whatever your future holds.

DIRECTIONS

1) Preheat oven to 325°F. Set aside a roasting pan large enough to fit the veal shanks in a single layer. 2) Dry veal with paper towels. Place flour, 1 tsp each salt and pepper in a small dish. Dredge shanks in flour mixture to coat, shaking off excess. In a large heavy skillet, heat half of the vegetable oil (2 tbsp) over medium-high heat. Add 3 veal shanks to the pan and sear on all sides until nicely

Gremolata

¼ cup finely chopped
fresh flat-leaf parsley

1 tbsp olive oil

1 tsp grated lemon zest

¼ tsp kosher salt

¼ tsp freshly ground
black pepper

browned, for a total of about 10 minutes. Place in roasting pan and repeat with remaining oil and veal. **3)** In a large bowl, combine onion, carrots, celery, garlic, sage, rosemary, parsley, salt, pepper and red pepper flakes. Spread mixture on top of seared veal and around the roasting pan. Pour diced tomatoes, wine and chicken broth over veal and vegetables. Cover ¾ of the roasting pan with aluminum foil and place in oven for 2¼ hours – 2½ hours, until meat is easily pierced with a fork. Using a slotted spoon carefully transfer veal to a serving plate. Cut off and discard kitchen string. With the slotted spoon, remove vegetables and place on serving platter along with veal. Pour remaining sauce into a medium saucepan and bring to a boil, reduce heat to medium and simmer for 10 minutes. Pour over veal and vegetables.
4) For the gremolata, just before serving the veal, in a small bowl combine parsley, olive oil, lemon zest, salt and pepper. Sprinkle a small spoonful over each serving.

Serves 6

BITE ME BIT

"Everyone has a purpose in life. Perhaps yours is watching television."

– David Letterman, talk show host

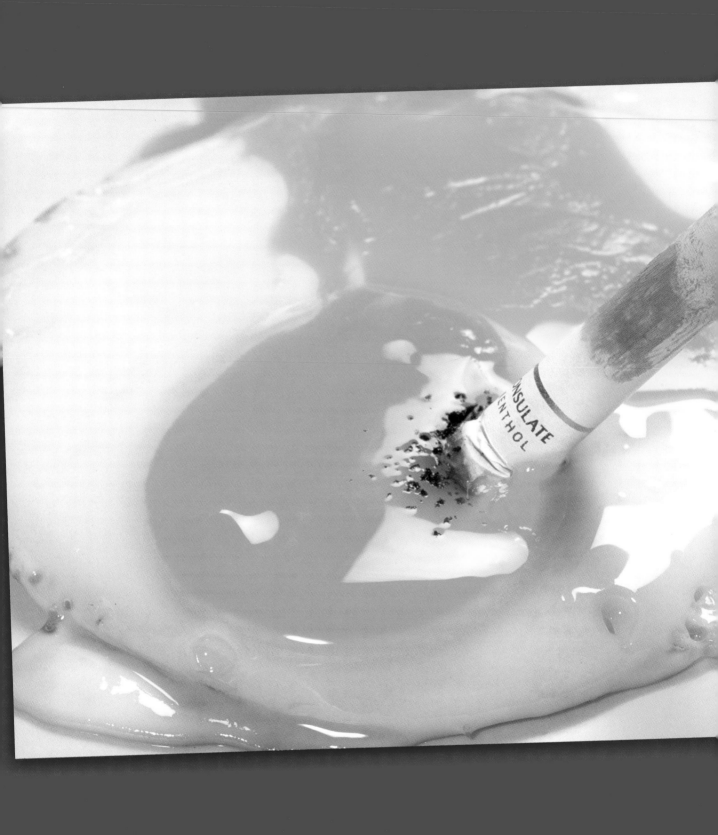

Join me

The Morning After

SUPERCAL...ISTIC STICKY FRENCH TOAST with CANDIED RICE KRISPIES

INGREDIENTS

Candied Rice Krispies

½ cup sugar

2 tbsp water

4 cups Rice Krispies cereal

French Toast

2 egg breads (challahs), crusts left on and cubed (approximately 14 cups)

1 (8oz/250g) package cream cheese, softened

6 large eggs

1½ cups milk

½ cup half-and-half cream

½ cup maple syrup

1 tsp vanilla extract

Caramel Topping

1½ cups packed brown sugar

½ cup butter

3 tbsp corn syrup

Mary Poppins played a game with kids called "Well Begun is Half-Done." Ain't that the truth. Easily assembled, this decadent French toast soufflé soaks overnight and is finished by drizzling it with caramel sauce, topping it with candied Rice Krispies and baking it to a golden dome. Yes, you get a spoonful of sugar in every sticky, scrumptious bite.

DIRECTIONS

1) For the candied Rice Krispies, in a large pot (that is both deep and has a wide bottom), bring the sugar and water to a boil over medium heat. Boil for 1 minute without stirring. Gently stir in Rice Krispies and continue to cook over medium heat, just until they are golden, about 5 minutes. Remove from heat and immediately pour Rice Krispies onto a baking sheet to cool. Once cooled they can be stored in an airtight container for up to 2 weeks. 2) For the French toast, coat a 13x9-inch baking dish with non-stick cooking spray. Place cubed bread evenly throughout the dish. 3) Place the cream cheese in a large bowl. Using an electric mixer, beat cream cheese at medium speed until smooth. Add one egg at a time, mixing well after each addition and making sure to scrape down the sides of the bowl with a spatula. Whisk in milk, half-and-half, maple syrup and vanilla until incorporated and smooth. Pour over bread cubes to moisten evenly, pressing lightly to submerge the bread. Cover and refrigerate at least 8 hours and up to 24 hours. 4) Once ready to bake, remove baking dish from refrigerator and preheat oven to 350°F. 5) For the caramel topping, in a small saucepan, combine brown sugar, butter and corn syrup. Cook over medium heat, stirring constantly until well combined, about 2 minutes. Immediately pour over French toast and cover with candied Rice Krispies. Place baking dish on a rimmed baking sheet and bake until puffed and golden, about 40-45 minutes.

Serves 8

BLINTZ SOUFFLÉ with STRAWBERRY SAUCE

INGREDIENTS

Sweet Cheese Filling

2 (8oz/250g) packages cream cheese, softened

3 cups ricotta cheese

2 large eggs

½ cup sugar

2 tbsp orange juice

1 tsp vanilla extract

½ tsp orange zest

Blintz Batter

½ cup butter, softened

½ cup sugar

6 large eggs

1 tsp vanilla extract

1 cup flour

2 tsp baking powder

1½ cups sour cream

½ cup orange juice

Strawberry Sauce

2 pints fresh strawberries

½ cup sugar

¼ cup water

1 tbsp fresh lemon juice

1 tbsp cornstarch

The Eastern European cousin of the crepe, a blintz is a thin pastry wrapped around a filling. As much as we love them, we also love not spending all our time rolling, folding and frying each individual blintz. Instead, we're doing blintzes freeform. We've transformed a 13x9-inch baking dish into one giant, creamy, sweet-cheese-filled blintz. All of the flavor and none of the labor, this puffy and golden soufflé is served topped with sweet strawberry sauce.

DIRECTIONS

1) Preheat oven to 350°F. Coat a 13x9-inch baking dish with non-stick cooking spray. 2) For the cheese filling, in an electric mixer, beat the cream cheese until smooth. Add the ricotta, eggs, sugar, orange juice, vanilla and orange zest. Beat thoroughly on medium speed until the mixture has a smooth, creamy consistency. Place in a medium bowl and set aside. 3) For the batter, in an electric mixer, cream butter and sugar until light and fluffy. Add the eggs one at a time, mixing well after each addition. Add vanilla and continue to mix. On low speed add the flour, baking powder, sour cream and orange juice, mixing just until combined. 4) To assemble, pour half the batter in the prepared baking dish. Add the filling by placing spoonfuls on top of the batter, gently spreading. Place the remaining half of the batter over the cheese filling. 5) Bake 65 minutes or until puffy and golden. Serve with sour cream and strawberry sauce. 6) For the strawberry sauce, wash strawberries and remove stems and cores. Thinly slice the berries and place 2 cups in a medium bowl. Set the remaining strawberries aside. 7) Mash the 2 cups of strawberries and pour into a medium saucepan. Add sugar, water, lemon juice and cornstarch. Bring to a boil over medium heat. Once the mixture has come to a boil, stir constantly for 1 minute or until thickened. Remove from heat and stir in remaining berries. Yield: 3 cups

Serves 8-10

BERRY STUFFED-and-SAUCED FRENCH TOAST SOUFFLÉ

INGREDIENTS

2 egg breads (challahs), crusts removed and cut into ½-inch thick slices

1 cup cream cheese

1 cup strawberry jam

3 large eggs

4 large egg whites

1½ cups milk

2 tbsp melted butter

2 tbsp sugar

1 tsp vanilla extract

½ tsp kosher salt

Berry Sauce

1 cup sugar

1 tbsp cornstarch

¼ cup orange juice

3 cups frozen unsweetened berries, either mixed, blueberries or raspberries

3 cups strawberries, quartered

All you have to do with this gorgeous dish is sleep on it. This overnight French toast does the work for you as the sweet egg bread, mounded with cream cheese and strawberry jam, is left to soak up a buttery mixture. After you wake and bake, you'll have an elegant, effortless brunch.

DIRECTIONS

1) For the soufflé, coat a 13x9-inch baking dish with non-stick cooking spray. Lay a single layer of bread slices along the bottom of the dish. Spread cream cheese on each piece. Spread strawberry jam on the remaining slices and lay to face cream cheese, creating sandwiches in the baking dish. 2) In a medium bowl, whisk eggs, egg whites, milk, melted butter, sugar, vanilla and salt. Pour over sandwiches and turn to coat. Cover and refrigerate for several hours or, for best results, overnight. Bring to room temperature before baking. 3) Preheat oven to 350°F. Bake uncovered for 35-40 minutes. 4) For the berry sauce, in a medium saucepan, combine sugar and cornstarch. Stir in orange juice until smooth. Add frozen mixed berries and heat to a boil over medium heat stirring constantly until slightly thickened. Remove from heat and stir in fresh strawberries. Allow to cool and serve berry sauce spooned over individual portions.

Serves 8-10

BITE ME BIT

"I went to a restaurant that serves 'Breakfast at any time.' So I ordered French Toast during the Renaissance."

— Steven Wright, comedian

SWEET NOODLE PUDDING – EXPOSED!

INGREDIENTS

1 (13oz/375g) bag wide
egg noodles

2 tbsp margarine

2 cups cottage cheese

2 cups sour cream

4 large eggs, lightly beaten

¾ cup sugar

1 tsp vanilla extract

1 cup raisins

Topping

1½ cups crushed corn flakes

¼ cup packed brown sugar

2 tbsp melted margarine

1 tsp ground cinnamon

By revealing this sweet, raisin-loaded noodle pudding we're breaking an unspoken code held by generations of Jewish women – you can kibitz about Auntie's moustache, kvetch about cousin's wet kisses, but, under no circumstances should you be a yenta about your secret noodle pudding recipe. We're taking a risk, but we think the public has a right to know.

DIRECTIONS

1) Preheat oven to 350°F. Coat a 13x9-inch baking dish with non-stick cooking spray. 2) Cook noodles according to package directions. Drain well and mix with 2 tbsp margarine. Set aside. 3) In a large bowl, combine cottage cheese, sour cream, eggs, sugar and vanilla. Add noodles, gently tossing to coat. Fold in raisins and spoon mixture into prepared baking dish. 4) For the topping, in a small bowl, combine corn flakes, brown sugar, margarine and cinnamon. Spread on top of noodles and bake covered for 30 minutes. Remove the cover and bake an additional 10-15 minutes, until the top is golden brown. Allow to cool before cutting.

Serves 8

BAGEL and LOX STRATA

INGREDIENTS

6 large eggs

1½ cups milk

1 cup sour cream

¾ cup smoked salmon, cut into matchsticks

¼ cup chopped fresh dill

1 tbsp fresh lemon juice

2 tsp lemon zest

½ tsp freshly ground black pepper

6 plain bagels, cut into ½-inch cubes

Garnish

½ cup sour cream

2 tbsp capers, drained and chopped

1 tbsp chopped fresh dill

1 tbsp fresh lemon juice

A HEBRAIC HAIKU

Oy! Oy! No schmear here
Bagel, lox, sour cream and dill
In each bite. Eat! Eat!

DIRECTIONS

1) Preheat oven to 350°F. Coat a 13x9-inch baking dish with non-stick cooking spray. 2) In a large bowl, whisk eggs, milk and sour cream. Stir in salmon, dill, lemon juice, lemon zest and pepper. Add the bagel pieces and toss to coat. Transfer to prepared baking dish and bake 45-50 minutes, until golden. 3) Let rest 10 minutes. Dollop sour cream on top and garnish with capers, dill and lemon juice.

Serves 10

NY PICKLED SALMON

INGREDIENTS

2 lb salmon fillet, skinned, rinsed and pat dry

1 cup water

1 cup white distilled vinegar

3 tbsp sugar

2 tsp mustard seeds

1 tsp black peppercorns

2 dried bay leaves

¼ tsp kosher salt

2 large sweet onions (Vidalia), sliced ¼-inch thick

Here's my question – if smoked salmon is SO great, why is it always buried under a pile of cream cheese, tomato, onion, capers and lemon? To us, the true gem of the brunch world is pickled salmon. Much like what you'd find at the Upper West Side landmark, Zabar's, salmon and onions are "cooked" in a zippy sweet and sour marinade. The resulting tender pink salmon needs no disguise – maybe just a nice slice of pumpernickel for this Broadway star.

DIRECTIONS

1) Cut salmon into 1-inch by 2-inch cubes, making sure to clean off any brown parts. Set aside. 2) In a large pot, combine water, vinegar, sugar, mustard seeds, peppercorns, bay leaves and salt. Bring to a boil over medium-high heat. Reduce the heat to low, add the salmon and sliced onions, cooking uncovered for 5 minutes. Transfer salmon, onions and marinade to a glass container. Let cool at room temperature. Cover and refrigerate at least 2 days before serving. To serve, pour off the liquid and arrange the salmon with pickled onions. Keeps in the refrigerator up to 1 week.

Serves 6-8

BITE ME BIT

"New York is a diamond iceberg floating in river water."

– Truman Capote, writer

POTATO, SPINACH and GRUYÈRE FRITTATA

INGREDIENTS

2 tbsp butter

10 (10oz/285g) small red potatoes, sliced ⅛-inch thick

½ tsp kosher salt

¼ tsp freshly ground black pepper

4 cups fresh baby spinach, stems removed

8 large eggs

3 tbsp melted butter

½ tsp kosher salt

¼ tsp freshly ground black pepper

½ lb (approx. 3 cups) shredded Gruyère cheese

When it comes to breakfast and eggs, some countries like to play the heavyweights. The French with their finicky Hollandaise and fussy soufflés. The Brits with their deep-fried Scotch eggs. So, what's the Italians' secret for La Dolce Uovo? The easy-going frittata: a thick, hearty, open-faced omelet that can be served at any temperature, eaten at any meal, and, best of all, filled with whatever you like. We love this combo, but also adore peas, feta and mint... red peppers, onions and goat cheese...

DIRECTIONS

1) Preheat oven to 350°F. 2) In a deep 10-inch ovenproof skillet, melt butter over medium-high heat. Add the potatoes, salt and pepper, sautéing until cooked through, 8-10 minutes. Remove from skillet and set aside. 3) Using the same skillet, add spinach leaves over medium heat, cooking until wilted, about 2 minutes. Remove from pan. When cool, squeeze spinach to drain excess liquid. Chop spinach and set aside. 4) In a large bowl, whisk eggs very well. Whisk in melted butter, salt and pepper. Spread cooked potatoes and spinach evenly on the bottom of your 10-inch skillet. Sprinkle Gruyère evenly over potatoes and spinach. Pour egg mixture in skillet and place in oven. Bake until golden brown around edges and just firm to the touch, 23-25 minutes. Remove from oven and let stand 5 minutes. Run a spatula around the skillet edge to loosen frittata and invert it onto a serving plate.

Serves 4-6

BITE ME BIT

"It may be the cock that crows, but it is the hen that lays the eggs."

– Margaret Thatcher, politician

THE BIG CHEESE and MACARONI

INGREDIENTS

2 large eggs

2¼ cups evaporated milk

2 tsp Dijon mustard

1½ tsp kosher salt

½ tsp freshly ground black pepper

⅛ tsp hot sauce

1 lb elbow macaroni

4 tbsp butter

2 cups shredded cheddar cheese

1 cup shredded Monterey Jack cheese

Breadcrumb Topping

8 slices white bread, crusts removed

2 tbsp melted butter

1 tsp kosher salt

½ cup shredded cheddar cheese, for topping

As lovers of movies on the W Channel, we have no problem with cheese – it's how you serve it up that counts. To get the creamiest noodles, we melt everything together on the stove, transfer the cheesy mixture to a baking dish and finish it in the oven with a tasty golden cover of crunchy breadcrumbs.

DIRECTIONS

1) Preheat oven to 375°F. Coat a 13x9-inch baking dish with non-stick cooking spray. 2) In a medium bowl, whisk eggs, evaporated milk, Dijon mustard, salt, pepper and hot sauce. Set aside. 3) Bring a large pot of water to boil over high heat. Add macaroni and cook until pasta is tender. Drain pasta well and return to pot. Add butter over low heat to melt. Stir in egg mixture, cheddar cheese and Monterey Jack cheese. Continue stirring until creamy, about 5 minutes. Transfer mixture to prepared baking dish. 4) For the breadcrumb topping, pulse bread in food processor until coarse crumbs. In a small bowl, toss breadcrumbs with melted butter and salt. Evenly top macaroni with remaining cheddar cheese and buttered breadcrumbs. 5) Bake in preheated oven for 10 minutes or until the breadcrumbs are golden brown. Cool 5 minutes and then serve immediately.

Serves 6-8 as main course, 10-12 as side dish

SPOT-ON CHOCOLATE CHIP SCONES

INGREDIENTS

3¼ cups flour

½ cup sugar

2 tsp baking powder

1 tsp baking soda

½ tsp kosher salt

¼ tsp ground cinnamon

¾ cup cold butter, cut into small cubes

1½ cups semi-sweet chocolate chips

1 cup buttermilk

¼ tsp vanilla extract

Sugar Topping

2 tbsp melted butter

2 tbsp sugar

When it comes to sugary snacks Lisa and I can go either Yiddish or British. We'll gleefully indulge in a little babka or rugelach, but when 4 p.m. rolls around, we suddenly fancy our 4 p.m. cuppa with cucumber and cream cheese finger sandwiches, followed by a freshly baked scone. Sweet and flaky, our scones are bang-on, slathered in creamy butter, strawberry jam and, dare we say, a dollop of clotted cream.

DIRECTIONS

1) Preheat oven to 425°F. Line a baking sheet with parchment paper. 2) In a large bowl, sift together flour, sugar, baking powder, baking soda, salt and cinnamon. Cut in butter using a pastry blender or rubbing between fingers, until mixture resembles coarse meal. Stir in chocolate chips. Add buttermilk and vanilla, stirring just until moistened. 3) Turn dough onto a lightly floured surface and knead briefly, 5 or 6 times, to gather into a large ball. Do not overwork the ball or the result will be tough scones. Divide the ball of dough in half and gently pat each into 8-inch flat rounds. Brush the top of each with melted butter and sprinkle with sugar. 4) Using a sharp knife, cut each circle into 6 even triangles and place on prepared baking sheet, about 1 inch apart. Bake 16-18 minutes until tops are golden.

Yield: 12 large scones

BITE ME BIT

"It's the face powder that gets a man interested, but it's the baking powder that keeps him home."

– Buck Barrow (actor Gene Hackman) in the 1967 movie "Bonnie and Clyde"

WHOLESOME HONEY-BAKED GRANOLA

INGREDIENTS

4 cups old-fashioned
large flake oats (not
quick cooking)

1 cup slivered almonds

1 tsp kosher salt

½ tsp ground cinnamon

½ cup melted butter

½ cup packed brown sugar

¼ cup honey

1 tsp vanilla extract

1 cup dried cranberries

½ cup raisins

I'm elated. I can now join the poncho-wearing pack. For years I had granola-envy but refused to eat the highly caloric, preservative-laden boxed oats and nuts. Hemp sneakers now firmly on my feet, I'm running to get a bowl of this nourishing, crisp-baked and clustered granola overflowing with golden almonds and plump dried fruit.

DIRECTIONS

1) Preheat oven to 300°F. Line a baking sheet with parchment paper. 2) In a large bowl, combine oats, almonds, salt and cinnamon. 3) In a small bowl, combine melted butter, brown sugar, honey and vanilla. Whisk well and pour over oat mixture. Toss to combine and spread granola on prepared baking sheet. Bake 20 minutes, stir carefully and then continue to bake for another 15 minutes. Remove from oven, transfer to a large bowl. Add dried cranberries and raisins, mixing to combine. Cool completely and store at room temperature in an airtight container for up to 1 week.

Yield: 7 cups

APPLE STREUSEL MUFFINS

INGREDIENTS

2½ cups flour

1 tsp baking soda

½ tsp kosher salt

½ tsp ground cinnamon

2 cups peeled and diced
Granny Smith apples

1½ cups packed brown sugar

1 cup buttermilk

½ cup vegetable oil

1 large egg

1 tsp vanilla extract

Topping

½ cup packed brown sugar

½ cup flour

¼ tsp ground cinnamon

¼ cup melted butter

Still obsessed with "Seinfeld" after all these years, Lisa was sick of me "pulling an Elaine" – I'd buy a few muffins, eat off the tops and toss the dry bottoms. Determined to put an end to my cruel decapitations, she created these super-moist apple cinnamon muffins, delectable from the golden-crusted lid to the stray crumbs on my plate.

DIRECTIONS

1) Preheat oven to 350°F. Coat a 12-cup muffin tin with non-stick cooking spray. Lightly dust cups with flour, shaking out the excess. 2) For the muffins, in a large bowl, combine flour, baking soda, salt, cinnamon and diced apples. Gently toss to combine. 3) In a medium bowl, whisk brown sugar, buttermilk, vegetable oil, egg and vanilla. Gently stir into flour mixture just until blended. Spoon batter into prepared tin, dividing evenly among muffin cups. 4) For the topping, in a small bowl, mix together brown sugar, flour and cinnamon. Add melted butter and toss with a fork until it resembles coarse crumbs. Sprinkle topping over muffin cups. 5) Bake for 23-25 minutes, until the muffins spring back when gently pressed. Remove from oven and let cool for 10 minutes before removing from pan and placing on a wire rack.

Yield: 12 muffins

BITE ME BIT

"Some people...some people like cupcakes exclusively, while myself, I say there is naught nor ought there be nothing so exalted on the face of God's grey Earth as that prince of foods...the muffin!"

– from the 1975 Frank Zappa song "Muffin Man"

PERSONALS

GOLDEN-TOPPED, FULL-FLAVORED MUFFIN SEEKS HUNGRY DINER – Height: 2½-inches. Weight: ¼ pound. I have an eye-catching golden exterior and a warm, plump blueberry interior. When I'm hot, I exude an intoxicating aroma. I'm looking for a long-term relationship and holding out hope that, one day, I'll have my own batch of mini-muffins. If you're that special someone, call me at 1-888-GR8-BITE.

BERRY BURST MUFFINS with CRUMBLE TOPPING

INGREDIENTS

2 cups flour

¾ cup sugar

1 tsp baking powder

1 tsp baking soda

¼ tsp kosher salt

2 cups fresh blueberries

½ cup melted margarine

1 cup sour cream

1 large egg

1 tsp vanilla extract

1 tsp lemon zest

Topping

½ cup flour

¼ cup sugar

2 tbsp margarine

DIRECTIONS

1) Preheat oven to 375°F. Coat a 12-cup muffin tin with non-stick cooking spray. Lightly dust cups with flour, shaking out the excess. 2) For the batter, in a large bowl, combine flour, sugar, baking powder, baking soda, salt and blueberries. Gently toss to combine. 3) In a small bowl, whisk melted margarine, sour cream, egg, vanilla and lemon zest. Gently stir into flour mixture just until blended. Do not overmix – the batter is supposed to look lumpy. Spoon batter into prepared tin, dividing evenly among muffin cups. 4) For the crumble topping, in a small bowl, use a fork to mix flour, sugar and margarine until it resembles coarse crumbs. Sprinkle topping over muffin cups. 5) Bake 23-25 minutes, until muffins spring back when gently pressed. Cool 10 minutes in the muffin tin before removing to cool on a wire rack.

Yield: 12 muffins

Top 10

Crème de la Crème

MUSICAL ACTS THAT BELONG IN THE KITCHEN

Meatloaf

Bread

Red Hot Chili Peppers

The Cranberries

Hall & Oates

Cream

Martha and the Muffins

Peaches

T-Bone Walker

Rosemary Clooney

MUSICAL ACTS YOU'D KICK OUT OF YOUR KITCHEN

Meat Puppets

Meat Whiplash

Smashing Pumpkins

Limp Bizkit

Hootie & the Blowfish

Poison

Dead Milkmen

Virgin Prunes

Psychotic Pineapple

Skankin' Pickle

TOOLS WE CAN'T LIVE WITHOUT

Kitchen shears

Microplane grater

Silicone spatula

Silicone-covered wire whisk

Silicone baking mat

Citrus press

Olive/cherry pitter

Hand held blender

Digital timer

Meat thermometer

MOVIES TO SATISFY YOUR APPETITE

Big Night

Moonstruck

Tampopo

Chocolat

9 ½ Weeks

Supersize Me

Babette's Feast

The Waitress

Willy Wonka & the Chocolate Factory

Who is Killing the Great Chefs of Europe?

SONGS TO MAKE YOU HUNGRY

Candy's Room, Bruce Springsteen and the E Street Band

Grits, James Brown

Honey, Moby

American Pie, Don McLean

Big Cheese, Nirvana

Quiche Lorraine, The B-52's

Tangerine, Led Zeppelin

Tacos, Enchiladas and Beans, Doris Day

Cheeseburger in Paradise, Jimmy Buffett

Buttered Popcorn, The Supremes

DUST-COLLECTORS IN THE KITCHEN

Flavor injector

Apple corer

Mini whisks

Avocado slicer

Electric knife

Egg cooker

Honey dribbling stick

Banana hanger

Shrimp deveiner

Iced tea maker

EUPHORIC LEMON LOAF

INGREDIENTS

Lemon Loaf

1½ cups flour

1 tsp baking powder

¼ tsp kosher salt

½ cup butter, softened

1 cup sugar

2 large eggs

½ cup buttermilk

Zest of 1 lemon

Lemon Glaze

⅛ cup fresh lemon juice

⅓ cup sugar

Take a big inhale. Yes, that's right. In aromatherapy, lemon lifts your mood and calms your stress. So let's take this balm of serenity out of the realm of wind chimes and Enya tunes and onto a plate — one bite of this zesty lemon loaf, drizzled with tart lemon glaze, will have you downright chilled.

DIRECTIONS

1) Preheat oven to 350°F. Coat a 9x5-inch loaf pan with non-stick cooking spray. 2) In a small bowl, combine flour, baking powder and salt. Set aside. 3) In an electric mixer, cream together butter and sugar on medium-high speed until light and fluffy. Beat in eggs, one at a time, until incorporated. On low speed, alternate adding flour mixture and buttermilk, ending with the flour. Stir in lemon zest. 4) Pour into prepared loaf pan and bake for 45-48 minutes or until golden around the edges and just cooked through. Remove from oven and let cool for 5 minutes before removing from pan. 5) For the glaze, in a small bowl, stir together lemon juice and sugar. Gently pierce the top of the loaf several times with a fork and pour glaze over.

Yield: 12-14 slices

BITE ME BIT

"We are living in a world today where lemonade is made from artificial flavors and furniture polish is made from real lemons."

– Alfred E. Neuman, MAD Magazine

CRANBERRY ORANGE BREAD

INGREDIENTS

2 cups flour

¾ cup sugar

1½ tsp baking powder

1 tsp lemon zest

½ tsp baking soda

½ tsp kosher salt

¼ cup butter, softened

½ cup orange juice

¼ cup cranberry juice

1 large egg

1½ cups chopped cranberries, fresh or frozen

2 tbsp cinnamon sugar

Lisa and I speak on the phone at 8:32 every morning. If she's perky, I know she's started her day with a large slice of our citrus-flavored, cranberry-studded loaf. If she's grunting one-word answers, I know her husband took the last piece or her jeans shrunk in the dryer.

DIRECTIONS

1) Preheat oven to 350°F. Coat a 9x5-inch loaf pan with non-stick cooking spray. 2) In a large bowl, combine flour, sugar, baking powder, lemon zest, baking soda and salt. With a fork, cut in the butter until the mixture is crumbly. 3) In a small bowl, whisk orange juice, cranberry juice and egg. Pour over the flour mixture and add the cranberries. Gently stir until the flour disappears. Pour into the prepared loaf pan and sprinkle with cinnamon sugar. Bake 55-60 minutes or until a toothpick inserted comes out clean. Allow to cool in the pan for 10 minutes before removing and cooling on a wire rack.

Yield: 10 slices

CINNAMON SWIRL BREAKFAST BREAD

INGREDIENTS

½ cup butter, softened

1 cup sugar

2 large eggs

2 tsp vanilla extract

1 cup sour cream

2 cups flour

1 tsp baking powder

½ tsp baking soda

¼ tsp kosher salt

Cinnamon Swirl

½ cup sugar

1 tbsp ground cinnamon

2 tbsp melted butter

Contrary to popular belief, you don't need fresh cut flowers or a coat of paint to sell your house. Heck, you don't even need a real estate agent. The homey aroma of this cake-like loaf is the ultimate welcome mat — once buyers catch the irresistible scents of spicy cinnamon and bread baking, their olfactory euphoria will blind them to any leaky faucet or drafty corner.

DIRECTIONS

1) Preheat oven to 325°F. Coat a 9x5-inch loaf pan with non-stick cooking spray. 2) For the batter, in an electric mixer, cream together butter and sugar on medium speed until well blended. Add the eggs one at a time, beating well after each addition. Add the vanilla and sour cream and mix on low speed for 30 seconds. Using a wooden spoon, stir in flour, baking powder, baking soda and salt just until moistened and the flour has disappeared. 3) For the cinnamon swirl, in a small bowl, stir together sugar and cinnamon. 4) Spoon half of the batter into the prepared loaf pan and sprinkle with half of the cinnamon sugar mixture. Pour remaining batter over the top. Sprinkle with remaining cinnamon sugar and drizzle with melted butter. 5) Place the loaf pan on a rimmed baking sheet to catch any drippings. Bake for 55 minutes. Let cool in the pan 10 minutes before removing. Serve warm.

Serves 12

CHOCOLATE CHUNK BANANA BREAD

INGREDIENTS

1 cup sugar

½ cup butter, softened

2 large eggs

1½ cups ripe bananas (3-4), mashed

½ cup sour cream

1 tsp vanilla extract

2½ cups flour

1 tsp baking soda

¼ tsp kosher salt

1½ cups chopped semi-sweet or milk chocolate

It's not just good things that come to those who wait. Especially where your bananas are concerned. Be patient and let them ripen to perfection – their natural sugars will take over, guaranteeing a big taste of sweetness in this moist, chocolaty loaf.

DIRECTIONS

1) Preheat oven to 350°F. Coat a 9x5-inch loaf pan with non-stick cooking spray. 2) Using an electric mixer, cream together sugar and butter on medium speed until well blended, about 1 minute. Add the eggs, one at a time, beating well after each addition. Add mashed bananas, sour cream and vanilla. Beat on low speed until blended, about 30 seconds. With a wooden spoon, stir in flour, baking soda, salt and chocolate chunks just until moistened and the flour has disappeared. Spoon batter into prepared pan. 3) Bake 70 minutes, until lightly browned on top and cooked through. Cool 10 minutes in the pan before removing to cool on a wire rack.

Yield: 14-16 slices

BITE ME BIT

"Intellectual property has the shelf life of a banana."

– Bill Gates, Microsoft founder

CHOCOLATE BAR COFFEE CAKE

INGREDIENTS

Chocolate Topping

2 cups chopped milk chocolate

1 cup packed brown sugar

2 tbsp cocoa powder

1 tbsp ground cinnamon

Cake Batter

1 cup sugar

6 tbsp margarine

2 large eggs

1 tsp vanilla extract

1 cup sour cream

1 tsp baking soda

1⅓ cup flour

1½ tsp baking powder

On the days we're short on sweetness and long on appetite, this is our go-to dessert. A perfectly luscious cake that's overrun with creamy chunks of chocolate, you'll be able to get it from pantry to oven in less time than it takes to brew a pot of coffee.

DIRECTIONS

1) Preheat oven to 350°F. Coat a 9-inch square baking pan with non-stick cooking spray. 2) For the topping, in a small bowl, combine milk chocolate, brown sugar, cocoa powder and cinnamon. Set aside. 3) For the cake, in a food processor, combine sugar, margarine, eggs and vanilla. Process for 2 minutes. 4) Mix sour cream with baking soda in a measuring cup. Let stand for 30 seconds. 5) Add sour cream to food processor and mix 3 seconds. Add flour and baking powder, pulsing 4 times or until flour disappears. 6) Pour half of the batter into the prepared baking pan. Cover with half of the topping. Repeat with remaining batter and topping. Bake for 40-45 minutes.

Serves 8-10

BITE ME BIT

"And above all...Think Chocolate."

— Betty Crocker

TWINKORETTE PEACH CRUMB CAKE

INGREDIENTS

1 cup sour cream

1 tsp baking soda

2¼ cups flour

1 cup sugar

¾ cup butter, softened

2 large eggs

1 tsp vanilla extract

1 tsp baking powder

¼ tsp kosher salt

2½ cups canned sliced peaches, drained well

For years I kept my self-destructive habit a secret, burying them in shopping carts, stashing one or two in the glove box for that easy-access quick fix. I couldn't let anyone know I was addicted to Twinkies – I'm a grown woman for goodness' sake! I thought I had it under control until that fateful early morning Lisa caught me ducked down in my car, crumbs flying and a telltale smear at the corner of my mouth. Ignoring my declarations of willpower, she spent endless hours in the kitchen concocting a cure for my cravings – this golden crumb cake that tastes like my beloved 4-inch long, cream-filled ladyfingers mingled with juicy peaches. Hello, my name is Julie and it has been 6 months, 22 days since my last cello-wrapped Twinkie.

DIRECTIONS

1) Preheat oven to 350°F. Coat an 8-inch square baking pan with non-stick cooking spray. 2) In a 2-cup measuring cup, combine sour cream and baking soda. Set aside. 3) In a food processor, combine flour, sugar and butter. Pulse on and off until blended and crumbly, 10-15 seconds. Remove and set aside 1 cup of the flour mixture for the cake topping. 4) Add the eggs, vanilla, baking powder, salt and sour cream to the remaining mixture in the food processor. Pulse 4 times on and off, scraping down the bowl once or twice. Do not overmix. 5) Spread half of the batter in the prepared baking pan. Place sliced peaches atop and cover with remaining batter. Sprinkle reserved crumbs to cover the top of the cake. 6) Bake 48-50 minutes or until the cake is lightly browned around the edges. Note that testing the center of the cake with a toothpick won't give an accurate result as the peaches are wet and the toothpick will come out wet even when the cake is fully baked.

Serves 10

GOOEY MONKEY BREAD with CARAMEL GLAZE

INGREDIENTS

Dough

¼ cup warm water

1 tsp sugar

1 package dry active yeast
(not rapid-rise)

¾ cup milk

¼ cup butter

¼ cup sugar

1 tsp kosher salt

2 large eggs

3½ cups flour

Sugar Coating

½ cup sugar

½ cup packed brown sugar

½ tsp ground cinnamon

5 tbsp melted butter

Glaze

1 cup packed brown sugar

¼ cup butter

2 tbsp heavy cream

Icing

1¼ cups icing sugar

2 tbsp milk

Yeah, monkey bread. But what do you expect when other 1950s recipes had such names as "Cantaloupe Pickles" and "Clever Judy Filling"? Also called bubble loaf or golden crown, monkey bread is pull-apart layers of sinfully sugared yeast dough dripping in sticky caramel glaze and topped with sweet icing. So addictive, even Nancy Reagan served it regularly at the White House.

DIRECTIONS

1) In a small bowl, combine warm water and 1 tsp sugar. Sprinkle yeast on top, cover and set aside for 10 minutes. 2) Meanwhile, in a glass dish, heat milk and butter in microwave until milk is warm and butter is melted. Pour into the bowl of an electric mixer. Add ¼ cup sugar, salt and eggs. Pour in yeast mixture and using a dough hook attachment, mix on low speed just to combine. Add flour 1 cup at a time, mixing on low speed. Once all the flour has been added, mix on medium speed for 3 minutes (or 8-10 minutes by hand on a lightly floured work surface) to knead the dough. Place dough into a lightly oiled mixing bowl. Cover with plastic wrap and set aside in a warm, draft-free spot to rise for 45 minutes. 3) While the dough rises, butter the inside of a 10-inch Bundt pan. 4) For the sugar coating, in a small bowl, combine sugar, brown sugar and cinnamon. In another small bowl, place the melted butter. Set aside. 5) When the dough has risen, turn it out of the bowl on to a lightly floured surface. Knead the dough for 1 minute. Cut off golf ball-size pieces of dough and roll each piece into a ball. You should have about 40 balls. Lightly dip each dough ball into the melted butter and then roll them in the sugar-cinnamon mixture. As you go, stack the balls of dough in the prepared Bundt pan. Once you've covered the bottom of the pan, start a new

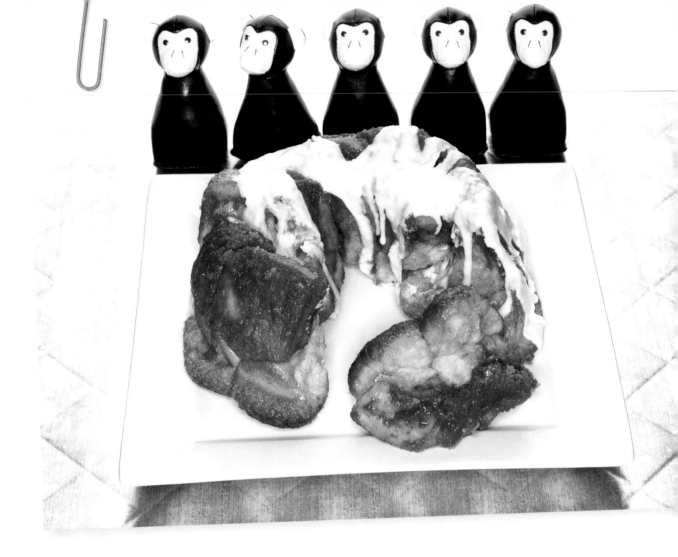

layer until all the dough is used up. **6)** For the glaze, in a small saucepan, add the brown sugar, butter and cream. Bring to a boil over medium heat, stirring constantly. Once the mixture has come to a boil immediately remove from heat and pour over the prepared dough balls. **7)** Cover the pan with a clean cloth or plastic wrap and set in a warm place to rise for 1 hour. **8)** Preheat oven to 350°F. Once the dough has risen and doubled in size, bake for 28 minutes or until golden brown. Remove from oven and allow to cool in pan for 5-10 minutes. Run a knife around the edges of the pan to allow for easy removal. Carefully flip onto serving plate and allow to cool completely before icing. **9)** For the icing, in a medium bowl, whisk together icing sugar and milk until smooth. Immediately drizzle icing over bread.

Serves 12

Fork me

Desserts for a Happy Ending

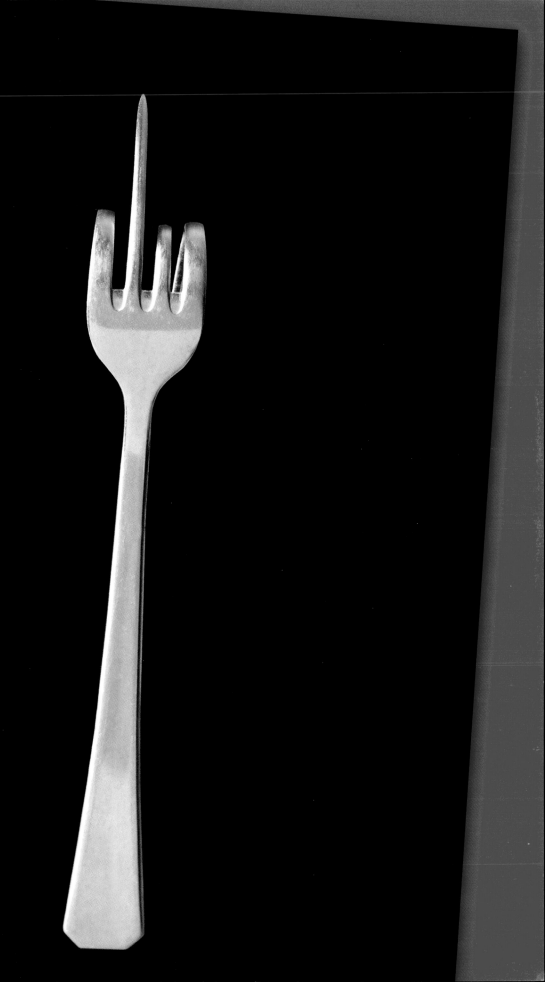

FUDGY DOUBLE CHOCOLATE LAYER CAKE

INGREDIENTS

Chocolate Cake

2 cups sugar

2 cups flour

¾ cup cocoa powder, sifted to remove lumps

1½ tsp baking powder

1¼ tsp baking soda

½ tsp kosher salt

2 large eggs

1 cup milk

½ cup vegetable oil

¾ cup boiling water

Chocolate Frosting

½ cup butter, softened

⅔ cup cocoa powder, sifted to remove lumps

6 tbsp milk

2 tbsp corn syrup

3 cups icing sugar

DIRECTIONS

1) Preheat oven to 350°F. Coat two 9-inch round cake pans with non-stick cooking spray. 2) Add sugar, flour, cocoa powder, baking powder, baking soda and salt to an electric mixer. Mix on low speed for 30 seconds to combine dry ingredients. Add eggs, milk and oil, beating at medium speed for 2 minutes. With a spatula gently fold in boiling water (note: the batter will be thin). Divide evenly into prepared pans. 3) Bake 23-25 minutes or until a toothpick inserted in the center comes out clean. Remove from oven and let cool for 10 minutes before removing cakes from pans. Completely cool layers on wire racks. 4) For the frosting, in an electric mixer, cream together butter and cocoa on low speed to combine. Add milk and corn syrup, continuing on low speed for 1 minute. Add icing sugar, 1 cup at a time, on low speed, making sure to scrape down the sides of the bowl. Once all the icing sugar has been added, turn speed to medium and beat until it is a smooth spreading consistency. 5) To assemble cake, place one cake layer on a serving dish and top with about ¾ cup of frosting. Spread evenly over cake. Top with remaining layer and use the remainder of the frosting over the top and sides of the cake.

Serves 10

NAUGHTY-TURNED-NICE CARROT CAKE with CREAM CHEESE ICING

INGREDIENTS

Carrot Cake

2 cups flour

¾ cup packed brown sugar

½ cup sugar

1½ tsp baking soda

1 tsp ground cinnamon

½ tsp kosher salt

½ cup vegetable oil

½ cup buttermilk

1 tsp vanilla extract

2 large eggs

2 large egg whites

3 cups shredded carrots
(approx. 6-7 carrots)

Cream Cheese Icing

3½ cups icing sugar

1 (8oz/250g) package cream
cheese, softened

½ cup butter, softened

1 tsp vanilla extract

As far as food folklore goes, "carrot cake is healthy" is right up there with "lobsters scream when boiled." SO not true. Until now. By cutting the oil in half, lessening the number of egg yolks and upping the carrot quotient, Lisa has once again proven the impossible.

DIRECTIONS

1) Preheat oven to 350°F. Coat two 9-inch round cake pans with non-stick cooking spray. 2) For the cake, in a large bowl, combine flour, brown sugar, sugar, baking soda, cinnamon and salt. Stir to combine. Make a well in the center and set aside. 3) In a medium bowl, whisk oil, buttermilk, vanilla, whole eggs plus 2 egg whites. Along with shredded carrots, add to flour mixture, stirring just until ingredients are incorporated and flour has disappeared. Divide batter evenly into prepared cake pans and bake 22-25 minutes or until a toothpick inserted comes out clean. Cool in pans for 10 minutes before removing and cool completely on wire racks before icing. 4) For the icing, in a large bowl beat icing sugar, cream cheese, butter and vanilla on low speed until blended. Scrape down the sides of the bowl and beat on medium speed for 30 seconds, until smooth and creamy. 5) To ice the cake, place 1 layer on a serving plate and spread with ¾ cup of the icing. Top with remaining cake layer and spread remaining icing over the top and sides of the cake. Store cake in refrigerator.

Serves 10-12

BITE ME BIT

"She's only eating carrots to increase the size of her breasts."

– Mike Baker (actor Justin Henry) in the 1984 movie "Sixteen Candles"

FROSTED APPLE CAKE

INGREDIENTS

Apple Cake

2½ cups flour

1 tsp baking soda

½ tsp ground cinnamon

½ tsp kosher salt

3 cups peeled and diced Granny Smith apples

¾ cup melted butter

1 cup sugar

½ cup packed brown sugar

½ cup apple butter (apple sauce can be substituted)

2 large eggs

1 tsp vanilla extract

Cream Cheese Frosting

1 (8oz/250g) package cream cheese, softened

½ cup butter, softened

Zest of 1 lemon

5 cups icing sugar

She used to pretend these mysterious disappearances were a figment of my imagination. Then she would say that she needed the fresh air and a chance to get away from it all. But I know why Lisa makes her pilgrimage to Chudleigh's apple orchard; I know why she adopted an apple tree. Because she's nuts. Every year she brings home her 42-pound box of hand-picked juicy apples and hits the kitchen. It could mean 15 quarts of apple sauce or gallons of cider. Last year's harvest yielded a chunky apple cake smothered in a smooth lemony cream cheese frosting. Now about all those secret trips to the pumpkin patch...

DIRECTIONS

1) Preheat oven to 350°F. Coat two 9-inch round cake pans with non-stick cooking spray. 2) For the cake, in a large bowl, combine flour, baking soda, cinnamon and salt. Add diced apples and set aside. 3) In a medium bowl, whisk melted butter, sugar, brown sugar, apple butter, eggs, and vanilla. Make a well in the center of the flour mixture and add butter/sugar mixture. Stir with a wooden spoon just until the flour disappears and all ingredients are combined. Divide batter between the 2 baking pans. Bake 15-20 minutes until golden on top and cooked through. Cool in pans 10 minutes before removing and allow to cool completely on wire racks before icing. 4) For the frosting, in an electric mixer, combine cream cheese, butter and lemon zest. Mix at medium speed until combined and smooth, making sure to scrape down the sides of the bowl during mixing. On low speed, gradually add icing sugar and mix until sugar is blended and you have a smooth icing. 5) To frost the cake, place 1 layer on a serving plate and spread with 1 cup of frosting. Top with remaining cake layer and spread remaining frosting over the top and sides of the cake. Refrigerate for 1 hour to allow the icing to set.

Serves 12

ENCHANTED COCONUT LAYER CAKE

INGREDIENTS

Coconut Cake

1¾ cup sugar

½ cup butter, softened

1 tsp vanilla extract

½ tsp coconut extract

4 large egg whites

2 cups flour

1 tsp baking powder

½ tsp baking soda

¼ tsp kosher salt

1⅓ cups buttermilk

½ cup flaked sweetened coconut

Coconut Icing

½ cup vegetable shortening

½ cup butter, softened

1 tsp vanilla extract

½ tsp coconut extract

4 cups icing sugar

3 tbsp milk

1 cup flaked coconut, sweetened or unsweetened

Once upon a time, in a land far, far away, lived a Queen. Every day she asked her magnifying mirror who was the fairest of them all? Despite her frown lines and crow's feet, the answer was always "You, my Queen, are fairest of them all." But, through the woods, a little distance away, lived an innocent maiden with 7 dwarfs and they all loved to bake. When the Queen next consulted her mirror she was taken aback – "You are no longer the fairest of them all...there is a snow white cake with thick swaths of ivory icing and sweet curls of coconut." At that, the Queen hurled her mirror in the trashcan and Heigh-Ho'ed it outta there to score a slice. THE END.

DIRECTIONS

1) Preheat oven to 350°F. Coat two 9-inch round cake pans with non-stick cooking spray. Dust pans with a few pinches of flour, tapping out excess. 2) For the cake, in an electric mixer, cream together sugar and butter on medium speed until well combined, about 1 minute. Add vanilla and coconut extract and continue on medium speed. One at a time, add egg whites, beating well after each addition. 3) In a separate bowl, stir together flour, baking powder, baking soda and salt. On low speed, add to the electric mixer in the following order: ⅓ of flour mixture, ½ of the buttermilk, another ⅓ of the flour, remaining ½ of the buttermilk, finishing off with remaining ⅓ of the flour. Beat just until combined – do not overmix. Gently fold in flaked coconut. Divide batter evenly into prepared pans and bake 22-24 minutes or until cake springs back when touched gently in the center. Cool in pans for 10 minutes before removing. Cool completely on wire racks before icing. 4) For the icing, in an electric mixer, cream together shortening, butter, vanilla and coconut extract on medium speed

for 30 seconds. Turn down to low speed, slowly adding ½ of the icing sugar and mixing until incorporated. Add milk and remaining icing sugar, continuing to mix until desired spreading consistency is reached. Fold in flaked coconut. 5) To assemble the cake, place 1 cake on a serving dish and top with 1 cup of icing, spreading it evenly over cake. Top with remaining layer and use the rest of the icing to cover the top and sides of the cake.

Serves 10-12

BITE ME BIT

"Your good friend has just taken a piece of cake out of the garbage and eaten it. You will probably need this information when you check me into the Betty Crocker Clinic."

– Miranda Hobbes (actress Cynthia Nixon) on the HBO series "Sex and the City"

Sara Lisa's ICED BANANA CAKE

INGREDIENTS

Banana Cake

2½ cups flour

2 tsp baking soda

¼ tsp kosher salt

½ cup butter, softened

1 cup sugar

¾ cup packed brown sugar

2 large eggs

1 tsp vanilla extract

⅔ cup buttermilk

4 medium-size ripe bananas, peeled and mashed

2 tsp fresh lemon juice

Banana Icing

¼ cup butter, softened

½ cup mashed bananas (about 1 banana)

½ tsp fresh lemon juice

½ tsp vanilla extract

3½ cups icing sugar

It's nice to know we're not alone. Countless others miss the irresistible "frozen fresh" taste of Sara Lee's Iced Banana Cake. In fact, there are chat rooms dedicated to immortalizing this aluminum pan sheet cake, its pronounced banana flavor and sweet rippled frosting. All you fans, you can finally log off and stop fantasizing about this bygone taste of childhood. We've brought you back in time – minus the propylene glycol esters.

DIRECTIONS

1) Preheat oven to 350°F. Coat a 13x9-inch baking pan with non-stick cooking spray. 2) In a small bowl, combine flour, baking soda and salt. Set aside. 3) Using an electric mixer on medium speed, cream butter, sugar and brown sugar until light and fluffy. Beat in eggs one at a time and then add vanilla extract. Alternate adding flour mixture and buttermilk until combined. Stir in mashed bananas and lemon juice. Pour batter into prepared baking pan and bake 35-40 minutes or until a toothpick inserted into the center of the cake comes out clean. Allow to cool in pan for 10 minutes. 4) For the icing, in an electric mixer, beat butter, bananas and lemon juice on medium speed until well combined. On low speed, slowly add icing sugar until a smooth consistency is reached, scraping down sides of the bowl once or twice. Spread icing on cool cake.

Serves 12

BREAD (& banana & cranberry) PUDDING

INGREDIENTS

1½ slightly hard/stale egg breads (challahs) crusts removed and cut into ½-inch thick slices

4 tbsp margarine

3 large eggs

¾ cup packed brown sugar

3½ cups milk

1½ cups mashed ripe bananas (4-5 bananas)

2 tsp vanilla extract

1 cup dried cranberries or dried cherries

Topping

1 cup flour

1 cup packed brown sugar

¼ cup margarine

Sorry pigeons. You're outta luck. We've found a new and improved way to use our crusty loaves. This dessert is the breadwinner...stale slices are soaked in a custardy mixture of eggs, milk and mashed sweet bananas then baked until golden and puffy.

DIRECTIONS

1) Preheat oven to 350°F. Coat a 13x9-inch baking dish with non-stick cooking spray. 2) Spread 4 tbsp margarine among bread slices and then cut bread into 1-inch cubes. Set aside. 3) In a large bowl, whisk eggs and brown sugar. Add milk, bananas and vanilla, whisking to combine. Add cranberries and bread, tossing gently to coat. Let stand for 10 minutes. Pour mixture into prepared baking dish. 4) For the topping, in a small bowl, combine flour and brown sugar. Cut margarine into mixture until crumbly. Spread crumble mixture evenly on top of the bread pudding. Bake 50-55 minutes or until golden.

Serves 8

BITE ME BIT

"On a traffic light green means go and yellow means yield, but on a banana it's just the opposite. Green means hold on, yellow means go ahead, and red means where the hell did you get that banana at..."

— Mitch Hedberg, comedian

INDOOR S'MORES

INGREDIENTS

Creamy Filling

2 (3.4oz/102g) packages instant vanilla pudding powder

1 (8oz/250g) package cream cheese, softened

3 cups milk

4 cups frozen dessert topping, defrosted

1 (14.4oz/400g) package graham crackers

Chocolate Topping

1 cup chopped milk chocolate

½ cup milk

½ cup miniature marshmallows

¼ cup butter

¼ cup honey

2 cups icing sugar

Aaah. No more Birk-wearing-Neil-Young-wannabes or roll-your-own tobacco-smoking canoe trippers. The only reason I endured campfires and rambling stories was to eat S'Mores, and now, thanks to Lisa, I can enjoy them in my house. My mouth sinks into layers of graham crackers, creamy vanilla pudding and marshmallow-infused chocolate sauce. This is the Sugar Mountain I wanted all along.

DIRECTIONS

1) Coat a 13x9-inch baking dish with non-stick cooking spray. 2) For the filling, in an electric mixer using the whisk attachment, combine vanilla pudding powder and cream cheese on the lowest speed for 1 minute. Add milk and continue on low speed until pudding mixture becomes firmer, 3-5 minutes. Gently fold in dessert topping to combine. Set aside. 3) For the chocolate topping, in a medium saucepan, combine chocolate, milk, marsh-mallows, butter and honey over low heat. Stir until melted. Remove from heat and whisk in icing sugar. Set aside. 4) In prepared baking dish, arrange one layer of graham crackers on the bottom. Spoon half of the pudding mixture evenly over crackers. Repeat with another layer of crackers followed by the remaining pudding mixture. Finish the top layer with graham crackers and pour the chocolate mixture over the top, covering the crackers. Refrigerate uncovered at least 2 hours before serving.

Serves 10

BITE ME BIT

Ham Porter: Hey, Smalls, you wanna s'more?

Smalls: Some more of what?

Ham Porter: No, do you wanna s'more?

Smalls: I haven't had anything yet, so how can I have some more of nothing?

– from the 1993 movie "The Sandlot"

FROZEN CHOCOLATE-BANANA-PB PIE

INGREDIENTS

Crust

1¼ cups finely ground vanilla wafer cookies (about 35)

¼ cup melted butter

2 tbsp sugar

Filling

1 cup semi-sweet or milk chocolate, melted

3 large bananas, sliced

1 cup packed brown sugar

1 cup smooth peanut butter

½ cup cream cheese, softened

½ tsp vanilla extract

4 cups frozen dessert topping, defrosted

½ cup chocolate sundae syrup, for topping

"I'd just like to be treated like a regular customer."
– Elvis Presley

He might have been able to swivel his hips and make women bawl, but really, Elvis was just your average Joe. I mean, look at The King's favorite food – a humble fried sandwich of peanut butter and banana. Not exactly regal. That said, this pie is our hunka-hunka-freezing-love tribute to him – a simple, velvety smooth icebox pie that would surely have elicited a "Thank you, thank you very much" from The Pelvis.

DIRECTIONS

1) Preheat oven to 350°F. Coat a 9-inch pie plate with non-stick cooking spray. 2) For the crust, in a medium bowl, combine vanilla crumbs, butter and sugar. Press against the bottom and sides of the pie plate to form a crust. Bake for 10 minutes. Cool completely before filling. 3) Cover the bottom of the crust with the melted chocolate and arrange banana slices on top of chocolate. 4) In an electric mixer, cream together brown sugar, peanut butter, cream cheese and vanilla on medium speed until smooth. Gently fold in whipped topping and spread over bananas. Drizzle top with chocolate sundae syrup. 5) Cover pie with plastic wrap and place in freezer for at least 3 hours before serving. For easier cutting, remove from freezer 10 minutes before serving.

Serves 8

DANGEROUSLY DELECTABLE PECAN PIE

INGREDIENTS

Crust

1½ cups flour

½ tsp kosher salt

2 tbsp sugar

½ cup butter, chilled

4 tbsp cold water

Pecan Filling

4 large eggs

1 cup corn syrup

½ cup packed brown sugar

3 tbsp melted butter

1 tsp vanilla extract

¼ tsp kosher salt

1 cup coarsely chopped pecans

Pecan Topping

⅓ cup packed brown sugar

3 tbsp honey

3 tbsp butter

1½ cups pecan halves

DIRECTIONS

1) Preheat oven to 350°F. 2) For the crust, in a medium bowl, combine flour, salt and sugar. Using your hands or a pastry blender, cut butter into flour mixture until it resembles coarse crumbs. Gradually drizzle cold water over flour mixture. Toss the mixture with a fork to moisten until the dough comes together. Gently gather dough into a ball. On a floured work surface, roll dough out into a circle that is 1-inch larger all around than an upside down 9-inch pie plate. Once rolled, ease dough into a 9-inch pie plate to evenly line the bottom and go up the sides. Fold overhanging dough under itself to form a rim. Transfer to freezer for 10 minutes while preparing filling. 3) For the filling, in a large bowl, whisk eggs, corn syrup, brown sugar, melted butter, vanilla and salt. Mix in chopped pecans and spoon into chilled pie crust. Place pie on a rimmed baking sheet and bake for 45 minutes. 4) While pie is baking, prepare topping. In a medium saucepan, combine brown sugar, honey and butter over medium heat. Cook for 3 minutes, stirring constantly until sugar dissolves and mixture is smooth. Stir in pecan halves and remove from heat. 5) Once pie has baked for 45 minutes, remove from oven and gently spoon topping over filling. Return to oven for 15-18 minutes baking until topping is golden. Cover the edges of the pie crust with aluminum foil if they are browning too much. 6) Cool pie completely before serving, allowing at least 3 hours to set.

Serves 8-10

⚠ WARNING

CONTAINS VAST AMOUNTS OF PREMIUM NUTS

DO NOT USE "PEH-KHAN" UNLESS SOUTH OF THE MASON-DIXON

NOT FOR WEAK-HEARTED – INTENSE CARAMEL-TOFFEE COVERS FLAKY CRUST

PRODUCT WILL BE HOT AFTER HEATING

NOT TO BE USED AS A PERSONAL FLOTATION DEVICE

BONA FIDE KEY LIME PIE

INGREDIENTS

Graham Crust

1¼ cups graham cracker crumbs

¼ cup sugar

6 tbsp melted butter

Lime Filling

3 large egg yolks

1¾ cups sweetened condensed milk

½ cup fresh key lime juice (if you can't find the golf ball-sized key limes, use traditional limes)

2 tsp lime zest

Meringue Topping

4 large egg whites

¼ tsp table salt

¾ cup sugar

On July 1, 2006, all eyes were on the State of Florida. New fashion in thongs? Winter weather? Lost ballots? None of the above. A tight race was dominating headlines – what would become the official state pie? After a real nail-biter, Key Lime beat out Pecan. Some attribute the victory to a fancy PR campaign, but when you're after some cool in the swelter of the Sunshine State no dessert can beat the tart and creamy custard and fluffy meringue cover.

DIRECTIONS

1) Preheat oven to 350°F. Coat a 9-inch pie plate with non-stick cooking spray. 2) For the crust, in a medium bowl, mix together graham cracker crumbs, sugar and melted butter. Press the mixture onto the bottom and sides of the prepared pie plate. Bake the crust for 8 minutes. Set aside and lower the oven temperature to 300°F. 3) For the filling, in an electric mixer, use the whisk attachment and beat the egg yolks on medium speed until fluffy, about 3 minutes. Gradually add the condensed milk and beat mixture for 4 minutes more. Add lime juice and zest and beat just until combined, about 1 minute. Pour the mixture into the prepared crust. 4) For the meringue, in a clean and dry bowl of your electric mixer, use the whisk attachment and beat the egg whites and table salt until stiff. Gradually beat in sugar and continue to beat until stiff peaks form. Spread meringue over the key lime filling and bake for 25 minutes until nicely browned. Remove from oven and let cool completely. Place in refrigerator at least 1 hour prior to serving.

Serves 8

STREUSEL-TOPPED BLUEBERRY PIE

INGREDIENTS

Graham Crust

2 cups graham cracker crumbs

2 tbsp sugar

½ tsp ground cinnamon

¼ cup melted margarine

Creamy Blueberry Filling

4 cups fresh blueberries

¾ cup sugar

⅓ cup flour

1 tsp lemon zest

¼ tsp kosher salt

2 large eggs, gently whisked

½ cup sour cream

½ tsp vanilla extract

Streusel Topping

½ cup flour

½ cup sugar

3 tbsp margarine

Fats Domino isn't the only one who found a little magic in a berry patch. Richie Cunningham, Little Richard and even Led Zeppelin also discovered ecstasy among the juicy purple orbs – and you can too. Hum along as you prepare this foolproof, sweet crisp-topped pie, so luscious it'll make the moon stand still.

DIRECTIONS

1) Preheat oven to 350°F. Coat a 9-inch pie plate with non-stick cooking spray. 2) For the crust, in a medium bowl, combine graham crumbs, sugar and cinnamon. Add margarine and mix until well blended. Press the mixture onto the bottom and up the sides of the pie plate. Bake for 8 minutes and set aside to cool. 3) For the filling, in a large bowl, gently stir together blueberries, sugar, flour, lemon zest and salt. Gently fold in eggs, sour cream and vanilla. Spoon mixture into graham crust. 4) For the topping, in a small bowl, combine flour and sugar. Using a fork, mix in margarine until crumbly. Spread topping over the pie filling. 5) Bake 40-45 minutes until lightly browned on top. Cool for at least 1 hour before serving.

Serves 8

BITE ME BIT

Mrs. Beauregarde: I can't have a blueberry as a daughter. How is she supposed to compete?

Veruca Salt: You could put her in a county fair.

– from the 2005 movie "Charlie and the Chocolate Factory"

MOM'S MILE-HIGH LEMON MERINGUE PIE

INGREDIENTS

Crust

1¼ cups flour

¼ tsp kosher salt

½ cup cold butter, cut into 6 pieces

¼ cup ginger ale

1 tbsp fresh lemon juice

Lemon Filling

4 large egg yolks

1 cup sugar

⅓ cup cornstarch

¼ tsp kosher salt

1½ cups water

½ cup fresh lemon juice

2 tsp lemon zest

3 tbsp butter

Meringue Top

6 large egg whites

½ tsp cream of tartar

¾ cup sugar

This pie often graced our childhood meals,
Luscious and towering, we were head over heels.
Yet the elation would last for only so long,
A few bites later, things would often turn wrong.

First we'd hoover the lemony bottom – so tart!
But here's where the bloodshed would always start,
All guarding our fluffy meringue to the end,
Upon each other's plates we'd fiercely descend.

Forks and knives flew, elbows raised high,
And with sleight of hand and blink of an eye,
Poor brother would lose his coveted prize,
As we sisters delighted in his sweet pie's demise.

DIRECTIONS

1) For the crust, place flour, salt and cold butter in food processor bowl. Process for 2 seconds at a time, 4 times, until mixture resembles coarse crumbs. In a small measuring cup, combine ginger ale and lemon juice. Add to machine while it is running. Process until dough gathers in a ball, about 10 seconds. Remove dough and press into a circular disk, about 1-inch thick. Wrap in plastic wrap and refrigerate at least 1 hour or overnight.
2) Preheat oven to 400°F. 3) On a lightly floured surface, roll dough into a 12-inch circle. Fold the circle in half and transfer it to a 9-inch pie plate. Trim off overhanging edges leaving about 1-inch excess. Fold under the excess dough and decoratively flute the edges. Line the pie crust with aluminum foil, waxed paper or parchment paper, then fill with pie weights or dried beans. Bake 14 minutes. Gently remove weights and foil, waxed paper or parchment from crust. Prick the bottom of the pastry all over with a fork. Continue to bake 12 minutes more or until evenly golden.

Cool for 10 minutes before adding lemon filling. **4)** For the lemon filling, place the egg yolks in a small bowl, whisk to combine and set aside. In a medium saucepan, combine sugar, cornstarch and salt. Stir in water and lemon juice until smooth. Bring to a boil over medium heat and stir continuously 1-2 minutes or until thickened. Remove saucepan from heat and add a small amount of the hot sugar mixture to the egg yolks. Stirring constantly, add the egg yolk mixture to the saucepan. Bring to a gentle boil over medium heat and stir for 2 minutes. Remove pan from heat and add lemon zest and butter. Allow filling to cool slightly and set aside. **5)** For the meringue, in a mixing bowl, beat egg whites and cream of tartar on medium speed until foamy. Increase the speed to high and gradually beat in sugar until stiff, glossy peaks form. **6)** To assemble, lower oven temperature to 375°F. Spoon the lemon filling into the baked pastry shell. Pile the meringue on top of the lemon filling making sure it touches the crust all around, otherwise the meringue will shrink away from the sides when it is baked. Using the back of a spoon you can create swirls and peak designs with the meringue. **7)** Bake 10-12 minutes, until the top is lightly golden. Remove from oven and let cool for at least 1 hour at room temperature before serving.

Serves 8

EASY as PIE STRAWBERRY APPLE CRISP

INGREDIENTS

6 cups peeled and cubed
Granny Smith apples

2 cups halved strawberries

¼ cup sugar

½ tsp ground cinnamon

Topping

1½ cups large flake oats

1½ cups flour

1½ cups packed brown sugar

1 tsp ground cinnamon

¾ cup margarine

When we were little I was kind enough to let Lisa brush my hair and scratch my back – hey, as her big sister, it was the least I could do. Now in adulthood, she owes me a few favors. Being a professional pastry chef was a start – Lisa was going to help me conquer my fear of baking. So, my little sister started me off slowly with this foolproof, fuss-free crisp of cinnamon apples and sweet strawberries under a thick, extra-crunchy topping. Lucky for her I'm no longer intimidated by baking so she can return to massaging my shoulders.

DIRECTIONS

1) Preheat oven to 350°F. Coat an 11x7-inch baking dish with non-stick cooking spray. 2) In a large bowl, toss apples, strawberries, sugar and cinnamon. Place in prepared baking dish. 3) For the topping, in a large bowl, mix oats, flour, brown sugar and cinnamon. Add margarine, mixing with a fork until crumbly. Sprinkle over fruit. 4) Bake uncovered for 25 minutes. Loosely cover crisp with aluminum foil and bake an additional 10 minutes.

Serves 6-8

BITE ME BIT

"Ducking for apples – change one letter and it's the story of my life."

– Dorothy Parker, writer

BUTTER TART SQUARES, EH?

INGREDIENTS

Shortbread Crust

½ cup butter, softened

¼ cup packed brown sugar

1 cup flour

Filling

1 cup maple syrup

⅔ cup packed brown sugar

¼ cup butter

2 large eggs

1 tsp vanilla extract

2 tbsp flour

½ tsp baking powder

¼ tsp kosher salt

⅔ cup currants

Y'know, there's more to Canuck cuisine than back bacon, poutine and prairie oysters. Well, hold on to your toque there because Lisa has created a wicked home and native treat. This nut-free, Northern cousin of the pecan pie has a flaky pastry crust topped with a gooey combo of brown sugar and maple syrup. Take off, pemmican – this is the new national delicacy.

DIRECTIONS

1) Preheat oven to 350°F. Coat an 8-inch square baking pan with non-stick cooking spray. Cover the base of the pan with a square of parchment paper and coat again with non-stick cooking spray. 2) For the crust, in an electric mixer, cream butter and brown sugar until light and fluffy, about 1 minute. Add the flour and beat just until flour disappears and the dough comes together. Press the mixture evenly into the bottom of the prepared baking pan. Bake for 18 minutes or until the crust is golden. 3) For the filling, in a medium saucepan, combine the syrup, brown sugar and butter over medium heat. Simmer for 5 minutes to dissolve the brown sugar. Remove from heat and allow to cool for 10-15 minutes. 4) In a large bowl, whisk eggs, vanilla, flour, baking powder and salt. Add maple syrup mixture, whisking well to combine. 5) Scatter currants evenly over baked shortbread crust. Pour the filling over the currants and return to the oven to bake for 28-30 minutes or until the filling is set and slightly browned on top. Allow to cool in the pan for at least 1 hour before removing.

Yield: 16 squares

C is for: cheesy, creamy, chocolaty, caramely, calories

H ello...there are toffee chunks in the batter

E xtreme opposite of beefcake

E stelle Getty & The Golden Girls ate tons of it

S o not lactose free

E ww...grossest pick-up line: "Show me a lil' cheesecake"

C heering at a Phish concert, yell "cheesecake" to fit in

A erosmith claims cheesecake is "looser than her sister"

K nown eatery (think: Factory) sells double-digit-priced-slice

E rroneous to call it a cake - technically, it's an unleavened pie

CHOCOLATE-CRUSTED CREAMY CARAMEL CHEESECAKE

INGREDIENTS

Crust

1½ cups Oreo baking crumbs

½ cup melted butter

¼ cup whipping cream

1 cup semi-sweet chocolate

Filling

4 (8oz/250g) packages cream cheese, softened

1 cup sugar

4 large eggs

1½ tsp vanilla extract

2 cups chopped toffee bits (Heath or Skor bar)

¼ cup purchased caramel sauce

DIRECTIONS

1) Preheat oven to 350°F. Wrap the outside of a 9-inch springform pan with aluminum foil. 2) For the crust, in a medium bowl, combine Oreo baking crumbs and melted butter. Press the mixture evenly and firmly over the bottom and halfway up the sides of the springform pan. In a small saucepan, bring the whipping cream to a simmer over low heat. Add semi-sweet chocolate and stir until melted. Remove from heat and pour evenly over the crust.

3) Chill crust in refrigerator to firm slightly while preparing the filling. 4) For the filling, using an electric mixer, beat the cream cheese on medium speed until smooth, scraping the bowl several times. Gradually add the sugar and continue to beat the mixture. One at a time, beat in the eggs, scraping the bowl as needed. Using a spatula fold in vanilla extract and toffee bits. Pour mixture into prepared crust. Finish by spooning caramel sauce over the top. Place pan on a baking sheet and bake 65-70 minutes. Remove from oven and let cool to room temperature. Cover with plastic wrap and refrigerate at least 6 hours before serving.

Serves 12

CHUNKY CHEWY BLONDIE BARS

INGREDIENTS

2 cups flour

½ tsp kosher salt

¼ tsp baking soda

2 cups packed brown sugar

¾ cup butter, softened

2 large eggs

2 tsp vanilla extract

2½ cups semisweet or milk chocolate chunks

We might have wanted Rod Stewart's body once upon a time – and we did think he was pretty sexy, but his contention that blondes have more fun didn't convince these two brunettes. We tried singing "Call Me" at the top of our lungs while we ran on the beach in our "Baywatch" bathing suits. Nope. No fun there. But just one bite of these golden-girl bars and we were reaching for the Clairol.

DIRECTIONS

1) Preheat oven to 350°F. Coat a 13x9-inch baking pan with non-stick cooking spray. Dust with a few pinches of flour, shaking out excess. 2) In a small bowl, stir together flour, salt and baking soda. 3) In an electric mixer, cream together brown sugar and butter until light and fluffy. Beat in eggs and vanilla, adding eggs one at a time until combined. Add flour mixture and chocolate chunks to the mixer, mixing on low speed just until the flour disappears. 4) Spread the batter evenly in the prepared pan. Bake 25 minutes or until lightly browned. Cool for 20 minutes before removing from pan.

Yield: 20-24 bars

BITE ME BIT

"I'm not offended by all the dumb blonde jokes because I know I'm not dumb... and I also know that I'm not blonde."

– Dolly Parton, singer

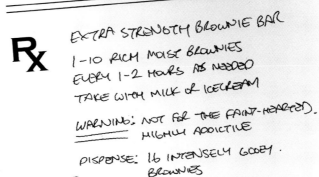

LIC. # ME 00001

DR. D. LICIOUS
TEL: (416) EAT-MORE   FAX: (416) CRA-VING

Rx

EXTRA STRENGTH BROWNIE BAR
1-10 RICH MOIST BROWNIES
EVERY 1-2 HOURS AS NEEDED
TAKE WITH MILK OR ICECREAM

WARNING: NOT FOR THE FAINT-HEARTED.
HIGHLY ADDICTIVE

DISPENSE: 16 INTENSELY GOOEY.
BROWNIES

(SIGNATURE)

REFILLS: 0 1 2 3 4 5 UNLIMITED

R$_X$ BROWNIES with FUDGE FROSTING

INGREDIENTS

Brownies

4 squares unsweetened chocolate, chopped

¾ cup butter

2 cups sugar

3 large eggs

1 cup flour

Fudge Frosting

½ cup sugar

¼ cup cocoa powder, sifted

¼ cup milk

2 tbsp butter

1 tbsp corn syrup

1 cup icing sugar

DIRECTIONS

1) Preheat oven to 350°F. Coat a 13x9-inch baking pan with non-stick cooking spray. Line with parchment paper. 2) For the brownies, in a microwave safe bowl, combine chocolate and butter. Melt on high heat for 1 minute, stir and melt for 30 seconds more or until the chocolate and butter are melted and smooth. 3) In a large bowl, whisk sugar and eggs. Add chocolate mixture and flour, stirring until flour has disappeared. Spread in prepared pan and bake 25-30 minutes. Let cool in pan for 15 minutes before removing. Cool completely on wire rack before frosting. 4) For the frosting, in a large saucepan, mix together sugar, cocoa powder, milk, butter and corn syrup. Heat to boiling, stirring frequently. Boil for 3 minutes, stirring constantly. Cool for 10 minutes. Whisk in icing sugar until smooth.

Yield: 16 brownies

GOOEY DOUBLE CHOCOLATY CHOCOLATE COOKIES

INGREDIENTS

1 cup butter, softened

1 cup sugar

½ cup packed brown sugar

2 large eggs

2 cups flour

⅔ cup cocoa powder

¾ tsp baking soda

½ tsp kosher salt

2 cups milk chocolate chips

Okay. The title of this recipe alone should have you running for the baking supplies. But if I must do a little sell-job, these decadent, oozing chocolate cookies have chocolate chips in them.

DIRECTIONS

1) Preheat oven to 350°F. 2) In an electric mixer, cream butter, sugar and brown sugar together on medium speed until light and fluffy. Add eggs and beat until well mixed. 3) In a small bowl, combine flour, cocoa powder, baking soda and salt. Using a wooden spoon, stir flour mixture and chocolate chips into butter mixture until blended. 4) Drop the batter by rounded tablespoon onto an ungreased baking sheet. Bake 8-10 minutes. Cool slightly on the baking sheet before transferring the cookies to a wire rack.

Yield: 35 cookies

CHEWY CHOCOLATE CHIP COOKIES

INGREDIENTS

2½ cups flour

½ tsp baking soda

¼ tsp kosher salt

1 cup butter, softened

1 cup packed brown sugar

½ cup sugar

1 tsp vanilla extract

1 large egg

1 large egg yolk

2½ cups milk chocolate chips

Dear Reader:

You're probably sick of my sister Julie by now, so I decided to try my hand at writing a recipe intro. I mean, how hard can it be? What's up with the tortured artist stuff? Dark nights of the soul? All you have to say is that these chocolate chip cookies are great. See?

Truly, Lisa

DIRECTIONS

1) Preheat oven to 325°F. Line 2 baking sheets with parchment paper. 2) In a medium bowl, combine flour, baking soda and salt. 3) In an electric mixer, cream together butter, brown sugar and sugar on medium speed until well blended. Beat in vanilla, egg and egg yolk until light and fluffy. On low speed, add flour mixture and chocolate chips, mixing just until flour disappears. 4) Drop dough by ¼ cup at a time, 2 inches apart on to the prepared baking sheets. 5) Bake for 15 minutes or until the edges are golden brown. Remove from oven and allow to cool a few minutes before transferring cookies to a wire rack.

Yield: 20-24 large cookies

BITE ME BIT

"...I believe in the sweet spot, voting every election, soft core pornography, chocolate chip cookies, opening your presents on Christmas morning rather than Christmas Eve and I believe in long, slow, deep, soft, wet kisses that last for 7 days."

— Crash Davis (actor Kevin Costner) in the 1988 movie "Bull Durham"

CHUNKY WHITE CHOCOLATE CRANBERRY COOKIES

INGREDIENTS

½ cup butter, softened

½ cup sugar

½ cup packed brown sugar

1 large egg

1 tsp vanilla extract

1½ cups flour

½ tsp baking soda

¼ tsp kosher salt

1½ cups white chocolate, cut into chunks

1 cup dried cranberries or dried cherries

"Bite Me" began with this recipe after I bought a cranberry and white chocolate cookie from a local bakery three years ago. I ate it, bought a dozen more, drove directly to Lisa's house and thrust the package at her. "Make these," I insisted. She sniffed them, did her little rabbit nibbles, closed her eyes, inhaled and said, "No prob." She made them. And then she created an irresistible cookie that far surpassed any we have ever eaten.

DIRECTIONS

1) Preheat oven to 350°F. Line a baking sheet with parchment paper. 2) In an electric mixer, cream butter, sugar and brown sugar together on medium speed. Add the egg and vanilla, beating until fluffy. 3) On low speed, add the flour, baking soda, salt, white chocolate and cranberries, mixing just until the flour disappears. Do not overmix. 4) Drop heaping tablespoons of batter on prepared baking sheet. Bake 10-12 minutes, just until the edges begin to brown. Cool cookies on a wire rack.

Yield: 16 large cookies

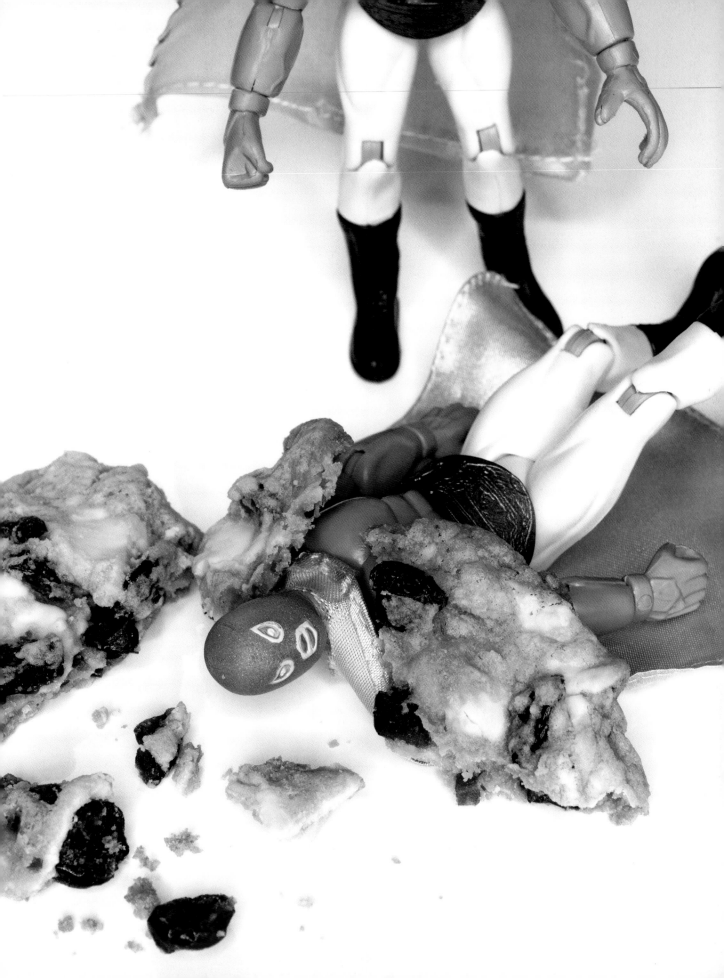

SOFT OATMEAL RAISIN COOKIES

INGREDIENTS

¾ cup butter, softened

¾ cup packed brown sugar

½ cup sugar

1 large egg

2 tbsp water

¾ cup flour

¾ tsp baking soda

1 tsp ground cinnamon

3 cups old fashioned large flake oats (not quick cooking)

1½ cups raisins or chocolate chips

Hi. We can't come to the phone right now. If you're calling to compliment our chewy, delicious cookies, press 1. If you're calling to leave a long, humble silence in homage to this great creation, press 2. If you're calling to pay tribute to one of the greatest gifts to mankind, or at least to snack time, press 3. Otherwise, hang up and try your cookies again.

DIRECTIONS

1) Preheat oven to 350°F. Line a baking sheet with parchment paper. 2) In an electric mixer, cream butter, brown sugar and sugar on medium speed until light and fluffy. Add egg and water, beating at medium speed until well mixed. 3) Add flour, baking soda, cinnamon, oats and raisins, mixing on low speed just until the flour disappears. 4) Drop dough by ¼ cup at a time on prepared baking sheet. Bake 12-14 minutes or until the edges are lightly golden. Cool slightly on the baking sheet before transferring the cookies to a wire rack.

Yield: 15 large cookies

BITE ME BIT

"I'm not really the heroic type. I was beat up by Quakers."

– Miles Monroe (actor Woody Allen) in the 1973 movie "Sleeper"

INSPIRING SUGAR COOKIES

INGREDIENTS

1½ cups icing sugar

1 cup butter, softened

½ tsp vanilla extract

1 large egg, lightly beaten

2½ cups flour

1 tsp baking soda

1 tsp cream of tartar

Calling all Pollock, Rothko and Mondrian wannabes: here's your chance to unleash your subconscious. Lisa, your artistic enabler, supplies the ideal canvas – a sweet, soft-centered, sugar cookie. You can cut, shape, drizzle, dip, ice and sprinkle to your heart's content or just be very "less is more" about it and let the buttery cookie shine au naturel.

DIRECTIONS

1) Preheat oven to 375°F. 2) In a large bowl, use a wooden spoon to mix together icing sugar and butter. Once incorporated, add vanilla and egg, stirring well to combine. Add flour, baking soda and cream of tartar, stirring until flour disappears. 3) Shape dough into a ball, cover with plastic wrap and refrigerate for 30 minutes to ensure easier handling. 4) After refrigeration, divide dough ball in half, keeping one half covered while working with the other. Roll out the dough on a floured surface to ¼ to ½-inch thickness. Cut into shapes with any cookie cutter. 5) Place cookies 1 inch apart on an ungreased cookie sheet. Bake 8-10 minutes until the edges are golden brown. Cool completely on a cooling rack.

Yield: 15 large cutout cookies or 30 small cookies

BITE ME BIT

"Women are not in love with me but with the picture of me on the screen. I am merely the canvas on which women paint their dreams."

– Rudolph Valentino, actor

Celebrate Thee

WE THANK

Our publisher Kyle Cathie for her "bloody brilliance," Anja Schmidt at Kyle Books, Ron Longe at Media Masters, Heather Reisman, Bruce Mau Design (Bruce Mau with Joanne Bell, Tom Keogh, Erik Krim, Laura Stein), Commerce Press and Estelle Elmaleh, Craig Offman, Ian Muggridge, Michael Alberstat, Phil Alberstat, Deanna Dunn, Penny Offman, Sheila Ryles, Nadia Olenchuk, Arren Williams, Big Red, The Immunity Idol, Dale Lastman, Ken and Jen Tanenbaum, our extraordinary grandmother Alice Lieberman, and of course, our parents Larry and Judy Tanenbaum for teaching us the love of family and food.

JULIE THANKS

Kenny A. for absolutely everything, Jamie for her kind touch, Perry for her crazy dances, Benjy for his sports updates, Dahra Granovsky, Richard Allen, Lisa Diamond, Laurence Loubieres and Sue Tanenbaum for brainstorming, Carolyn Offman for endlessly distracting me, Kevin Deonarine for my scapula, Cheryl Louvelle for babying me, Miriam, Andy, Estelle, Elise, Sacha, Wendy, Barbara, Penny and Kristi for all their sweetness.

LISA THANKS

Jordan for late night grocery runs and sampling meatloaf at midnight, Emmy for her enthusiasm, Lauren for her sweetness, Alex for her smiles, 3 Musketeers for your support, and of course, all my friends for loving my cookies.

Index

IMAGE SOURCES

All food photography by Michael Alberstat

Cover Image by Michael Alberstat Photography
p. 7 © Melvin Sokolsky / Marek&Associates
p. 8 © Gulliver Theis / Bransch New York
p. 10 © Miles Aldridge / trunkarchive.com
p. 12 © Image Source / Getty
p. 33 © John Springer Collection / Corbis
p. 34 © iStockphoto.com / abzee
p. 44 © Miles Aldridge / trunkarchive.com
p. 54 © Marissa Zarembsky / stockthatdoesntsuck
p. 81 © John Londei / stockthatdoesntsuck
p. 104 © Erwin Wurm / Courtesy of Galerie
    Krinzinger Vienna
p. 118 © Melvin Sokolsky / Marek&Associates
p. 123 © iStockphoto.com / tjhunt
p. 129 © Romain Laurent / Bransch New York
p. 158 © Horacio Salinas / Chris Boals Artists /
    trunkarchive.com
p. 169 © iStockphoto.com / abzee
p. 170 © DeBROCKE / Robertstock / Aurora Photos
p. 179 © David LaChapelle / Art+Commerce
p. 204 © Miles Aldridge / trunkarchive.com
p. 220 © Cheryl Koralik / Stockthatdoesn'tsuck
p. 233 © RK Studio / Kevin Lanthier / Getty
p. 262 © Laura Letinsky / Courtesy Yancey
    Richardson Gallery

CREDITS

Design
Bruce Mau Design

Printing
Commerce Press

Editor
Craig Offman

Copy Editor
Deanna Dunn

Food Photography
Michael Alberstat

Food Styling
Ian Muggridge

Prop Styling
Arren Williams

Image Sourcing
Art+Commerce

Typesetting
Richard Hunt

Indexing
Liba Berry